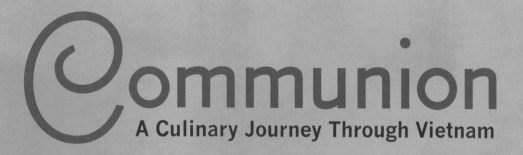

Communion

A Culinary Journey Through Vietnam

By Kim Fay

Photographs by Julie Fay Ashborn

Communion
A Culinary Journey Through Vietnam
By Kim Fay
Photographs by Julie Fay Ashborn

Cover and book design by Janet McKelpin
Copy-editing by Elizabeth Mathews
Book production by Paul Tomanpos, Jr.

For information regarding permissions, write to:
ThingsAsian Press
3230 Scott Street
San Francisco, California 94123 USA
www.thingsasianpress.com
Printed in Singapore
ISBN-13: 978-1-934159-14-9
ISBN-10: 1-934159-14-X

In food, as in death, we feel the essential brotherhood of man.

Vietnamese proverb

China

Hanoi

Laos

Gulf of
Tonkin

Vietnam Ma

Thailand

Hue

Hoi An

Cambodia

Nha Trang

Dalat

Gulf of
Thailand

Saigon

Phan Thiet

South China Sea

Introduction

Hanoi

HUE

HOI AN

NHA TRANG

Dalat

Phan Thiet

Saigon

Introduction

Of the hundreds of meals I ate during the four years I lived in Vietnam, it would be an exaggeration to say that I remember all of them. But I do remember most. I remember where I was and who I was with, and most especially, I remember the flavors. Those tangy, sweet, fiery flavors that are the essence of Vietnamese food.

At the age of twenty-eight, in the mid-1990s, I came to Vietnam from Seattle for the adventure of living in an exotic country, and to write a novel. Teaching English was my way of getting a visa and paying my rent while I wrote. A few months into my life in Saigon, the southern city officially known as Ho Chi Minh City, I moved from a hotel of dubious repute in the tourist district to a family-run guesthouse a few blocks away. It was late September, Saigon was just coming out of its rainy season, and the days weren't as humid as they had been when I arrived in June. After my morning classes, I would pedal my bike back to the guesthouse from the beautiful old French-colonial high school where I taught grammar, usage, and the occasional racy idiom to adults. During the lunch hour a woman wheeled an aluminum cart to the head of my guesthouse lane and surrounded it with small plastic stools and tables. I would lock my bike inside, then walk back to her cart.

I didn't know what the woman's food was called in Vietnamese, and I didn't need to. Like most street vendors, she sold only one meal. In her case, a pork chop with a side of water spinach, served on a bed of rice. I would take the plate up to my third-floor room and sit out on my balcony beside my little jasmine plant while I ate. The pork chop was slender, and tender to the bone, and it had a hint of sweetness that mingled addictively with the char from the grill. Softly sautéed in garlic, the water spinach was always fresh. The rice, though firm, seemed to melt in my mouth, and it left me satisfied and craving at the same time.

For three months I lived in the guesthouse, and for those three months I ate this lunch nearly every day. I never got tired of it, or of gazing down into the lane, where my neighbors nibbled their pork chops, while children and puppies tumbled like miniature circus acts and a trio of women sat propped against the wall outside their home doing piecework, sewing bindings for schoolbooks.

Teaching six separate classes a week meant that I had more than one hundred students, and it was inevitable that at least one would befriend me. A few years older than I, Dung was slim, pretty, and serious about making sure that I was taken care of, a single young woman so far away from home. One day she invited me to her family's house for lunch, where I met her parents and two sisters. From that day forward, we became four sisters. Six months later I moved again, this time into a little house affectionately called The Cave, just around the corner from Dung and her family.

Often after my classes, and before I wrote in the afternoons, I went to her house for lunch. Her mother's cooking was the best I'd had in Vietnam. Even the fresh vegetarian spring rolls she served for my first meal were memorable, laced with roasted rice powder, which gave them a hint of being toasted over an open fire. Occasionally, though, we sisters would forego our midday habit of lounging and gossiping around the house, climb onto a pair of Honda motorbikes, and venture out into the city. I always sat behind Dung, one of the worst drivers I have ever met, so I was busy hanging on and praying, and I couldn't begin to remember how to get back to any of the little cafés we visited, especially the tamarind crab shack in Cholon, Saigon's Chinatown district.

The heart of Cholon is a warren of winding streets that look the same, lined with similar-looking shops conducting the same type of business. Our tamarind crab shack was surrounded by a dozen others, all crowded with customers, and all sticky with tamarind sauce. Somehow, the sisters knew that this shack was the best of the bunch, and we sat around a table with a mound of unshelled crab on a plate at the center and one cold beer to share, because even though two of the sisters didn't drink alcohol, you "had to" drink beer with tamarind crab.

Once I started in on the crab, I was committed. I could not even tuck an annoying strand of hair behind my ear, because my fingers, my hands, and even parts of my wrists were coated in the sweet, tangy sauce, which is made from the pods of the tamarind tree. The crab was fried whole in a wok with garlic, sugar, and the tamarind paste, and its thick chunks of meat preserved the briskness of the sea within a warm caramelized glaze. We cracked the shells and tossed them, as everyone else was doing, on the crunchy, sticky floor. Conversation wound down as our attention was absorbed with slurping and gnawing, and the chilly comfort of the beer, whose bottle eventually felt as if it were slathered in honey.

By the time my first year in Vietnam came to its end, Dung had moved to Fort Wayne, Indiana, in an arranged marriage with a Chinese-Cambodian, and I had quit teaching to write for local newspapers and magazines. I was still spending a lot of time with the oldest sister, Duyen, but I had made a new friend, Huong, who, although ten years younger than I, was a kindred spirit. I had also fallen in love with a handsome Australian, so my meals were divided. Lunches were spent with my Vietnamese family or Huong, who introduced me to my favorite soup joint behind Ben Thanh Market, where at least twice a week we drizzled lime juice and chili paste onto steaming broth and savored the soothing swirl of chicken and noodles. Dinners were spent with Sam, the Australian, after he got off work, at the little French steakhouse at one end of Le Thanh Ton Street, or the Vietnamese café at the other end, where the deep-fried chicken wings were one of our many guilty pleasures. They tasted as if they had been bathed in butter, a flavor I now know comes from a cook who understands how to use fish sauce.

From teeny tubs of homemade yogurt after morning walks in my local park to midnight *pho* at an old Viet Cong hangout on Pasteur Street, food nurtured every aspect of my life in Vietnam. It cradled my relationships, not only with people, but also with the country, no matter how simple the dish.

Among my favorite meals was one I often indulged in when I woke early. There is a particular quiet in Vietnam that can be found only just before the day starts up with its motorcycle engines and chit-chatting street vendors, and I would toss on a T-shirt, shorts, and flip-flops and walk out into it. First, I went next door, to the rickety wooden lean-to attached to The Cave, where a very old man lived, his only furniture a hammock that he slept in most of the day. To support himself, he sold small, fresh baguettes from a basket each morning. Soon enough he got used to me, and he did not even bother to roll over in his hammock for our exchange of a thousand-dong note (about eight cents) for a warm loaf of bread.

Carrying the bread rubber-banded in newspaper, I shuffled the two or three steps across the lane to the corner shop, which was not a shop in any sense I had known before, but a niche in a wall where a woman rolled up a wooden awning and squatted on a shelf, surrounded by household necessities and a tray of eggs that had been gathered within the hour. I bought an egg and returned to The Cave, where I fried it, tucked it into the warm bread, and splashed it with soy sauce. Then I wandered to the shelf of cement that separated my house from the lane, squatted down across from an ancient woman squatting in her own doorway across from me, ate my sandwich, and watched as another day in Vietnam began.

During those four years in Vietnam, even though I consider myself a foodie, I did not learn how to cook a single Vietnamese dish. It wasn't for lack of interest. It's just that my mind and heart were preoccupied. I was writing a novel. I was navigating a relationship. I was building friendships. I was torturing myself with unsuccessful stop-and-start efforts to learn the language. I was discovering myself as an entirely new person living in a foreign land. Also, I could just walk out my front door at any hour of the day and trade a few cents for an amazing bowl of beef noodle soup spiked with cinnamon and star anise, or wander around the corner for the best home cooking in Vietnam.

Not long after I returned to America, I felt the ache that accompanies missing something very much. I missed the food of Vietnam, and the casual, conversational, make-yourself-at-home lifestyle that revolved around it. Although I was enjoying more than my share of wonderful meals with family and friends, I longed to sit down over a great big Vietnamese meal with those who were closest to me.

Having settled in Los Angeles meant that I was just north of Little Saigon, the largest Vietnamese community outside of Vietnam, where Duyen, the oldest of my Vietnamese sisters, had recently moved with her new husband. We would meet up for a *banh cuon* breakfast (minced pork in rice paper) or *bun thit heo nuong* for lunch (grilled pork on a bed of noodles), but because of typical L.A. freeway traffic, it was usually an hour-long drive each way, rather than just a quick, entertaining jaunt on my bicycle, and the restaurants were always tucked into strip malls, not wide-open to the busy, noisy streets like they were in the real Saigon. As my hunger grew, I began to realize that in order to get what I wanted, I needed to learn to make the food myself.

I bought cookbooks. I tried recipes. Things tasted fine, but nothing satisfied me. I even took a Vietnamese cuisine class at the New School of Cooking, but although I now knew how to make barbecued beef wrapped in rice paper and sea bass broiled in banana leaves, the yearning remained. Finally, it hit me. It wasn't any old Vietnam from a website or L.A. cooking class that I wanted to share with my loved ones. It was *my* Vietnam, and so that was where I had to go. I didn't plan on becoming an expert chef. Just expert enough to create a meal that I could serve in my own home in America.

I started researching cooking classes in Vietnam, little knowing the consuming curiosity this would induce. The more I researched, the hungrier I grew, not just to learn to cook a Vietnamese meal for my friends, but to know everything there is to know about Vietnamese food. I devoured books whole in one sitting and spent hours online. I learned the names of chefs, restaurant owners, winemakers, and even poets dedicated to the pleasures of the Vietnamese table. I grew fascinated with Vietnam's culinary past—the way that the country's food reflected its complex history—and curious about its future. Through its food, I realized that I could understand more than just the country's flavors. I could understand its culture, traditions, geography, and people. I wanted to gather everything I was discovering and put it all in a book. And I continued to crave more of the meals that had caused me to fall in love with Vietnam in the first place.

I began plotting a trip, which would begin in the north in Hanoi and wind down to my former home of Saigon in the south. I contacted chefs. I made lists of markets. I discovered a regional dish called *com hen* (clam rice) in the former imperial city of Hue and added it to my "must eat" list, along with *ragu* in the old French hill town of Dalat. One contact led to another, and I scheduled a class with the "Julia Child of Vietnam," dinner with the granddaughter of the chef of Vietnam's last emperor, a fish sauce tasting in the small beach town of Phan Thiet, and an entire day with my own Vietnamese mother, who would teach me to make the very spring rolls I had eaten for my first meal in her house. I decided that my younger sister, Julie, who had already photographed one book for me, should come along and take pictures. What better person to accompany me than the one I had eaten more meals with than any other in my life? Then it worked out that my dear friend Huong would join us for much of the trip to help translate. What better person for this than the one I had eaten countless meals with in Vietnam?

My first four years in Vietnam were a grand adventure, and I never thought I would be lucky enough to have such an experience there again. But ten years and four months after I first arrived in Vietnam, I returned to renew my relationship with the country I loved so much. More than one hundred years ago, in *The Physiology of Taste*, the gourmet Jean Anthelme Brillat-Savarin wrote, "Tell me what you eat, and I will tell you what you are." As I stepped off the airplane onto the tarmac in Hanoi, I lifted my face to the familiar humid air. *Tell me, Vietnam.*

Hanoi

Northern Vietnam

Hanoi•

•Hue
•Hoi An

•Nha Trang
•Dalat
•Phan Thiet
•Saigon

Open Your Eyes

When I was living in Saigon, I had a little market I liked to call my own. Cho Tan Dinh was just a ten-minute walk from my house. But I must confess that I never seriously investigated its mysterious herbs and vegetables. Nor did I gather up its bursting red chilies, fragrant garlic, and leafy mustard greens and take them back to my windowless kitchen, to wash them in the uneven tiled floor trench that served as a sink and experiment with them in a sauté of fish sauce on my two-burner gas stovetop.

Instead, on the day I moved away from Vietnam, the country's produce, when not presented as a fait accompli on a friend's table or at one of the food stalls at the end of my lane, was, for the most part, uncharted territory for me. I had adored my market and meandered its humid aisles nearly every day in search of bouillon, canned white beans, or Earl Grey tea—the comforts of home that I couldn't get on the streets. I used its familiar carrots, spring onions, and tomatoes to make vegetable soups that tasted as if they had been kissed by sunlight, and once I even dared to buy some skinny eggplants and concoct a kind of ratatouille, which I spread on slices of freshly baked baguette. But that was the extent of my culinary creativity. I didn't linger over Vietnam's exotic green leaves and wonder what I could turn them into. At that time in my life, I was too busy wondering what I was going to turn myself into. But with my return to Vietnam, my relationship with Vietnamese markets was about to change.

If I really wanted to understand Vietnam's cuisine, I needed to understand its markets—the intimate relationship between raw ingredients and each dish. My long-standing, nonchalant you-do-your-thing-I'll-do-mine enjoyment of the country's produce wasn't enough. That was why I chose to spend the first morning of my culinary rebirth with Didier Corlou, exploring a market in Hanoi.

Overseeing the pair of acclaimed restaurants at the Hotel Sofitel Metropole Hanoi, the French-born Didier came to Vietnam in 1990. His romance with the country included both a local chef, whom he soon married, and the local food, resulting in a career dedicated to the preservation of Vietnamese culinary traditions. Even though he was not Vietnamese, he was considered the country's foremost authority on its food, and it was a bonus for me that he spoke English. I had read in magazines and newspapers about his "inspired flair" and "remarkable devotion," and how he was "a mad scientist" and "enthusiastic, respected, fanatical, noisy, and passionate." I had read so much that I was understandably nervous. Meeting him face-to-face felt like going on a blind date with a person my friends had told me too much about.

Because Vietnamese markets spark to life at daybreak, our tour was scheduled for 7:00 a.m. Jetlagged and a little shaken from flying in the day before on the corrugated currents of Typhoon Damrey, Julie and I struggled to get out of bed. Our sluggish start ruled out stopping by the hotel café for breakfast.

"Even coffee?" Julie asked wistfully, having searched our hotel room and discovered that while it offered much by way of colonial charm, it did not have a coffeemaker.

I looked at the pretty bamboo clock and shook my head. "Sorry."

"So close and yet so far away. I've been craving Vietnamese coffee for weeks."

"I know." It was the best coffee I'd ever tasted, without a trace of bitterness. "Me too."

The Metropole was generously hosting us in one of the elegantly restored rooms in its historic wing, and we had only to walk downstairs for our meeting with Didier. We managed to make it to the lobby a little before seven. He had arrived even earlier. The first word I thought of when I saw him was "motion." Dressed in his kitchen whites, he was conferring with a member of his staff, and despite the early hour, he was talking as fast as a person can possibly talk, his arms keeping pace with his words. He was one of those people who would surely be struck mute if his hands were tied behind his back.

Didier was in his late forties and had the short, stocky body typical of the rugged Breton coast where he grew up. His hair and eyes were dark, and his skin flushed, as if from the heat of the kitchen. Because of his reputation, I feared a degree of standoffishness. After all, he had fed the world's leaders, including those from Vietnam's champions (Putin and Castro), as well as its former invaders (Chirac and Clinton). But he introduced himself as if continuing an unfinished conversation.

"And it is good to check on the fish," he said to Julie and me, heading out the door. "There hasn't been any seafood for five days because of the typhoon. This way, this way, over here." He motioned to a trio of cyclos.

Related to the rickshaw, a cyclo is a three-wheeled vehicle, in which the driver pedals behind the passenger, who sits in a bucket seat. As we climbed in, Julie glanced at me and smiled. How many times when she visited me in Vietnam had we spent a pleasant hour cruising around in cyclos? Being in them now felt symbolic. With Didier beside us explaining the disruption the typhoon had caused to his menus, and the tires of our cyclos whirring on the pavement, this trip that we had been talking about for months was officially underway.

There was little traffic as we passed the French-colonial-era buildings that sit with nostalgic dignity along the wide, tree-lined boulevards of Hanoi's central district. The air was honey-sweet from the powdery white blossoms of the *hoa sua* trees. Julie's cyclo fell back, and when I looked for her, her face was obscured by her camera. All I could see was her black T-shirt, red skirt, and long brown hair. Although she hadn't gotten her cup of coffee, she was alert, already absorbed in the details of the waking city.

A woman drifted near my cyclo on her old Chinese bicycle, a pot of bougainvillea strapped to the rack over the back tire. As she floated beside me, I could imagine the soft, green fragrance of the leaves. A checked scarf was tied over her nose and mouth, to protect her from motorbike exhaust, but when she looked at me, I could see her greeting in the curve of her eyes. I nodded good morning. She tipped her head before pedaling on, along the current of golden morning light, and I was reminded of why I had fallen instantly in love with this country when I first arrived. I had felt welcomed everywhere I went.

Our cyclos rolled to the curb outside Cho 19/12, the December 19 Market, which was named after the day in 1946 when the Vietnamese began their resistance against the French. This was appropriate, since a famine was one of the driving forces behind the rebellion. Julie and I were still climbing out of our cyclos as Didier moved toward the market's Soviet-style cement-block entrance, talking all the while. "My first time coming here was 1991. It was love at first sight. Back then, it was a black market."

Quickly, he walked inside, through an aisle of open stalls crammed with sundries, and I experienced déjà vu looking at the same Pantene shampoo, expired Nice 'n Easy hair dye, and watered-down Vaseline Intensive Care lotion that I had bought at my own market when I lived in Saigon. The scuffed tile floors were familiar, as were cubicles that seemed to overflow one into the next with brands I had resigned myself to buying because the ones I wanted weren't available. As we reached the produce area, I recognized the corroding hoses winding dangerously across the walkways, the fierce cleavers and aging scales and stark fluorescent lights. I marveled as I often did at the feeling of permanence, even though the market was made of crumbling cement and pitted tin propped up with rotting wood beams and rusty metal bars. But there was no time to reminisce if I wanted to keep up with Didier's rapid steps and speech.

I was still tuning my ear to his Gallic accent when he stopped at a stall, where wild little bundles of herbs were piled on a weathered wooden plank. The middle-aged woman behind the hills of greenery did not even glance at us as Didier plucked one of her *rau ram* leaves and said, "Herbs are the cuisine. In Vietnam, every herb has its dish." He pointed to the razor-edged leaves of the saw coriander in his hand and then to a banded bunch of feathery dill on a counter. "Dill is only in the north, with fish."

He crushed the *rau ram* between his thumb and middle finger and pressed the bruised leaf into my palm. His skin, like the air in the market, was hot and damp. I held the leaf to my nose and inhaled, recognizing the watery fragrance, although I wasn't sure why. "What is it used for?" I asked.

He rattled off a list of foods in Vietnamese, including *cha gio* and *banh xeo*. Spring rolls and shrimp crepes. The cozy flavors of these familiar fried dishes came to me, along with the cool, spicy taste of *rau ram*, which is served on a side platter among the many raw herbs and lettuces used to balance the weight and heat of such recipes. With Julie clicking away behind me, I stepped around the soupy water in the low depressions of the market's tiles and followed Didier, whose thin hair was lank against his forehead and whose temples were glossy with sweat. It wasn't even eight, but the market was obscenely hot. His whites, though, remained immaculate and his energy unflagging. I chased his words as if they were beads of mercury spinning through water. Picking up a stub of ginger, he declared, "You can tell its age, the same as with a person, by the elasticity of its skin." Sweeping his hand over a pile of galangal: "A natural complement to dog meat." Plucking an angry brown crab from a bucket: "My wife insists the female has more flavor than the male." High on my success of recognizing the *rau ram* leaf—maybe I wasn't so ignorant after all—I absorbed every word, dreaming of one fine day when I would know a Vietnamese market as well as he did.

We had drifted from the produce to the seafood area, where every surface was splashed with water and many of the creatures in their plastic containers were still alive. With their soft tiger stripes, prawns as translucent as glass lay piled in little bins, and one table held basket after basket of shiny brown snails. Small flat crabs tinted an astonishing shade of electric blue clambered atop one another in a wide pink tub. Catfish gaped open-mouthed, whiskers twitching, as if incredulous to find themselves so far from a river. Didier stopped to flick a frog's leg. "If it's fresh, it must ping," he insisted, moving on before I could ask him what "ping" meant. Peering over the old-fashioned wire-rimmed glasses that had slipped down the bridge of his round nose, he proudly pointed out "Madame Diep, queen of the fish market." The weathered old woman was sitting solemnly on a wooden chair held together with strips torn from a plastic bag. He checked one of her fish for what he called "glue" in its gills, and then noticed that he was still holding an herb in one hand. He pinched its odor loose, and in one of his energetic bursts, nearly stuffed it up my nose.

"To cook Vietnamese cuisine," he told us, earnestly, "you must know the product. Attitude is important. My attitude is very important. I work with what I have. I respect my environment. This is important not only when it comes to food, but in general, for life. This is something you must have inside you."

Although Didier's career required him to be indoors, his cheeks were ruddy, and I could just as easily imagine him out on a fishing boat as I could in front of a stove. I was developing a crush on this man who was so passionate about food. How could I not? What woman doesn't feel even the smallest flutter for a man who knows his way around a kitchen, let alone believes that a market is a metaphor for life?

I looked around and saw a decrepit electric fan strapped to a steel pillar with rusty wire. A clump of plastic bags hung from a hook on the wire, along with an old plastic pitcher. The fan was plugged into a socket half underwater, but it was not turned on, and the woman beneath it fanned herself with a piece of damp cardboard. This could have been a tableau from my own Cho Tan Dinh in Saigon. I found myself taking great comfort in the unchanging landscape of Vietnam's markets; in Didier's affection for them; and in being there with my sister, who had not put her camera down since we'd left the Metropole. Every once in a while she looked at me as if to say, "Do you think he'll ever hold still?" Just as I was having a hard time keeping track of Didier's words, she was having a hard time keeping him in focus, but we wouldn't have wanted him any other way. "Crazy charming," was how we later described him.

As we rounded a corner and returned to the produce, passing dead trussed pigs and plucked chickens hanging by their feet, his attention flew to yet another vendor in yet another stall, and he told us that he bought his lemongrass from her. "She grows it herself, you can see, do you see? It is small. Even though Chinese garlic is imported, garlic from Vietnam is more expensive because it's smaller. The Vietnamese, they understand. Chicken." He flung his hand back toward the poultry aisles. "Tomatoes." His head tipped toward glistening tomatoes the size of eggs. "Everything. Most foreigners want bigger, because bigger means better, but the Vietnamese know, with the small there is more flavor."

I thought about how I always chose the biggest golden delicious apple, Texas grapefruit, or Walla Walla sweet onion. I felt very American. Usually, this did not embarrass me, since living in Vietnam had cured me of the Communism-is-romantic/capitalism-is-evil college conceit. But this was one of those moments when I was humbled by it, even though Didier did not know that I am a "big fruit" eater. Nor would he, since I didn't plan on telling him.

"The difference between chefs around the world and chefs in Vietnam is *terroir*. The land, the *terroir*, is the product, do you understand?" He placed his hand over a potato, still gritty with the dirt of the Red River Delta. "I am in Vietnam. I must respect the pureness of the gastronomy."

Feeling sorry for my processed, bigger-is-better, preservative-filled American self, I mumbled, "It's so much easier here. At home, it's hard. We don't have—"

Sharply, he cut me off. "Everywhere there is much. You must learn to open your eyes."

His reprimand stung, but he had already forgotten it, captivated by a bin of star anise. He grabbed a small constellation of the dried brown spice. He held one out and invited me to examine it. "This is from the border of Vietnam and China. Young couples plant a star anise tree when the woman becomes pregnant. Fifteen years later, the tree is grown, and they sell anise to pay for the child's school."

I took the spice from Didier and rolled its sharp, parched petals between my fingers. I held it to my nose and breathed in the sweet, dusty smell. I looked around at the platters and baskets made of plastic and cane, piles of bitter melon, tamarind pods, mango, and chili like red flames within the endless green. I caught sight of a counter laden with tub after tub of rice. So many different kinds of rice, each with its own purpose and even its own legend. Despite my triumphant *rau ram* leaf moment, I wondered if I would ever reach a point where I understood how to choose rice for a meal.

As a kid, I ate Minute rice soaked in 2 percent milk and sprinkled with C&H sugar and Schilling cinnamon. Earlier, Didier had waxed poetic about the region where the cinnamon he used was gathered. I wasn't even sure if Minute rice actually was rice, and I certainly did not know where Schilling cinnamon was grown. When I was a girl, if you had asked me where spices came from, I would have answered, quite seriously, "A jar."

I gazed around at Vietnamese women picking through baskets of water spinach, spring onions, and *la lot* leaves, earnestly discussing quality and price with the vendors. I was filled with admiration and envy, for their intimacy with the sources of the food they ate. I thought about the foods I loved as a child. Canned Hormel tamales wrapped in buttered Wonder bread. My mother's Betty Crocker spice cake with brown sugar frosting. As a college student I lived on Rice-A-Roni, and I felt sheepish at how many boxes of Kraft macaroni and cheese I bought in my old market in Saigon. How could I possibly understand all of these ingredients that did not come labeled in boxes or cans?

Before despair could set in, my thoughts crept round a corner, and I remembered pies. I could not believe that I had forgotten pies. The raspberries picked by my mom, Julie, and me at U-pick lots all over Washington State. The blackberries picked by my dad. Not the big side-of-the-road blackberries, but the tiny wild ones. He would disappear into the woods for hours at a time, filling Folgers coffee cans hanging from twine over his shoulders. The flaky, golden crusts were made by my mom or my aunt Janice, and just the day before Julie and I flew to Vietnam for our trip, in a dairy town in the Cascade foothills outside Seattle, by my aunt Wilma.

My aunts, uncles, and dozens of cousins had gathered in Carnation for my grammy's memorial. Memorials in my family are always potluck (as are baby showers, wedding showers, and birthdays), and because my aunt Wilma knows how much I like raspberry pie, rather than the blackberry everyone else is so crazy about, she made a special one just for me. But pie in our family is fair game, so I wrapped a piece in foil and hid it behind the TV in the back bedroom, to eat after the service. I thought it was beating my cousin Tim out of that last piece that made it taste so good when I finally ate it, ever so smugly in Grammy's gazebo. Now, as I listened to Didier talk about the origins of each ingredient as if he were talking about the history of people he knew intimately, I could see how much more there was to it.

Like the grassy stalks of asparagus Julie and I had picked alongside irrigation ditches when we lived in Moses Lake, or the crisp apples snapped right off the trees when we lived in Wenatchee (the "Apple Capital of the World"), raspberry pie is a food that ties me to the place where I grew up. The Pacific Northwest. The *terroir* of my youth. Not just the physical *terroir*, but the emotional and spiritual *terroir*, as well. The landscape in which my grammy and all of my other grandparents were raised. Where my mother and father spent their childhoods. Where Julie and I were nurtured in the spirit of our family's history. With the *rau ram* leaves still damp in my palm, I felt a thrill. I had a *terroir*. Already, my eyes were opening, and it wasn't even nine o'clock.

Welcome to Métropole
Cooking Class

Time: 10 am → 13 pm
Teacher: Nguyễn Kim Hải

Menu

1/ Vietnamese banana flower salad
2/ Hanoi deep-fried "nem"
3/ Grilled beef on lemongrass
4/ Grilled pork in bamboo tupe
5/ Steamed fish with beer
6/ Sautéed pumpkin branches with garlic

Hanoi

Good Vietnamese Girls

In the lobby of the Metropole hotel, the heavy green fronds of the potted palms were as motionless as the two uniformed young bellboys flanking the front doors. Well-to-do travelers and businessmen milled around the check-in desk and concierge counter. Outside, the heat expanded with each passing minute, but inside the temperature remained cool and comfortable. My stomach grumbled with hunger. Julie and I had just returned from the market tour, with no time to grab a bite to eat before meeting up with Huong.

Julie went back to our room to get more film for the cooking class we were going to take that day, while I waited eagerly for Huong, who I had seen only twice in the six years since moving away from Vietnam. Despite our time apart, we were still the closest of friends. We met when I was twenty-eight and she was eighteen. She had been working in an embroidery shop that rented black-market movies on the side, using her job as a chance to practice English with the expatriates who came in for copies of Hollywood blockbusters shakily filmed from the back rows of American theaters and straight-to-video bombs no one had ever heard of back in the States. We chatted whenever I dropped in, and one day she offered to help me. Despite its fledgling embrace of capitalism, Vietnam was still very much a Communist country back then, and it was during the Marxist nightmare of trying to get towels embroidered for my Australian boyfriend's company golf tournament that Huong and I became friends. Among the many things we had in common, we discovered a love of eating, as well as a lack of natural talent in the kitchen.

The first time she stayed at my house, she announced that she was going to make her "specialty" for me for dinner. The front door was padlocked, the curtains drawn, and the Cranberries nearly inaudible on the stereo, because I hadn't registered to have an overnight guest with the neighborhood police, and I didn't want to get evicted for breaking the law. With pluck that put Julia Child to shame, Huong showed me how to open a can of corn and simmer the mushy yellow buds in water with a dab of margarine. She boiled a packet of instant ramen and added fresh chili. "The secret ingredient," she explained.

At some point, we heard pounding on the metal grate that served as a front door. We were sure that one of the lane's informants had tipped off my archenemy, the local policeman, who was a bitter, underpaid civil servant with beer breath and a chin mole that sprouted a foot-long hair. Huddled over the pan of corn, we kept clear of the windows and tried not to laugh, because we didn't want him to hear us and become even angrier than he no doubt already was. Finally, he gave up, and Huong and I howled with laughter before she served our meal on the coffee table in the living room.

Tucking into the ramen and canned corn, I studied my plate and said, "I have to be honest. I was expecting something a little more, well, Vietnamese. I thought all good Vietnamese girls know how to cook."

Smirking, she said, "Who said I am good?"

Huong has never lived that dinner down, even though by the time I moved back to America she had taught herself how to make a terrific Thai beef salad to impress dates. Her cooking skills were not all that had evolved over the years. In the early days of our friendship, she slouched around in rugby shirts and baggy overalls. Now, just off the plane from Saigon, walking toward me in the lobby of the Metropole, she wore a pair of fitted black capris with a backless orange silk blouse.

Despite her sophisticated look and her current job with Ogilvy & Mather, her smile was still the same. Engaging, and with a frisky hint of an underbite that set her apart from every other pretty Vietnamese girl her age. It was the smile that used to greet me every time I walked into the Kim Phuong embroidery shop to find out what new B movie had made its way into Vietnam. As I approached, she held out her arms and said, "You're going to cry, aren't you, darling?"

She knew me well. I cried, just a little, because I was tired and hungry, and because it felt so good to be back in Vietnam.

Huong and I are not the kind of friends who need to get used to one another after time apart, but it would have been nice to sit down and eat a meal together before we had to start working. There was no chance for that, though. We were scheduled for our cooking lesson at eleven. My focus in Hanoi was mainly on Vietnam's restaurant culture, but we were taking this one class in the capital city at the invitation of Didier.

Because of his heavy schedule, the class was led by his second-in-command, a middle-aged woman named Madame Hai. Julie, Huong, and I met her in a demonstration area in the depths of the hotel, which opened onto the kitchen that served Spices Garden and Le Beaulieu restaurants. The kitchen had the sort of stainless steel appliances and ample counters I dreamed about in my cramped little walk-through space back in Los Angeles. It was the kind I envied on television cooking shows, but with a few homey Vietnamese twists: a pair of heavy, charred woks and a crude, branchlike whisk, evidence of Didier's love of what he called "the kitsch" of Vietnamese kitchen tools.

Julie and her camera hovered in the background, while Huong and I took seats at a classroom table facing Madame Hai, who stood behind a metal counter. The white tiled walls were hung with framed, multilingual articles about the Metropole's restaurants, the cooking class, and Didier. We were given a packet of recipes that included the familiar, such as Hanoi deep-fried spring rolls, beef on lemongrass, and sautéed pumpkin branches with garlic, and a few that were new to me, including marinated pork grilled in bamboo, steamed fish with beer and herbs, and banana flower salad. I wondered how long the class was going to take. I was starving, and we had been told that we would eat everything that Madame Hai prepared for lunch.

Reading through the recipes, I noted ingredients that might be difficult to find in Los Angeles—perfumed mushrooms, probably, and the pumpkin branches—as well as those that nearly every dish had in common: garlic, chili, and fish sauce. The ingredients had already been measured out, with a small tray set up for each recipe. Madame Hai, too, looked as if she had been readied for us, with her tall paper chef's hat, fitted white jacket, and cloth wrapped like a dashing cravat around her neck. Her hair was tied into a low bun, and she wore discreet gold hoops in her ears.

She began with the banana flower salad, explaining in soft-spoken Vietnamese the mixing of chili, crushed peanuts, sesame seeds, and *rau ram* herb for the dressing. Despite the fact that the Metropole's cooking class was the most high profile in the country, Madame Hai was unlike any cooking teacher I knew from schools or television shows back home. Although she was pleasant, she was quite reserved. She seldom smiled, and there were spans of time as she cut the chicken meat or marinated the star fruit in a bit of sugar when she did not speak at all. In the hush of our classroom, I began to feel as if I had crept into her home and was peeking round a corner, spying on her as she gently peeled back the violet outer layer of a teardrop-shaped banana flower to reveal the white bulb within.

In this demonstration class setting, I found my mind wandering in a way not possible in a hands-on class, where my attention would have been preoccupied with an attempt to replicate Madame Hai's expert slicing of the banana flower bulb into thin, concentric rings. I was thinking not just about the dish, but about Madame Hai. She seemed to be in her late forties or early fifties, about twenty years older than Huong, of a generation of females that cooked because it was an integral and expected part of a woman's life. Traditionally in Vietnam, a girl did not learn how to make banana flower salad in a classroom, or even from a recipe book. She learned it at her mother's side. By watching, by doing, and by repeating during the course of daily cooking.

I could envision Madame Hai in the market we had toured with Didier that morning, seeking the most delicate stalks of lemongrass, the most fragrant little cloves of garlic. The skill of choosing the freshest fish would have come into her life as naturally as puberty. Perhaps this was the reason for her lack of polish in the classroom. How do you explain a skill to others that you have never needed to explain to yourself? Also, cooking instruction was a new, artificial activity in Vietnam, unlike in America, where many women my age and younger didn't pick up kitchen basics at home, and where learning from TV shows has become a way of life. Watching Madame Hai douse the marinated fish in a can of 333 beer while she quietly explained, as if to herself, that she was going to steam it along with julienned leek, carrots, and celery, I could only imagine how much harder it must be to teach in a language that is not your own, and also from a perspective developed in a country that was closed off for decades from the Western world and its culinary expectations.

Madame Hai's paradigm was so different from that of her foreign students, particularly the Americans and English accustomed to chefs who were celebrities, cheerleaders, and quasi-confidantes all at the same time. Through Huong I learned that she had worked at the Metropole since 1978, which meant that she cooked in this kitchen—or some form of it—during Vietnam's first years united under Communist rule. She cooked here during the country's postwar shortages and failed socialist agricultural experiments and gradual but uneven exposure to the West. Although she was too modest to say it, she was more than just a teacher for entertainment-seeking tourists. When it came to food, she was historically significant. She was among the few who had cooked professionally during one of Vietnam's most difficult culinary eras.

I wondered what it had been like, but no matter how much I wanted to ask if she ever felt conflicted, cooking for government fat cats and visiting Eastern European diplomats while thousands died of starvation, I wouldn't. I couldn't. What was considered normal journalism in America was more than just rude in Vietnam. Most anywhere in Asia, asking such a direct, confrontational question would cause the person being asked to lose face. I knew enough about Vietnam's struggles after the war to know that Madame Hai did not deserve to lose face because of my curiosity. I knew more than enough about its individual hardships, beginning with the friend sitting next to me.

For all that Huong and I had eaten and laughed about and shopped for together, she didn't invite me to her home until I had been living in Saigon for nearly three years. I had seen the impoverished houses of my neighbors and a few of my students, but Huong was so savvy, modern, and generous that I was not prepared for the meager, two-room apartment with scarcely any furniture that she shared with her mom and stepsister. By that time Huong was already a close friend, but the moment I was served a simple meal on her living room floor, the moment she allowed me to see the genuine poverty that was the reality of her daily life, our friendship shifted and became something deeper, irrevocable.

The years after the American war were harsh to the Vietnamese, and twenty years later, when I came to learn to cook, many people were still recovering, if not financially, then emotionally and spiritually. Who was I—a woman raised on milk and beef and all the vegetables I could possibly want, and often as a little girl didn't—to question the sober rather than dog-and-pony teaching skills of a chef whose country included a recent history of famine? No matter how noble my intentions were, I could not bring myself to question her conscience for taking a good job when times were tough.

Finally, the food was ready, and we gathered around the table to eat. The fish was delicate in its soft steam of beer and dill. The pork was grassy and sweet from being encased in bamboo. The beef rang with the zest of lemongrass and ginger, and the deep-fried spring rolls were both hearty and light, with their blend of black mushrooms, sweet turnip, bean sprouts, and young papaya. Sautéed pumpkin branches delivered the healthy satisfaction that only dark green vegetables can provide, but it was the banana flower salad that won our hearts. And it was Julie who won the salad, while I was off guard, happily recognizing the flavor of the *rau ram* leaf among its chopped herbs.

She had put her camera down and was eating any of the dishes that did not include beef and pork. She had been a quasi-vegetarian since she was a little girl, making her preferences known by stuffing baloney sandwiches down the toilet or feeding them to her horse. "This one," she murmured, claiming the salad. "I want to learn to make this one."

There was a chalky texture to the crisp banana flower rings. They tasted clean, a tabula rasa where traditional ingredients come to mingle: lime juice, fish sauce, and the sour star fruit that was in season while we were there. Pepper and chili kept our taste buds alert, and because of the chopped peanuts and sesame seeds mingling among the rings, variations of crunchiness were layered within each bite.

"It's fresh," Huong commented with wonder, as if she did not eat fresh Vietnamese food every single day.

"Have you ever had it before?" I asked her.

"Yes, but not like this. Madame Hai really knows what she's doing."

"I hope we can get banana flower at the Bangkok Market," Julie said, referring to a grocery store near our apartment in Los Angeles that sold Vietnamese ingredients.

Wistfully, I took another bite of banana flower salad. Not only had Julie and I eaten thousands of meals together but we had also cooked countless meals together, and somehow over the years we had fallen into an arrangement. If I made a dish, she didn't. If she made a dish, I didn't. We each had our specialties. Because we lived together and went to most of the same dinner parties, we rarely overlapped. I knew from the look of concentration on her face that the salad already belonged to her. At least I had the consolation of knowing that when it came to cooking, Julie always gave it her best effort. If anyone was up to the task of channeling a good Vietnamese girl and re-creating the intricate beauty of Madame Hai's dish back in America, my sister was.

Julie's Banana Flower Salad

Using recipes from our cooking classes at the Metropole in Hanoi and the Cargo Club Cooking School in Hoi An as a base, Julie perfected this salad. Highlighted by the hot-tart play of chili and lime off the crisp rings of the banana flower, it is a refreshing dish that is perfect for a hot summer day. If banana flowers are unavailable, a good substitute is peeled and shredded green papaya.

SALAD INGREDIENTS:
2 banana flowers, thinly sliced (see directions)
2 tbsp. peanut oil
Scant 1/4 cup shallot, coarsely chopped
1/2 cup roasted peanuts, chopped
1/2 cup fresh mint, coarsely chopped
1/2 cup fresh Thai basil, coarsely chopped
3 tbsp. lime juice + 1 lime for the bowl of water
Large bowl of room temperature water

DRESSING INGREDIENTS:
3 tbsp. lime juice
2 tsp. brown sugar
1 red Thai chili, chopped
2 tsp. fish sauce
2 cloves garlic, chopped

DIRECTIONS:

1. Heat the peanut oil in a large skillet. Sauté the shallots until golden brown. Leave them in the oil, and set aside to cool.
2. Squeeze fresh lime juice into the bowl of water. This will be used to prevent the banana flower slices from turning brown.
3. Peel back the dark purple layers of the banana flower until you reach layers with just a hint of purple. Using a mandoline, slice the banana flower into thin rings, beginning at the point and slicing about three-quarters of the way down. The rings will look similar to onion rings. Immediately soak the rings in the lime water until ready to use. Set aside.
4. Once the oil is cool, mix in half of the mint leaves and half of the Thai basil with the sautéed shallots.
5. Mix the dressing ingredients in a separate bowl. Heat lovers will want to add more chili.
6. When you slice the banana flower, you will end up with small bits from the center of the flower. Strain these out using a spoon. Don't worry if you don't get all of them. Remove the banana flower from the water, and combine with the shallot/mint/basil mixture, chopped peanuts, and remainder of the fresh mint and basil.
7. Toss in the dressing, and serve.

Serving: 4 as a side or 2 as a main dish for lunch.

ARÔME CUISINE
Badiane
55°
Echantillon
KUMQUAT 29°
Fût de chêne
08.04
Arôme renforcé

Delicious Flavor

As I sat through Madame Hai's class, I was grateful for the research I had done before my trip. Along with all of its ingredients, Vietnamese food is a product of history, geography, and even a bit of science, and the more a person knows about any of this, the more satisfying it is to learn to make each dish.

Typically, Vietnam's long S-shape is compared to a traditional *don ganh*, a yoke with a basket hanging from each end that resembles the scales of justice. Street vendors carry the *don ganh* balanced over one shoulder, and although it is not used much in the cities these days, it is still common in rural areas, to convey vegetables, fruit, and even small, itinerant coffee or soup cafés. The baskets are said to represent the Red River Delta in the north and the Mekong Delta in the south, where rice crops are grown. The yoke illustrates the mountainous central region.

The idea of Vietnam as a culinary triptych, with distinct southern, central, and northern territories, has been emphasized to me by everyone from my former students to my old cyclo driver. I do not know when this view originated. Over the past few thousand years, the country's partitions have shifted regularly. What is known as present-day Vietnam came into being for the first time only under the Nguyen Dynasty in 1802. Not long after that, it was taken over by the French. Then it split in two with the dissolution of French Indochina in 1954, and was once again reunited under a Communist government in 1975. This, though, is only political flux. Through it all, geography and microclimates remained static.

During the course of my culinary exploration of Vietnam, I planned to visit all three regions. Of the three, I was most familiar with the south, which is home to Saigon; somewhat familiar with the center, where I had done a bit of traveling; and least familiar with the north and Hanoi, where I had been only once before. Unlike the balmy south, the north gets a fiercely cold and damp winter. Because of this, and because the north borders China, it offers more stir-fried dishes and hearty soups and stews. Different landscape and climate mean that pepper gives heat to food in the north, while chilies are more common in the south. And less agricultural variety in the north means that food is simpler there. For example, *pho*, which originated in Hanoi, is the country's ubiquitous noodle soup. In Hanoi it is not typically garnished with herbs, unlike in the more plentiful south where it is eaten with *mui ta* (long coriander) and *hung* (basil), as well as bean sprouts.

Poetic types will claim that the soil of the Red River Delta is responsible for the rich flavor of northern veggies, making Hanoi food better than any other in the country. In the "garden city" of Dalat in central Vietnam, exceptional flavor is attributed to the cool air and altitude. In the south, the abundance of spices and sweeter flavors, products of the early spice-trade routes, are the key. It is always fun to ask my Vietnamese friends about the cuisine of their hometowns, particularly if more than one region is represented at the table. Most Vietnamese I know are inherent foodies, and while they all appreciate the cuisines of other areas, they inevitably champion the dishes they grew up with, just as in the United States those of us from the Pacific Northwest defend our alder-smoked salmon and Southerners argue for their fried chicken.

One of the things that makes Vietnamese food interesting is that despite clear regional distinctions, there is a common denominator in most dishes. Part of this is due to the philosophy of umami. Originating in Japan, the word *umami* translates literally into "delicious flavor." Having captured the imaginations of Western cooks in recent years, umami is considered the palate's fifth food sense, an amplification of the basic four: salty, sweet, sour, and bitter.

Umami was formally identified and given its name in the early 1900s by Dr. Kikunae Ikeda of Tokyo Imperial University, who extracted glutamate from *konbu* (kelp) and found that this active ingredient gave the plant its intensified flavor. Glutamate is found naturally in a wide variety of foods, from mushrooms to the milk of cows, goats, and sheep. As well, its function as umami is the principle behind products developed as flavor enhancers, the most well-known being MSG. Others include ketchup, because tomatoes have a strong concentration of glutamate, and Worcestershire, whose umami factor is caused by the anchovies that are among its ingredients, making it distant kin to that most essential element in Vietnamese cooking: fish sauce.

That said, umami cannot exist in a dish just by including a glutamate-laced ingredient. I don't think anyone would argue that French fries become a perfectly balanced food simply by being doused in ketchup. And no one in her right mind would dump fish sauce on any food to bring out its essential flavor. The magic in fish sauce is that just a few drops of something that smells so terrible, blended with a little chili and lime, can give even a mild strand of banana blossom clarity. Umami is about the incisive harmonizing of a dish's ingredients, and Vietnamese food is about finding the alchemy—the umami—in each dish. Therein lies the art.

Add to this the freshness of the ingredients and the synchronicity of soft, crunchy, silky, and chewy, and you have the beauty of Vietnamese food. There are few experiences more satisfying than sitting at a sidewalk table watching early morning traffic pass by, taking a bite of *banh cuon* steaming off the grill, and letting the layered flavors of this savory crepe work their way over your tongue. Testing the chewiness of the soft rice-flour paper that is wrapped so snugly around the filling. Lingering over the fragile crunch of fried shallots against the mushrooms and minced pork. Catching your breath at the electrifying snap of chili.

To understand these basic inner workings of Vietnamese food is to begin to understand how even the simplest dish represents a perfect life: balanced and refined. Grasping the foundations enabled us to replicate Madame Hai's banana flower salad—even though we weren't clear on all of her instructions— once we were back home in our own kitchen, far from the markets of Vietnam, using hand-raked salt from the Camargue, chilies from an El Salvadoran market down the street, and *nuoc mam* smuggled back in our suitcase, despite Vietnam Airline's ban on carrying firearms, drugs, and fish sauce onto its planes. It was also necessary, as I would learn from Didier, for appreciating not only where a cuisine has come from but also where it can go.

Didier leaned forward in his chair. His hands fiddled with a pen, tapping it against a calendar of upcoming interviews with journalists from South Africa, Thailand, France, and Canada. He declared, "People evolve, yes? Why not the food? *Alors*, don't put it in a museum! Let the young people have a chance to create. Because the country has been closed for so long, the whole world is new to them."

Following a postlunch tour of Didier's garden on a patch of the hotel roof, I had set Julie and Huong free so that I could conduct an "official" interview in his office. Located just off the hotel kitchen, the windowless room was small and very white, its paint and tiles made even brighter by the flickering fluorescent lights overhead. As he talked about the changing face of Vietnamese food, I studied the shelves and a large metal file cabinet that were cluttered with reused glass jars and plastic water bottles, hand-labeled and filled with herbs, spices, and liquid concoctions—ingredients for his experimentations with what he called "aroma cuisine." Other than a few awards hanging on the wall, the office offered nothing to advertise his prestige. It gave no evidence of the immensity of his passions, which he could talk about for hours. He had already waxed poetic about brewing his own fish sauce, which he would infuse with wood ear mushrooms, the way those in the West infuse olive oil with truffles. And he had explained how he was making his own cheese, using milk from a model farm at nearby Ba Vi Mountain, where the goats ate sugar cane and jackfruit leaves. My crush on him was blooming into a more serious form of admiration as he briskly pointed out that when he talked about letting young people create, "Of course, I am talking about innovation, not fusion. Fusion is confusion."

That darling of the modern food world, fusion is credited to chef Wolfgang Puck, who famously created Japanese dishes with California produce and French techniques in the 1980s at his Chinois on Main restaurant in Santa Monica, California. Perhaps the most overrated culinary movement, fusion—despite its basic principle of blending ingredients—is very different from umami. Umami underpins a dish. Its result, and not its orchestration, is what is tasted. Fusion, on the other hand, makes its mixtures clear. As a concept, it anchored nearly every description I had read in newspapers and magazines about Didier's food, which me made all the more fascinated to hear him denounce it.

"Fusion unites the preexisting. Innovation is about creating the new," he explained.

"But so much of Vietnamese food is taken from other cultures. China and Thailand. And Cambodia. I'm not sure I understand the difference," I said.

Ensnared in his own train of thought, he was oblivious to my lack of comprehension. He said, "Naturally, heritage is important, too. Sometimes it feels at risk of being lost." He tossed the pen aside and reached toward the corner of his desk for a plastic jar half-filled with peppercorns. He screwed the lid on, screwed it off, and screwed it on again. "For forty years, gastronomy was not a priority in Hanoi. During the war, nobody had time or resources to think about the value of the cuisine. I talk with the grandmother of Mai, my wife, and she tells me that before 1945 there was a very interesting cuisine here in the north. Now, well." He scowled. "We have museums for culture, arts, paintings. Food should be the same. For the young people, we need to preserve."

"But you just said not to put it in—"

"Phht."

I contemplated his Gallic gust of dismissal. The question his contradiction raised. How can the past and future coexist? This was one of the issues Didier had devoted himself to, and his answer was education. Just a week earlier more than one hundred local and foreign chefs met in Hanoi to discuss the establishment of a chef's association in Vietnam. Its many unprecedented functions would include teaching young professional chefs the foundation of Vietnamese cuisine and providing them access to techniques from around the world so that they could build on that foundation. Didier—no surprise—was one of the instigators of the project.

"I think there will be good chefs in the future. I am not talking about home cooks, but chefs. But it will take time, much time. Look at this beautiful product," he said. He yanked the lid from the jar, and peppercorns sprang into the air, bouncing like tiny black pebbles across his desk and onto the floor. We jumped from our chairs to salvage what we could, and as he crouched beneath his desk he said, "There are eighty million people in this country, and I am the first chef to think of working with this minority spice. This is about a way of thinking." He reemerged, plucked a peppercorn from the corner of his appointment calendar, and thrust it at me.

I bit into it, and instead of the black-pepper taste I was accustomed to, my mouth burned with an acrid, aniselike flavor.

He looked at me expectantly. "Do you understand?"

I imagined him traveling around the country, encountering this spice for the first time, and I thought how quickly his mind must have set to work, envisioning it into his recipes. How exhilarating to know a cuisine so well that he felt such confidence in taking it to the next level. I nodded.

"There are two kinds of chefs," Didier told me, sitting back down, even though there were still stray peppercorns scattered around the office. "Chefs who work, and chefs who mix. It is the same with music and art. Of course, I respect the worker, the guy who makes *pho* on the street, but I like to push Vietnam at the same time. I spent thirty years cooking around the world, but here, it is different. There is so much to work with. Heritage. The ingredients.

After fourteen years in Vietnam, I am still curious." He dropped a handful of peppercorns back into the jar and paused, one of the few times I had seen him hold still that day.

I was grateful for the break as I tried to assimilate what he was telling me about potential with all that I had already learned about the traditions of Vietnamese cuisine.

"The world is big," he finally said, "and we are not finished. The migration of food is good. Food moves. It is alive. Three hundred years ago, you did not have wine in California. I remember in the South Pacific when I first worked with lobster and vanilla. Five years later, chefs in other countries were making scallops with vanilla. Centuries ago, white pepper was considered exotic, but now." He rolled his eyes to indicate how common white pepper had become. "I would like to have one laboratory, just to make my experiments."

"You have Vietnam," I said.

He smiled and nodded in agreement. He rolled a small, hard peppercorn between his thumb and forefinger. "Respect the culture. That is what you must do. Know it, respect it, and then move on. The world changes. Whether for right or wrong, cuisine follows these changes. This is what's coming in Vietnam, this mixed culture, and it's exciting."

Class & Status

There are chronicles of dining establishments serving a variety of foods from written menus as far back as China's Song Dynasty (960–1279), and I unearthed a claim that the oldest still-in-business eatery is a chicken restaurant founded in Kaifeng, China, in 1153. The *Guinness Book of World Records* cites Madrid's Sobrino de Botin as the oldest continuously operating dining establishment in the world, dating back to 1725. But it is the French who usually get the credit for the restaurant as we know it today, because the word originated in Paris when a soup maker set up shop in 1765 and described his selection of potage with the word *restaurer*, which means to restore.

Then in 1782 the first restaurant given credit for an à la carte menu opened in Paris. In tandem with the French Revolution, The Grand Taverne de Londres transformed the world of dining out. With the end of the French monarchy came the breakup of the royal catering guilds. No longer were France's culinary artisans restricted to their specialties. Rather than just prepare roasted meats, a *rotisseur* could now bake a loaf of bread or make a custard, and better yet, this combination of foods could be served to the public in a single venue.

As for the history of restaurants in Vietnam, I was not able to find much. In Vietnam, street stalls and small cafés usually serve a single dish, and restaurants offer a banquet's worth of selections. I assume the country's dining culture took its cues from China and France, both of which wielded great culinary influence during their respective thousand- and hundred-year dominations. I was told that nearly all of Hanoi's restaurants shut down after 1954, when the country declared its independence from France and the Communists' pursuit of nationalism wiped out such bourgeois enterprises. During the American war that followed until 1975, and the lean decade after the war's end, dining out in restaurants in the north, even at street stalls, was almost nonexistent, except for the privileged few and visiting dignitaries, such as those Madame Hai probably cooked for at the Metropole.

It makes sense that restaurants proliferated after the revolution in France as a backlash to absolute authority. There are few more empowering ways of expressing personal freedom than by choosing what and how you eat—rather than letting the state choose for you. Vietnam experienced the same sort of reaction, although it got off to a rocky start. In 1986, after ten years of failed agricultural collectivization attempts, the government introduced *doi moi*, a policy shift intended to loosen the Communist party's tight economic grip. The policy would allow free enterprise—including restaurants—but unlike the French monarchy, whose culinary guilds had produced chefs of exquisite skill, Vietnam's totalitarian government had the opposite effect. It had shut down most of the restaurants, and this, combined with the food shortages and famines that North Vietnam had suffered for four decades, resulted in the neglect of culinary traditions that Didier had mentioned in our interview.

In Hanoi, an entire generation was born into and raised in an environment where food as enjoyment was taboo. Along with restaurants, traditional festivals and celebratory feasts were abolished, and food became a reason for begrudging and mistrusting your neighbor. By the time *doi moi* came along, this malnourished generation was well into adulthood. With few pleasurable food memories, many were unfamiliar with how it felt to simply enjoy a meal.

For imagining what it was like in Hanoi as the 1980s drew to a close, I suggest reading Duong Thu Huong's once-banned-in-Vietnam novel, *Paradise of the Blind*, which takes place in North Vietnam during that era. In one scene, the main character, teenage Hang, brings food from her shopkeeper mother (considered a wicked woman for her mercantile ways) to her aunt and uncle, who are pious Communist party officials. When the aunt serves the food, Hang says, "She gestured to the closed windows. 'So they won't see,' [my aunt said]. I suddenly understood why, when I brought out the gifts, she had shot me the anxious look of a shoplifter. This was the way they lived here, vigilant, spying on each other, each keeping watch over his neighbor. One mouthful too many, and the others might turn you in as a potential threat to the collective."

I cannot fathom what it must have been like to have lived in such an atmosphere. And then, as if roused from a nightmare, to suddenly no longer live with the fear that the escaped odor of contraband chicken would cause a neighbor to report you to the police, when just a year before such a thing was a certainty. What was it like to have spent decades thinking one way, only to be told by the very people who enforced that way of thinking that it was now acceptable, and even encouraged, to think otherwise? To be told—as implied by the policy changes—that the old way of thinking, the very thinking on which you based your life, was flawed?

How greedily and yet suspiciously Hanoi must have approached the buxom fruits and iron-rich vegetables returning to the markets in the late 1980s. The smoky, carnal aroma of grilled pork drifting democratically through the streets. The lascivious availability of nourishment when to be nourished had long been considered a deviancy, proof that you had something tasty to hide.

Those traveling through Vietnam nowadays might have a hard time grasping what the country has been through. Food stalls, stands, and carts populate sidewalks and street corners even in the smallest towns, and upmarket restaurants serving food ranging from tapas to sushi can be found in Hanoi and Saigon. Vietnam is a foodie's paradise of astonishing flavors, colorful markets, and people eating just about everywhere it's possible to set up a stove and a few stools. You cannot interact with a stranger without being invited to share a meal. Even in the middle of the night, if you cruise around most cities, you will find someone tending a vat of steaming broth and a few customers slurping quietly in the dark.

The food revolution happened fast. In 1990, four years after the introduction of the government's official change in policy, Barbara Cohen wrote *The Vietnam Guidebook*, the first English-language guide to the country published after the war. In it she recommended only five restaurants in Hanoi and described eating at the Thang Loi Hotel in the company of "animated Cubans, dour Soviets, and some two hundred thumping Bulgarians." When I arrived in the south just five years later, the country was flourishing. During my first year in Saigon there were more than thirty Japanese restaurants in the city, and as a writer for *Vietnam Today*, I reviewed places serving Swiss, Argentinean, Russian, and even Tex-Mex cuisine.

For me Saturday nights meant choosing from a menu of five different sauces and a small but smart wine list at a favorite French steakhouse near the New World Hotel. Dining out with girlfriends involved the Russian buffet in an elegant old French villa, or Cal-fresh appetizers and jazz at Buffalo Blues. I found comfort in the gooey mac-and-cheese at Brodard on Dong Khoi Street; sustenance at the cart selling grilled pork just outside my guesthouse; and conviviality at the seafood restaurants of Thi Sach Street, which were crowded every Friday night with low-level local government drones blowing their meager paychecks on prawns and beer.

From Buddhist cafés to Russian teahouses to a weekly mosque buffet, I ate out regularly in 1995, and this was not because I was a privileged Westerner. My Vietnamese friends, most of whom were poor, ate out regularly, too. And I knew from reading the Timeout entertainment section of the *Vietnam Investment Review* that people were also dining out—a lot—up north in Hanoi.

In a Communist society, gathering for reasons other than party purposes is a serious hammer-and-sickle no-no. What else do we do in restaurants but gather? Mandy Thomas, PhD, sums it up best in his must-read essay, "Transitions in Taste in Vietnam and the Diaspora." "By eating in imaginative new ways, Vietnamese in Vietnam are resisting state control through the senses ... [They] are eating out and choosing restaurants and foods as a way of marking out class and status." It is intriguing that a country can make a statement about what it is and what it wants simply by the way it eats. Vietnam is a perfect example of how food can not only reflect change but also engender it.

To discover what kind of class and status the Vietnamese were marking out for themselves, I wanted to eat at Restaurant Bobby Chinn. Since its opening in 2002, it had been praised for its "inventive menu" and hailed as "the talk of the town." *The Wall Street Journal Asia* even named it "one of the best Western restaurants in Asia."

By the time Bobby Chinn's arrived, Vietnam already had Didier's inventive menus at the Metropole hotel, plenty of nouvelle Vietnamese bistros, and the aforementioned sushi joints and tapas bars, but arguably chef/owner Bobby Chinn was the first to bring hip-haute dining to Vietnam. It is the kind of experience that has become expected in major metropolises, from New York to

London to Dubai, combining come-hither signature dishes, a svelte ambience, and the chef's charismatic personality. While such things may have been old hat back home in Los Angeles, in Vietnam they represented the new dawn.

A few hours after my interview with Didier, Huong, Julie, and I arrived at Bobby Chinn's for dinner with my publisher, Albert Wen, who had flown in from Hong Kong, and his friend Suzanne Lecht, the owner of Art Vietnam, a prominent Hanoi gallery. They had not yet arrived, so we took seats at the bar and ordered a gentle Pinot Noir from Paso Robles.

"All this way for a wine from Paso," Julie laughed, raising her glass to toast the familiar. Encountering food and drink from halfway around the world always amused us. Paso Robles is just three hours north of Los Angeles, and we drove up there regularly to visit friends and tour the wineries.

We had scarcely taken a few sips when Bobby crossed the bar to greet us. I had not corresponded with him, so he did not know that we were coming, or why we were there, but I recognized him from photographs I had seen online. Half-Egyptian and half-Chinese, he was slender, lithe, and handsome. I was sure that women fell for him regularly, and probably a few men, too. He introduced himself, examined our wine choice, approved of it, and asked us what we were doing in Hanoi. Upon hearing about the book I was writing, he was off and running.

From the lack of skilled waitstaff in Vietnam to the "real cooks" out on Hanoi's city streets, Bobby was very opinionated, as I have discovered that most chefs are. He was a local star. Everyone from a rough-and-tumble Australian building contractor to a pretty Vietnamese-American Fulbright scholar swung by to say hello and bask in his glow during the fifteen minutes of conversation that passed until Albert and Suzanne arrived. Suzanne and Bobby knew one another as certain high-profile expatriates always do and cheek-kissed before he led us to a center-of-attention table on a dais in the middle of the dining area.

Roses were suspended from the ceiling over our table like baroque raindrops, and the space around us was framed in gauzy, artistically knotted curtains. It felt as if we were in a midsummer night's dream. As we admired the stylish decor, I was curious to know if the food would live up to it. I was a bit reluctant about eating at Bobby Chinn's. Vietnam is marvelously skilled at counterfeiting—it's the perfect place to buy a reproduction of your favorite Monet—and because its standards for this kind of dining experience were practically nonexistent, I doubted the restaurant would be as terrific as all the reviewers claimed. If Bobby was going to do this kind of thing in the country I loved so much, I wanted him to do it right. I didn't want the Vietnamese to get stuck with something second-rate and think it was first, just because they had nothing else to compare it to.

Menus were handed out. *Long Live the Cock!* This brassy headline acknowledged the year's Chinese zodiac sign. Drinks were saucily designated *Stages of Inebriation*, and cigarettes fell under *Cancer Sticks and Water Pipes*. Among the side dishes: "We tell you that 'you are beautiful' all night long, $2.00." A little too coy, perhaps. Perusing the selections, Huong declared, "I don't eat much rice anymore. I've been eating it for twenty-nine years, and I'm tired of it. It has too many carbs." As Albert read through the side dishes, including apple risotto, lemon-scented couscous, and wasabi mashed potatoes, he unknowingly echoed Didier by announcing, "Fusion? I think it's confusion."

If Bobby Chinn's represented a new era of dining in Vietnam, our table of five represented its new era of diners. Huong was from Vietnam. Julie and I were from America. Albert and Suzanne offered further contrast. The soft-spoken owner of ThingsAsian Press, Albert was of Chinese descent, but he had been born in Vietnam, had moved to America in his youth, and now lived in San Francisco and Hong Kong. Born in America, Suzanne took the opposite path, moving to Japan with her husband, and after his death, to Vietnam. She had the blond hair and tan skin of a Southern California beach girl, but wore the luminescent orange *ao dai* (a traditional tunic and trousers) that she had been photographed in for a recent article in *Travel + Leisure* magazine. Huong, on the other hand, was dressed up in an embroidered halter top and black miniskirt. Add to this that we would be eating dishes from a chef descended from Egypt and China, and our group could not have been more international. Vietnam had certainly come a long way from its lean, homogenous postwar days. How satisfying it felt to not just witness, but to be part of, the "mixed culture" that Didier had talked about in his office that afternoon.

Our food arrived. I had ordered "Symphony of Flavours, A Selection of the Chef's Signature Bite Size Appetizers." Wanting desperately to be impressed, I poked my fork at each of the tidbits on my plate before stabbing a grape enveloped in goat cheese and crushed pistachios. A smooth, grassy buffer rested between the juiciness of the plump red grape and the parched pistachios. The cheese melted softly on my tongue, followed by a burst of flavor as the fruit and nuts came together. I tried to imagine what it would be like for a Vietnamese diner who had never before eaten such a combination. Would it come as a shock? A delight? Or would it seem, somehow, innately familiar, because after all, Vietnamese food is all about intertwining flavors?

With the juice of the grape cool in my mouth, I looked around, watching as Julie, Huong, Albert, and Suzanne took their first bites, of Moroccan beet salad with hazelnut-crusted goat cheese, pan-roasted salmon on wasabi mashed potatoes, grilled jumbo prawn with sweet coconut sticky rice, and blackened barramundi on braised banana blossoms. We were all silent as we passed through the stages of tasting identified by the gourmet Jean Anthelme Brillat-Savarin. First, the direct stage, when food touches the tongue, and second, the complete stage, when it passes to the back of the mouth and connects with the sense of smell. Then comes the third phase: reflection. That moment when opinion is formed.

I don't remember who spoke first, but our conversation erupted something like this: *Oh, wow, this is great. How's that? Excellent, want to try it? Here, would you like some of this, it's amazing.*

Good manners and our center-stage table be damned as we poked our forks into one another's plates. I was relieved. The Vietnamese weren't being conned. Nor was I, who had been disappointed by my fair share of haute-hip establishments during a stint working for a restaurant reviewer in Los Angeles. For a moment I thought about Didier. There was no denying that Bobby's food was fusion cuisine. The effort was there for all to see. It was about showmanship and fireworks, with all of its attendant oohs and ahs. There was nothing subtle about it. And still I liked it.

The sake struck its high note against a steamed clam. Red curry clashed playfully with sticky rice soaked in coconut milk. The best dish, though, was the banana flower. Although it was called a banana blossom on the menu, it was the same ingredient that Madame Hai had prepared for us at the Metropole. The same humble purple pod found in markets throughout Vietnam. It had been braised to highlight its naturally crisp texture and then drizzled in a vinaigrette that was mellow with turmeric and bittersweet with balsamic vinegar. Banana flower, I happily discovered, was like a pretty country girl with a glamorous alter ego.

As with all good meals, our shared appreciation for the food, combined with another bottle of wine, drew us closer, and conversation about chipotle broth evolved into conversation about life. We talked about the current fascination with blogs. We discussed Albert's first visit to Hanoi's oldest restaurant, Cha Ca, back in 1990. Suzanne told us that she moved to Vietnam because of a photo that she saw in Cathay Pacific's in-flight magazine, of two bearded old men in pajamas, sitting on a bench in the rain in Hanoi. "It captured for me the beauty and sadness of life." More wine was drunk. A few secrets were spilled. Around us, tables were filled with young Vietnamese, dressed like their counterparts in the West. Lots of black.

Although I am generally more low-key in my restaurant tastes, I understood why the Vietnamese were so enamored with this place. Class, status, and good food aside (that all seems obvious), for a citizen of a country in which the government had controlled so much for so long, to be at Bobby Chinn's with whomever you chose, laughing and drinking good wine and saying whatever you pleased, eating as much as you wanted, not just because you could afford to, but because you felt like it, was freedom in its purest form.

Outside, we dispersed. Suzanne headed back home, and Julie, who was coming down with a cold, returned to the Metropole with Albert. Ready to relax and finally catch up, Huong and I took a cab to Sloppy Joe's, a pub that was owned by her friend Thong. Beyond the dartboard, standing behind the bar, Thong called out to me. Her throaty voice was rinsed in the *g'day mate* inflections of the Australians who had taught her English. "Long time," she laughed.

A forgotten memory rushed over me, from my first months in Saigon, when Sundays were spent eating lunch at 180 Restaurant. Lunches that lasted for hours, with my then-boyfriend Sam, his Scottish business partner, his partner's Vietnamese wife, and their gorgeous toddler, Fiona. We would appropriate a large table in the covered patio section, try to catch the breeze from the fan, drink too much coffee, read the *International Herald Tribune*, and let the afternoons drift lazily by. A young waitress would come to our table and turn bright red every time the guys flirted with her, which was every time she approached—she had the most beautiful smile, and they loved to tease it out of her. Back then she always wore a traditional white *ao dai* and was incredibly shy. Now, Thong was wearing low-rise jeans and a snug T-shirt, welcoming me with a hearty hello, inviting me to belly up to her bar so she could mix me a margarita.

I hadn't seen Thong in nearly ten years. As I watched her slosh lime juice with tequila, it seemed appropriate that I would run into her just after eating at Bobby Chinn's. The restaurant may have represented change, but Huong, Thong, and their friends embodied it. Thong ground the rim of a glass into a plate of salt and poured me a margarita that would make Tijuana proud. Full and tired, I sat and sipped between Huong and another of her good friends, Trinh. Unlike Huong and Thong, who are from the south, Trinh was born and raised in Hanoi. She too had a deep, sultry voice, although hers was more mature, which suited her northern demeanor. She was not matronly, but of the three, she was the one you would call first in an emergency. We talked about the men we loved or had loved, because that's what girlfriends do over tequila at bars like Sloppy Joe's. Then we got around to talking about Bobby Chinn's restaurant.

"I know Bobby," Thong said, and I was not surprised. She was smart and beautiful, and hip circles in cities like Hanoi are small. "I like him."

"Why?" I asked. "For you, what's his appeal?"

"Young people have never seen anything like him before. He's irreverent. Uninhibited. His restaurant is new and exciting. We admire him."

As she spoke I realized that Bobby's place was more than just a novelty. Coming from the outside world but sanctioned by the government, it validated the nontraditional lifestyles that young Vietnamese were beginning to choose. For them, Bobby's mischievous—and risqué—*Long live the cock!* and truffle crab espresso offered hope that one day they would be able to not only speak as freely as he but also break through the iron curtain of their upbringings and think as freely, as well.

The midnight hour arrived, and I had another full day coming up, beginning with a breakfast interview with a local foodie. Thong offered to drive me back to the hotel on her Honda. I hugged Huong goodnight and hopped on the back of the bike. Hands loose on the handlebars, Trinh balanced on the front. We buzzed through the vacant streets, passing a lone food stall, where a woman stood over an aluminum pot that steamed in the warm night air. The three plastic stools at her cart were empty. I caught a whiff of the hot, nourishing broth that would be gone before dawn. I had two favorite times in Vietnam. Very late at night and very early in the morning. Everyone is asleep. It is almost possible to remember what coolness feels like. The silence is so thick I can feel it on my skin. The world is at rest, and it is one of the few times when I can rest, too.

Cheap & Nice

"Why didn't you tell me that he's an old man?" Huong muttered in the midst of translating a story about life as a soldier in the jungles during the American War. "I would have worn something different."

"This is an interview," I whispered back, smiling so that seventy-eight-year-old Nguyen Dinh Rao, who spoke no English, wouldn't suspect that we were talking about him. "Who wears a miniskirt to an interview at nine in the morning?"

"I thought he'd be somebody like Bobby."

"Mr. Nguyen is *nothing* like Bobby."

In his grandfatherly windbreaker, Mr. Nguyen was the antithesis of hip. By way of introduction, the elderly gentleman had shown us a black-and-white photograph, protected in a plastic sleeve, of himself as a young North Vietnamese soldier standing beside General Giap, Ho Chi Minh's right-hand man and the military leader responsible for Vietnam's defeat of France and America. While we passed it around, he stood at attention, his expression illuminated by a shy, touching pride. Even Huong, who had no love lost for the Communists, was impressed. "Wow," she said, "Giap is a really important man."

It was the morning after our dinner at Bobby Chinn's, and we were gathered in the courtyard café of the Metropole hotel, our low table cluttered with coffee cups. I had originally planned to hit the streets for *banh cuon*, the minced pork crepe that had been one of my favorite breakfasts when I lived in Saigon, or *bun cha*, the grilled pork on cold vermicelli that is a Hanoi specialty, but my culinary treasure hunt was derailed by this appointment that Didier eagerly set up for me with Mr. Nguyen, the president of Vietnam's UNESCO Gastronomy Club. Julie had gone her own way, to photograph street food scenes, but my publisher, Albert, was with us, his interest piqued after I told him how highly Didier spoke of Mr. Nguyen's importance as a keeper of culinary tradition.

The only problem was that as the interview proceeded we couldn't figure out what exactly this role was or what the club did. Huong had asked Mr. Nguyen directly, but after listening to him speak steadily in Vietnamese for quite some time, she said, uncertainly, "Well, you see, his club doesn't have very much money, so ... They need money."

"That's what he's been talking about for so long?" I asked.

She nodded.

"But what does his club do?" I asked.

She seemed puzzled. "I don't know."

I remained silent.

"Okay, okay." She turned back to Mr. Nguyen. Her voice remained soft and courteous as she asked once again. She nodded politely when he replied, punctuating his pauses with attentive "ohs" and "mmms." Then she translated. "The club needs funding to accomplish its goals."

"But what are its goals?"

"He didn't really say."

More questions. More answers. Finally Huong was able to tell me, "He has this club with his friends. They get together and talk about food and cuisine and that kind of thingie. You know, the old days."

"Am I missing something in this translation?"

She shook her head.

"But he talked for so long."

"Uh, well, he says that when he was in the military, he had to go fighting and stuff in the jungle, and sometimes they don't have food, so whatever they find in the jungle, they eat it. Sometimes they eat, you know, *mang*, which is young bamboo. And sometimes when they come to the village, the people make him a special cuisine from their area. He can eat lots of things that nobody knows about."

Observing from a chair set back from our small table, Albert was holding back a smile. I was appalled that he was observing this demonstration of my journalistic incompetence. "That's interesting," I said, "but it doesn't really answer my question."

She shrugged.

I hoped Mr. Nguyen could not sense my frustration. Especially since I shouldn't have been frustrated. I knew better. I had lived in Vietnam for four years, and during that time I'd had many a rambling discussion that never got to the point, especially with people from the north. Some Westerners I know define these kinds of conversations as "very Asian," and others call them "very Vietnamese." But what those terms mean to me is the Asian conversation as a form of ceremony: the honorific greetings, the litany of obligatory questions about your health and the health of your family, and then the slow, ritualistic procession toward the subject at hand. This situation was different. What I was experiencing with Mr. Nguyen is something I call "very Communist."

Often, as an English teacher in Vietnam, when talking with one of my adult students whose life had been shaped by Communism, I felt as if I were trapped in the land of non sequitur. Somehow, it was possible to spend an entire conversation talking all the way around a subject, but never actually addressing it. How hard is it, I would find myself thinking, to just say yes or no? But as I got to know the country, I began to suspect that this was a means of self-preservation. In certain environments, such as a Communist society, a person learned not to answer a direct question with a direct answer, because he never knew what might implicate him in whatever crime the state dreamed up on any given day. Circumspection becomes a habit, so even when you are asked about something as benign as your gastronomy club, you are unable to give a straight answer. Combine this with a traditionally elusive conversational style and a get-to-the-point Westerner like me, and the result is an impasse.

Sitting across the low table from Mr. Nguyen, who was forty years older than I and not from a country that loves frank talk, I felt a kind of determination growing within me. A need to rise to the occasion. Determined, I forged ahead. "Let's try something else. Ask him if he thinks that traditional Vietnamese cuisine is at risk."

Dutifully, Huong conveyed my question. Mr. Nguyen replied, talking again without pause for nearly ten minutes, with Huong nodding and muttering lots of "ahs" and "I sees" in a way that buoyed my spirits. She was smiling. She was interested. At last he finished. I gripped my pen.

"He says that when foreign investors come to Vietnam, they have a lot of money to advertise their cuisine. So it gets people's attention more than traditional cuisine. But traditional cuisine will not disappear, because the beauty of the tradition comes from nature and the body."

"Nature and the body?"

"Hold on," she said. "There's more."

I sat forward, eagerly.

"He says that himself, he would love to publish his own book, but he doesn't have the money."

I set my pen and notebook in my lap. I glanced at Mr. Nguyen, who was gazing back at me with his patient, rheumy eyes. All the patience in the world. Communism had also taught him this.

I tried to imagine what was going through his head, as he sat in a luxurious colonial-style hotel that was a tribute to the nation he spent his youth fighting against. Behind him, I could see a shapely Vietnamese woman sipping her morning coffee while she sunbathed in an itty-bitty hot pink bikini. A Western couple played with their newly adopted Vietnamese daughter on the steps of the swimming pool. Overlooked by guestrooms that cost hundreds of dollars a night, the shallow pool was located above a former bomb shelter that had most likely harbored some of Mr. Nguyen's comrades when the United States bombed the hell out of Hanoi during the Christmas holidays of 1972. As for the city just outside the hotel, Hanoi was changing more rapidly than it ever had before. Bobby Chinn was just the beginning.

I realized that if I was going to get anything from our meeting, I could not force it. No matter how much I loved and knew about Vietnam, Mr. Nguyen and I were from different planets. I needed to just let him talk and see where he would take us. The following hour meandered through the topics of fish sauce, eating dog, and a particular kind of crispy duck that Mr. Nguyen had once tasted in the highlands near the Chinese border. "The best duck he has ever eaten," Huong assured me, offering tidbits she hoped might leave me satisfied with this interview. At one point, Albert leaned forward and said, "In America, when we say Vietnamese food, what we mean is *pho* and then *cha gio*." He was speaking of Hanoi noodle soup and fried spring rolls. "That's really the only Vietnamese food we know about. Does Mr. Nguyen think these dishes are a fair representation of his country?"

As Huong discussed *pho* with Mr. Nguyen, she shifted to keep her skirt modestly in place. She told us, "He said a dish that's really special, too, that's the *nom*. The salad, like the one Madame Hai made in our class."

"And it represents Vietnam?"

"Well, not exactly."

"Then that doesn't—"

"I know," she cut me off. "That doesn't answer your question." She lowered her eyes, like a weary prizefighter gathering energy, knowing he is about to get pushed back into the ring.

"For example," I continued, "people think America, and they think hamburger. The hamburger represents America. It's big and meaty and fast, and a little bit unhealthy. For the rest of the world, *pho* is Vietnam. *Pho* is a simple and elegant dish. Does Mr. Nguyen think it fairly represents Vietnam? And if not, what does?"

"He says *pho* is very popular in Vietnam because we can get it anytime, anywhere. He compares it to McDonald's in America."

"How about this? If Mr. Nguyen was a poet and he was going to write a poem about Vietnam and use just one food to symbolize the country, what would the subject of the poem be?"

"Actually, he said that this idea, writing a poem like this, it has already been done by other people."

The woman in the bikini was gone. The couple with the new daughter was gone. The entire breakfast crowd was gone. The four of us were alone in the lounge. I had vowed to go with the flow, but at heart I'm just not that kind of person. "But in his opinion, I want his opinion."

"In his opinion," Huong finally said, "he would write about the vegetables cooked with river crab."

Success! I grinned. "Why?" I asked.

"Because, in the old days, everybody can eat it. It's cheap and nice."

"That's what he thinks of Vietnam? Cheap and nice?"

Apologetically, she said, "Vietnam's not really cheap anymore."

Mr. Nguyen was a man who had fought alongside General Giap for his country's freedom from foreign rule. Didier, Vietnam's great culinary preservationist, respected him. UNESCO, which was dedicated to saving cultures around the world, lent its name to his gastronomy club. I looked at Mr. Nguyen. His expression was attentive. Nothing in it suggested that he was deliberately trying to thwart me. He looked as if he hoped that his answers pleased me, and I realized that my frustration lay not in his avoidance of my questions, but in my not accepting his answers. I was being "very American." Wanting everything spelled out. Maybe his gastronomy club was about saving the ethnic dishes he had learned about in the jungles when he was a young soldier. Maybe he chose vegetables cooked with river crab because "cheap and nice"—or high-quality, affordable food for everyone—was the principle he spent his youth fighting for. And maybe, just maybe, his obsession with funding was his way of telling me that saving the old ways from the encroachment of the modern machine required so much more than just getting together with his old friends and talking about food and cuisine and that kind of thingie.

Dining Is Living

After the interview with Mr. Nguyen, Huong and I met up with Julie in our hotel room. We flopped side by side across the cool cotton bedspread. Soft light eased through the shutters, painting a ladder of thin, luminous lines across the tobacco-colored hardwood floor.

"It's hard taking photos here," Julie said, when we asked her how her morning had been. "Hanoi's different from Saigon. It's so reserved."

"Yeah," Huong said, "I know what you mean. I feel that when I'm here. Hanoi's quieter than Saigon."

Julie said, "I always ask before I take someone's picture, but a lot of people said no today. I felt like I was invading their privacy."

Lazily, in air-conditioned comfort, we discussed the differences between the two cities. Hanoi, with its cold, wet winters and elegant but aloof beauty. It's possible to get to know Hanoi, friends who lived there had assured me, but it takes time, unlike balmy Saigon, with its eager, puppy dog friendliness. Because my stomach was rumbling after two cups of coffee and no breakfast, I changed the topic to what I still wanted to accomplish in Hanoi, food-wise, before the following night, when we would catch a train south to the former imperial city of Hue. Along with the special tasting dinner that Didier was preparing for us at the hotel's formal Le Beaulieu, "I *must* eat at Cha Ca La Vong," I told them. Cha Ca was the city's oldest restaurant.

"Oh yeah," Huong said, rolling languidly onto her side. "I almost forgot. The owner of Cha Ca is Trinh's godmother." Trinh was the friend I had met at Thong's bar, Sloppy Joe's. "Trinh can be there at one thirty today if you want to meet her. Do you want to meet her?"

I swatted her thigh. "What do you think?"

Since it was not yet eleven and we were starving, we decided to go to Ngon, another restaurant I wanted to visit. It had originated in Saigon a few years earlier, and because of its popularity, it recently opened an outpost in Hanoi. It re-created the country's diverse street stall scene in a single venue, and I wanted to know how—or if—it was serving to bridge the gap between street cuisine and the fast-growing, high-end dining scene.

For every Didier Corlou or Bobby Chinn, there were thousands of local cooks manning stalls and carts on street corners around Vietnam. There is a rustic grace to street cuisine, a balladry to the lone cook setting up at the head of a narrow lane, preparing just *pho* or *bun cha* using little more than a sharp knife and a small brazier. The way diners sit around the cooking pot on short plastic stools makes it feel as if the cook is hosting an intimate party, rather than just the day's customers.

Vietnamese street dining is communal, out in the open, and it's something I miss when I am back in America. Sometimes, to ease my homesickness for Vietnam, I will drive around downtown L.A. at dinnertime, until I find the Mexican and El Salvadoran women standing over grills cradled in the beds of shopping carts. Wrapped tightly in corn husks, their tamales look like small gifts. Flanking the carts, diners sit on folding lawn chairs with paper plates propped on their knees, chatting as if the sidewalks are their front porches. There is something about the way everyone gathers, the availability of what they are eating to anyone who happens to be walking by, that makes me feel close to this city I inhabit. Vietnam's street stalls have the same effect on me. When I eat at one, it bonds me to the country.

I like that when it comes to eating in Vietnam, there are few boundaries between public and private. Dining is living. With a folding front grate rather than a solid front wall, even the average neighborhood café is fully exposed to passersby. While working, selling clothing, or perhaps fixing a watch, shopkeepers eat and gossip, and even share what they are eating with their customers. Homes, too, are often open to the street. It is not uncommon to pass a house and look in on a family around a table eating dinner.

As Julie, Huong, and I walked into the vast, tree-shaded courtyard of a beautiful, tall French villa that served as Ngon's main dining area, I reflected on how Vietnam's distinctive indoor-outdoor dining experience was being captured within the walls of this restaurant. Stations were set up around the perimeter of the courtyard to resemble street stalls—very clean and picturesque street stalls, with dark wood counters, clay-tiled roofs, and each stall's specialty hand-painted on a flat basket hanging from a pillar beside the cooking area. The stalls were run by young women wearing olive-colored silk tunics and black trousers.

Given Ngon's gimmicky premise, I thought it might turn out to be a place for tourists who wanted the novelty of trying Vietnamese street food but didn't trust the local hygiene. To my surprise, the place was packed with locals. Julie and I were the only foreigners there. Later, when I mentioned this to a stylish Vietnamese friend, the owner of three trendy restaurants, she told me that she had been to Ngon twice that week. "I don't have to sit near sewage while I'm eating. I can get fruit juice or coffee, or even both if I want, and I can eat all sorts of different foods. My kids can have one thing, and I can have another. Maybe it's not the best, but we can each have whatever we like. And when we leave," she added, smiling, "my hair doesn't smell like cuttlefish."

But isn't sitting at a stall that sells only one dish, sucking up the exhaust of Honda motorcycles, what makes street food what it is? Isn't part of the essential experience the smell of cuttlefish that lingers in your hair long after the meal is through? I wondered about this as Julie, Huong, and I sat down at the end of a table in the shade of a large white parasol. Unlike the child-size tables usually found in street cafés, this one was of normal height and did not require us to squat on small stools. We studied the list of dishes on the menu. I had been told that the cooks preparing the food were recruited from the streets, to ensure authenticity. Julie and I ordered a tasty tamarind crab in memory of the crab shack in Saigon where I had eaten with my Vietnamese sisters so many years ago. Huong ordered *bun bo Hue* (beef noodle soup) and *bun rieu cua* (minced crabmeat with rice vermicelli soup), two foods that are never found served at the same stall, and often not even on the same street.

Glistening golden-orange on its bed of lettuce, the crab was sweet, sticky, and satisfyingly rich, but somehow it wasn't as good as the version I'd had in Saigon. I couldn't pinpoint why, and I couldn't decide if it was the crab itself, or the fact that everyone around me was eating with chopsticks and forks. No one else, aside from Julie and me, was up to her wrists in tamarind sauce.

Huong, who considered herself a bit of an expert on *bun bo Hue*, declared this version "good," and her *bun rieu cua* "all right."

"Not the best?" I asked.

She shook her head. "But not bad. I'd come here again. It's clean. I like that."

I nodded at the bowl of *bun bo Hue*. "What would make it better?" I asked.

"This one seems like it's for foreigners. It needs more flavor. More shrimp paste."

This was my concern. A sanitized setting leading to the sanitization of flavor. I understood why the Vietnamese wanted cleaner places to eat, but at the same time, I worried that cleanliness would extend to the hot, sour, salty, and sweet of the food itself. Someday, people might think they know what *pho* is because they had a bowl at a branch of Pho 24, a new, sterile, McDonald's-like chain that Huong said was okay if you were drunk and needed to soak up some alcohol, but that one of my favorite food magazines in the United States had actually—unbelievably—recommended in an article about eating street food in Vietnam.

Of course, the issue is far more complex than stalls = good and chains = bad. When it's excellent, Vietnamese street food is better than anything I have ever tasted. But not all street food is that good. I am a believer in street food, but when I lived in Vietnam, eating on the streets, I encountered more mediocre dishes than I did exceptional ones. Crouched beside dented metal carts, I had at times found myself eating grainy gray beef, stringy chicken, gristle, unidentifiable crunchy bits, wilted greens, MSG-laden broth, and slimy noodles. If I had to choose between any of those street meals and Ngon, there is no question which way I'd lean. And I'm not the only one.

I was surprised to read that Vietnam's critical street food aficionado, the blogger Noodlepie, declares himself a fan. He wrote that, like on the street, "There are some dishes that are noticeably better than others." He raved about the eel rice porridge and fried shrimp cakes, and even said the latter are better than those served at a Hanoi institution specializing in them. "Plus," he added, sounding like my friend who owns the upscale restaurants, "there are no rats, no crappy chairs, no knackered tables, no hordes of roaring drunks or floors littered with dinner debris."

Part of the pleasure of the pork chop stall where I bought lunch the first months I lived in Saigon was the dish itself. The food was fresh and, though simple, excellent. The other part was its hidden, shady spot beneath the balcony of my guesthouse apartment, encircled by the daily life of my neighborhood. But I was also taking pleasure in the peaceful surroundings of Ngon, with its friendly waitresses, potted palms, and good, if not excellent, food. The plates and cutlery were clean, and the iced tea thin and refreshing, just like on the streets, but with trustworthy ice. And for all of its manipulated quaintness, and the lack of motorcycles revving past just inches from our table, I did not, in the end, feel entirely distanced from the traditional outdoor dining culture of Vietnam.

When Julie vacated her chair to take photos, a nicely dressed, middle-aged Vietnamese woman quickly sat down. As if we were at a sidewalk stall in a small back lane, her family crowded around her. They hovered, waiting to take over our end of the table, even though Huong and I were still eating and there was still food on Julie's plate. No waitress came along to shoo them away. Huong did not seem to notice or care that they were there, although the woman was just inches from us, leaning so close that I could hear her breathing as she scrutinized our half-eaten dishes.

From the Heart

After we finished one lunch at Ngon, we headed across town to the historic Cha Ca restaurant for yet another. In the narrow, crisscrossing lanes of the Old Quarter, Cha Ca is located on what used to be known as Hang Son, or Paint Street. That was back when the street was lined with shops selling paint. Now, because it is home to numerous restaurants—all imitators selling Cha Ca's signature fish dish—it is called Cha Ca Street.

Depending on whom you asked, Cha Ca has been in business since 1871 or 1899, and Trinh's godmother, Mrs. Loc, is the great-great-granddaughter of the founder ... I think. As Trinh introduced us to Mrs. Loc, the debate about the number of greats was long and filled with much laughter and digression, all in Vietnamese. Eventually, Huong informed me that I would have to be happy with two greats because "it's close enough, isn't it?"

We climbed the solid, ladderlike stairs to the dining room on the second floor, where Mrs. Loc had staked out a table in the center of the small room. The chalky, aqua-blue walls looked scorched from the mildew seeping through the paint near the ceiling A modest family altar with tea, rice, orange slices, and incense; cabinets cluttered with porcelain figurines; and promotional Carlsberg beer insignia gave no indication of how famous this place was.

Mrs. Loc helmed the table. She was in her midfifties, but when she smiled, which was often, you could see the impish twenty-year-old girl she had once been. She had the kind of high cheekbones that wear well into old age. Her polyester blouse and trousers were typical for a middle-aged woman, although her black top wasn't the usual muted earth tones, but instead shone with garlands of fuchsia-colored hibiscus. As I set up my tiny tape recorder, which was out of its league in the clamor of the lunch hour, Thong from Sloppy Joe's arrived and immediately leaped into a discussion with Huong, Trinh, and Mrs. Loc about what to order. It was an unusually long and heated discussion, considering that the restaurant served only one dish, *cha ca.*

Because Mrs. Loc's time was limited, I wanted to get straight to the questions that most interested me—Cha Ca's history within the framework of Vietnam's twentieth-century history—and I asked if Cha Ca had ever closed.

"Yes," Trinh said, without bothering to confer with her godmother.

"When?" I asked.

"Oh, well, that," she said, uncertainly. She turned to Huong and they chatted, laughing the whole time. With Huong wearing a little orange tank top and Trinh in a sleeveless black blouse, they could easily have been out at a bar,

Julie pushed a frog leg away, Huong scowled and said, "I don't understand. It comes from the water, and it tastes like chicken. Why can't you eat it?"

"Good point," I said, grinning. There was no way Julie would eat a frog leg.

Huong said, "Don't think about the throw up thingie. Think about the beauty of the food."

"Nice try, but no thanks." Julie smiled, admirably unapologetic about the foods she does not like. I had eaten mine just to be a good sport. To my relief, she gave the springy little leg to Huong.

Delicate, Thumbelina-sized flowers and the coy, curled ends of bean sprouts adorned the plates, which continued to arrive with a steadfastness that reminded me of *The Sorcerer's Apprentice*. It seemed impossible to eat everything, but a crime not to. As we sampled what Huong described as "posh *mien cua*," an upscale version of a street favorite, crab on glass noodles, I was already stuffed, and while she took a call from Saigon, I sipped a mellow rice wine digestif and grew genuinely worried about how I was going to make room for the green pepper sherbet and sea bass cheek in an herb crust with caviar that was next on the menu.

Fortunately, the culinary gods took pity on me, granting me a second wind, and I relished not only the sea bass but also fried and smoky soft-shell crab with a fresh coconut heart spring roll, and a memorable variation on the street stall pork-and-noodle favorite, *bun cha*: a pork nougat accented with wild pepper and kumquat. No matter how unexpected and innovative each dish was, no matter how influenced by the techniques of Didier's home country, the food was ultimately a tribute to his love for the herbs and spices, fruits and vegetables, and fish, fowl, and meats of Vietnam. It was a mouthwatering illustration of his advice to respect the culture, and then move on. Best of all, as Huong pointed out, gazing glassy-eyed at our empty plates, "Didier is like Mrs. Loc. The heart is in the food."

Hue

Central Vietnam

Hanoi•

Hue
•
•Hoi An

•Nha Trang
•Dalat

•Phan Thiet
•Saigon

Famine & Feast

As our train chugged toward Hue, Julie and Huong lay comatose on their bunks, Julie curled up below and Huong sprawled out above, both of them blindfolded with scarves to fend off the invading dawn. As I stole out of our compartment into the corridor, I swayed against the rhythm of the train for balance. I craved a sticky-sweet iced coffee, or steaming cup of jasmine tea, anything with caffeine. But this wasn't the Orient-Express, so I remained half-asleep as I looked out at the landscape veiled in haze.

Limestone outcroppings flanked the train tracks. As we traveled toward the former imperial city, they rose and fell, as if the land was inhaling, exhaling, heavily. The sun perked up behind a peak, then dropped back down, then emerged full in the sky, then disappeared. The hills parted to reveal a man patiently following a crude wooden plow behind a buffalo through a green field. Farther on, at another small farm, a young boy laughed as he chased a renegade cow.

The low cliffs closed back in, and the vegetation thickened. Vines spiraled down from treetops, each dripping the dusky purple pendant of a banana flower. They would be perfect for the salad that we had watched Madame Hai make at the Metropole. The tart-spicy flavors of our new favorite dish rushed back to me. Although Thong had fed us her addictive *nuoc mam* fried chicken wings at Sloppy Joe's just before we caught our train the night before, plus given us two tubs of her homemade fried rice to take with us, I was starving. I wanted to jump out and slurp a bowl of soup at every stall that whisked past.

Fields gave way to an inlet dappled with old timber fishing boats. Two women rowing a small craft glanced up at the train, and one era darted past another, as if intersecting in a time travel machine. Land reappeared, and with it life and death. Ancestors inhabited eternity in a small cemetery, surrounded by the living, who waded knee deep in lemony rice shoots iridescent in the rising sun. Each small farm possessed its own wood plow, worked by a farmer whose muscled forearms were roasted brown. Buffalo squirmed on their backs like puppies in a bed of mud.

As the train traveled through the countryside, Vietnam was a place whose fertile landscape and constant activity of its farmers belied its past. Staring out, I found it hard to believe that throughout the past century, as recently as twenty years earlier, deprivation, constant hunger, and even famine was a way of life for many Vietnamese.

Famine. According to the World Health Organization, it is "regional failure of food production or supply, sufficient to cause a marked increase in disease and mortality due to severe lack of nutrition and necessitating emergency intervention, usually at an international level." According to my girlfriends who lived through the 1980s in Vietnam, famine and its poor relation, the food shortage, are the ache of hunger every day, without relief. It is eating not enough spongy rice and taro, and being sickly all the time, and hearing your mother cry quietly at night when she thinks you are asleep. It is a blister in your stomach that does not go away, following you even into your dreams and waiting for you to wake each morning.

I remember once, the oldest sister in my Vietnamese family looked at me while a single tear slipped down her cheek as she said, "We were just so hungry all the time."

Famine is not always about lack, though, as French colonial rule in Vietnam attests. It can be the result of policy, about who controls what is available, and how they distribute it. During the hundred years of French colonialism, from the mid-1800s to the mid-1900s, the French government provided the Vietnamese with many wonderful things: sensuous architecture, the École Supérieure des Beaux-Arts de l'Indochine, and baguettes. But these were not symbols of benevolence. They were not gifts. They were part and parcel of Gallic sovereignty. They came at a price of *mission civilitrice*, and it was the Vietnamese who paid it.

Precious land and manpower were commandeered to exploit natural resources and produce crops such as cotton, jute, and oil-bearing plants, rather than food for the local population. In the north, an area that could easily have supported its own, rice had to be imported from the south. In *Shadows and Wind: A View of Modern Vietnam*, Robert Templer writes, "A region whose economy … was a considerable distance from any alternative source of food was always susceptible to the political and economic forces that create famines."

The Japanese occupation during WWII aggravated an already dangerous food situation, as more land was given over to industrial crops. Peasants were forced to sell their harvests at unreasonably low prices. The government hoarded rice, turned it into ethanol to fuel engines, and refused to release it even though thousands of people were dying of hunger.

Between October 1944 and May 1945, up to two million people died of starvation in Vietnam. The year 1945 was the same time Ho Chi Minh declared the country's independence. The French challenged the new national government, but the resistance of the Viet Minh, the nationalist organization led by Ho Chi Minh, had gained strength, due in large part to a revolution that was fed on lack of food.

Nutritional injustice and a famine were not the only reasons a large portion of the Vietnamese population loathed their former rulers, but they played a critical role. Templer writes that agricultural policies "helped strip the French of their colonial pretence to a higher morality and doomed their rule." As Nguyen Cong Hoan's 1938 novel *Impasse* illustrates, the colonial-era French flourished while Vietnam's peasant population lived at subsistence level, at best. Making things worse were the Vietnamese mandarins who served as the link between the French government and the Vietnamese peasants. They were underpaid and treated like servants by their French leaders, so they meted out punishment to those beneath them, often taking crops and land for personal gain.

While *Impasse* does not end happily for the peasant farmer Pha, whose wife and infant son die due to the barbarity of policy and the venality of the policy makers, it does show—when Pha finally lashes out at his aggressors—that few things anger a person more than an empty stomach. On the other hand, as Angelo Pellegrini writes in *An Unprejudiced Palate*, "Give a man bread, woolens against the cold, labor that he enjoys, and you may open wide the doors to the futile agitator or riots and revolutions … It is everlastingly true that a social order endures so long as the pantries of its citizens are stocked with good food."

So believed the Viet Minh. Even before the French were ultimately defeated in 1954 and evicted from the country, the Viet Minh undertook their first land reform campaign. From 1953 to 1956, inspired by policies in China that had not yet proven to be abysmal failures, they forcibly redistributed privately owned land to more than 1.5 million peasant families.

The program did not succeed. One interesting aspect of this experiment was the Vietnamese government's recognition that it was a failure. But although it was followed by a public apology and a "Rectification of Errors" campaign, the north was still far from feasting. When the French left, the country officially divided into North and South Vietnam. Soon the American War was gaining momentum, cutting North Vietnam off from surplus agricultural imports from the south. Meanwhile, the south lived relatively well-fed under an American-backed Vietnamese government.

In an attempt to get food on every table in the north, cooperatives were started in 1959, and by 1965 nearly all of the peasant households were organized into collectives. But collectivization was no more successful than land redistribution, for the same sorry reasons. Templer writes, "Farmers found they were producing crops at low prices for government collectors who to their mind were becoming suspiciously similar to the old landlords and their hated agents."

The North Vietnamese resigned themselves to this demoralizing déjà vu. After all, they were accustomed to bearing the brunt of government policy. It had become a way of life. Southerners were another story. After the American departure and South Vietnam's defeat in 1975, followed by the reunification of Vietnam, the Communists' agricultural collectivization program was introduced in the south. Southerners resisted, not only because theirs was a culture in which a man earned from his own land, but also because—although the battles and bombings were over—the Communists were still considered adversaries. Their policies were a manifestation of the very ideologies the south had been fighting against.

The Communist government tightened the screws, but this only made things worse. Although the country was seeing more land cultivated than ever before, somehow less food was being produced. Then there was a drought in 1977; typhoons and flooding in 1978; and the strain on resources from invading

Cambodia to fight the Khmer Rouge, also in 1978. This invasion led to a border war with Pol Pot's ally, China, in 1979, and resulted in the Chinese cutting off much-needed food aid to Vietnam. Because Vietnam was subjected to sanctions and trade embargoes by much of the Western world, there were other influential scarcities as well, including chemical fertilizers, pesticides, and the spare parts needed to repair farm machinery. With only a few mutinous Western countries helping out, along with strapped Soviet and Eastern Bloc nations, the whole of Vietnam was tumbling into a culinary and nutritional Dark Ages.

Almost everyone I've talked to who lived in Vietnam in the early 1980s has a story about ration coupons and food lines. Lines that a person could wait in all day, only to have the poor-quality rice run out before he got his share. Famine was a constant threat, and according to Templer, by 1985 the inability to meet its promise to feed the nation became a source of shame for the Communist party. Things got so bad that for the first time Vietnam's National Assembly began publicly criticizing everything from skyrocketing prices for basic goods to the underproduction of export crops like sugar and coffee.

It had to have been disappointing (and humbling) to give up on policies that had started off as an idealistic dream. But the government didn't mulishly stick to its guns as North Korea has disastrously done. In the mid-1980s, it began its reforms, allowing farmers to possess their land and sell crops for a profit. The combination of hunger and freedom proved to be a powerful motivator for the Vietnamese. By 1986, agriculture was responsible for more than 40 percent of the national income, compared to an average of 10 percent in developed nations.

But the country was deeply wounded, and despite shifts in policy—and more importantly in practice—it experienced another famine in 1988. It was the shock of this that really propelled Vietnam forward. From being a country unable to feed itself, in little over a decade it became the third-largest exporter of rice in the world.

I believe this says much about the Vietnamese people—about their strength, determination, and work ethic. For a traveler, to know this history of triumph over adversity is to know how precious a single serving of rice can be. It is to look out a train window at a farmer plowing his lush green field and understand the great respect that the food bounty of Vietnam has earned.

Don't Be a Follower

While I was standing out in the corridor of the train, watching the morning pass by, Huong woke and lured me back into our compartment with the tub of Thong's should-be-famous chicken and mushroom rice. Julie, too, was awake and hungry, propped up against the thin pillow of her bunk. The rice had had all night to yield to the soft spices, and now had a soothing, steeped, lukewarm quality that would make it the perfect dish for a snowy winter day or postbreakup blues. Once every grain was consumed, the three of us took turns rubbing our fingers along the inside of the plastic tub, until the sheen of grease and the last of the flavor was gone.

Sleepy again, Huong lay back on her bunk. Julie sat cross-legged on hers, opened her camera bag, and dumped out the twenty-plus rolls of film she had taken in Hanoi. She dug out her notebook and began to organize the rolls, noting which ones contained Old Quarter sidewalk cafés and which ones the kitchen at Cha Ca La Vong, which had seduced her lens with its photogenic rusticity. "I've never seen anything like it," she had said to me, with wonder, as she took shot after shot of charred clay braziers, chipped porcelain plates, and basket after basket piled with dill—all through the haze of stifling, smoky air.

I wandered back into the corridor, to keep tabs on the waking day. I was full, and yet I was still incredibly hungry, because I knew what lay in store. Once the country's imperial capital, Hue was famous for its signature dishes, which included celebrated street foods, plus remnants of the old royal cuisine. Visiting Hanoi had been about exploring the evolution of Vietnam's restaurant culture; Hue was to be about discovering regional cuisine—in a region all my Vietnamese friends had told me was one of the most appetizing in the country.

The official grand opening of Hue's La Residence Hotel & Spa was still months away, and so there were few guests, giving it an abandoned air. The gardens that surrounded the Art Deco former governor's residence were thoughtfully designed, but somehow felt on the verge of turning into jungle at any moment. The infinity pool did not look sleek or cutting edge, but rather as if it were going to overflow into the unruly vegetation that separated the hotel grounds from the Perfume River.

As we made our way to our room, I indulged myself with visions of the lethargic journalists biding time at the French embassy in Phnom Penh in the

Huong wrapped a leaf with some pork and rice paper and tried it. "Mouthwash herb," she declared it, scowling with disgust.

I disliked it, too—it was too strong—until I took a bite without it, and then another, and another. I realized I was bracing myself for it, anticipating it, enjoying the element of risk. Was it going to appear in the next bite or not?

While I played spearmint roulette, Huong asked the waitress for an order of *nem chua Hue*, another of her favorite Hue specialties, which she explained was good everywhere, but only great in Hue. The restaurant did not serve it, but because Vietnam is a place where people will constantly go out of their way to be helpful, the young girl offered to run down the road and buy some from a nearby street vendor who was known for it.

I had devoured half a dozen rolls and was slowing down, contemplating the contrast between the chewy rice paper, the charred pork, and the slices of fig, which had a pleasantly chalky texture, when the girl returned with a bundle of packets wrapped in banana leaves and tied together with red plastic twine. Huong offered me one of the wedges of sour, pressed pork before gnawing on her own. Because I have never cared for *nem chua Hue* and its many Spam-like relatives, and because I was perfectly happy with my *nem lui* and didn't want to spoil the aftertaste, I politely nibbled off a corner and then set the hunk down beneath the rim of my plate. *Nem chua Hue* is made of pork, so Julie escaped having to try it. But she could see its value for Huong's new anticarb lifestyle. "It's Atkins friendly," she said, telling Huong about the protein-centric diet fad that was born in the early 1970s and had recently experienced a resurgence in America.

"Mmm," Huong agreed, peeling back the creamy skin of another banana leaf. "Just protein. Oh, I love this one. It's really good."

"Then you can have them all," I said. "Lucky you."

Beneath us on the sidewalk, plastic tables from a child's birthday party were being cleared away. Silence rested patiently in the boughs of the tree next to us, like solemn little birds, waiting to take flight and fill the night air. In just a few hours, I had fallen in love with Hue. I sat back in my chair, content, looking at the walls of the restaurant, which were covered with graffiti. I considered the words scrawled behind Julie's head. *Also eat at places outside of the tour guide. Don't be a follower. (Great food here. ☺)*

True, I thought. Lac Thien's *nem lui*, *tom lui*, and *bun bo Hue* were wonderful. But I was ready to heed the sensible advice: eat beyond the guidebooks. It was time to move away from the pack, and I knew exactly where I wanted to start. Among Hue's many specialties was a dish called *com hen* (clam rice). It was not mentioned in any of my guides, and the moment I first came across it in my research, the moment I learned that there is an entire street in Hue devoted to it, I became obsessed. I explained to Julie and Huong that first thing the following morning, we would eat *com hen*.

Clam Rice

A cold that had nipped at Julie in Hanoi struck her down our first morning in Hue. Lying in bed, she looked forlorn and more than a little devastated to miss out on the search for clam rice. Clams were within her dining sphere. It wasn't fair! I felt guilty. She is the kind of person who will forge on through the plague, so I knew she must be really sick. But we had only three full days in Hue. We offered to stay in with her, but she shook her head valiantly and said, "No, no, it's just the flu. Have fun." We promised that if clam rice was any good, we would go back as soon as she felt better. She nodded, but food—any food, but particularly a food as distinctive as clams—did not sound appetizing at that moment. She rolled over and fell asleep.

"No," said Mike, our hotel's good-looking executive chef, "no, I don't."

Sebastien, the resident manager, whose physique called to mind Ichabod Crane, echoed Mike with a definitive "no."

Nicolas, the general manager, and the most aloof of the trio, nodded in agreement.

Before Huong and I could go in search of clam rice, I had to meet with the hotel management. It was one of the trade-offs for getting a reduced press rate for a room. We were seated in the lobby. Huong and I were on a sofa on one side of a low table. On the other side, the three men had assembled in a semicircle of chairs, like a small European council. The lobby was grand in a sleek, geometric, Art Deco way. I might have been able to imagine Catherine Deneuve striding through in her fiery red *Indochine* dress were it not for the loud pop music coming from the ceiling speakers and a tourist couple, wearing shorts and T-shirts, checking in at the front desk.

The men were smoking, which made them appear trapped inside an overcast day. Outside, the morning's white haze refused to lift. Shrouded, the lawns insinuated the wilderness this place would surely become were it abandoned for even a month. The question that I had just asked Mike, the chef, was if he liked the food in Hue. After a resounding no not only from him but also from the other two men, I asked, "Why not?"

"It's no good," Mike declared, unapologetically. "I was very surprised. I came here from Thailand. The Vietnamese food in Thailand is excellent."

Nicolas added, "My wife is from Lac Cai, in the north near the Chinese border. She had heard so much about the food in Hue. She was disappointed when we moved here."

Given that my only meal in Hue so far had been at a tourist restaurant, I did not feel qualified to argue, and I could not decide if I should worry about what they were telling me, or if they were merely jaded expats. When one is a jaded expat (just one of many varieties of expatriates that exist), it is requisite to hate everything about the place where you live.

"But the food of Hue is famous," I said. "How can it be that bad?"

From inside his capsule of smoke, Sebastien offered, "There are not many people left here who are originally from Hue. Many people moved away, especially during the war."

The men agreed that the best Hue food was found in Hanoi and Saigon, in Bangkok and Paris. Not only because of the people from Hue who had migrated to those cities, taking their skills with them, but also because of access to fresher, better-quality ingredients.

With a grimace, Sebastien said, "Most people who live here now have come from the countryside."

This comment reminded me of a Vietnamese woman I had met, who told me about her mother's village in a rural area outside Hue. When the woman, a chef, visited her mother's hometown, the villagers begged her to teach them to cook something other than the bland fish and boiled ginger they had lived on for as long as they could remember. Combined with what the men were saying, this did not bode well. "So," I said, "you're telling me that I'm out of luck? You can't recommend a single good restaurant."

"This is because restaurants are different in Vietnam," Nicolas said, lighting up another cigarette. "It is not like Europe, where you linger. Here, you go in, you eat, you go out. That is all."

Huong, who had a proprietary claim to this subject, remained tactfully silent. I followed her lead and did not insist that my Vietnamese friends loved to loiter around the table, both at home and in restaurants. I could recall meals that had lasted for hours—sometimes for an entire evening. Instead, I took a philosophical approach and asked, "Do you think this is because the Vietnamese were not allowed the luxury of enjoying themselves in public for such a long period of time?"

"No," said Nicolas, without even thinking about it.

Mike stamped his cigarette in the ashtray. Sebastien was finishing a stubby little cylinder of tobacco and would surely start on another as soon as he was done. Looking at the men, I thought about how expats are such an unusual breed. The farther you go from the main cities and the more isolated from other expatriates the outposts, the more peculiar they get. They also become franker. I was in Hue not only to write about food. As long as I was there, I was also going to write about this new hotel for a French guidebook. It seemed that these men would want to make a good impression. Instead, they smoked like fiends, dismissed my questions, and insisted that Hue food was terrible.

I liked them. A lot.

I felt like a Pollyanna as I told them that, well, I appreciated their opinions, but I was here to eat good food, and by golly, I was off now to find some, and even though I had been there less than twenty-four hours, and they had lived there for months, I was going to prove them wrong. To their credit, they humored me. They wished us luck and offered to take us to dinner that night at a little hole-in-the-wall, a *bun bo Hue* place, "behind a big tree, that isn't too bad."

Huong and I rented bikes from the hotel and pedaled slowly up Le Loi Boulevard. We rode side by side, chatting about nothing in particular, like we used to do when I lived in Saigon, me on my maroon bicycle, she keeping pace on her Little Green Machine, a dubious midget of a motorcycle that always felt on the verge of a nervous breakdown. Although we were in no rush, it took us less than ten minutes to reach Truong Dinh Street, which will forever be known in my heart as Clam Rice Street. It was quiet, dusty, and stark in the midmorning light, reminding me of a ghost town I had visited in Montana when I was a kid.

Near an intersection, we saw a trio of scruffy, open-faced restaurants—two on one side, and one on the other. Their rusted, scratched signs all advertised *com hen*. No one was eating at any of them. Huong glided up to a teenage boy standing in front of one of the shops. After asking a few questions, she informed me, "*Com hen* is usually for breakfast. You can have it for lunch, too, but not now." It was 10:30. She and the boy discussed which *com hen* joint was best. We expected him to peddle the one he appeared to be affiliated with, but he directed us to the restaurant across the street. We decided to come back in a few hours.

We had already eaten runny eggs and greasy little knobs of sausage at the hotel before our meeting with the managers, because breakfast was free and we needed something in our stomachs. We decided to tide ourselves over just a little bit more at Am Phu, which had been recommended by a chef in Saigon, the granddaughter of the head chef of the last Vietnamese emperor. I had found the woman during an online search and asked Huong to call her to get some suggestions. She told Huong that Am Phu was Hue's oldest continuously operating restaurant, dating back to 1947. For fun, I ordered *nem lui*, to compare it to Lac Thien's.

Just as the night before, the ingredients were set out before us on the table: a dish of peanut sauce and plates of greens; rice paper; and pressed, grilled pork. There were small differences from Lac Thien, such as the addition of bean sprouts, and the absence of star fruit because of the heavy rains in the night. Also absent was the herb *cai cuc*, and in its place the softer, curly *rau muong bao*. I prepared a roll and took a bite.

I can't say how I knew, but I did: this *nem lui* was better. Much better, even though I had liked Lac Thien's. The pork tasted fresher, lighter and cleaner. The peanut sauce was thick and substantial, nearly a dish in its own right. Without the citric tang of star fruit, I could taste each herb individually. I thought about the men back at the hotel. Had they never been to this place? If they had, then how could I trust them? If they hadn't, I wondered why not. I dipped another roll of rice-paper-wrapped pork into the peanut sauce and ignored the drumlike tightness of my belly. Already, their curmudgeonly opinions were losing credibility.

As we pedaled back to the clam rice restaurant, the heat was intense but not miserable, as it can often be as noon approaches. A motorcycle buzzed past, but otherwise, there were no vehicles on the streets. With its single-story buildings and lack of pop music blasting distorted from every shop, Hue felt as if it had been forsaken by the twenty-first century. Where were the endless Internet cafés that populate even the most remote tourist outposts? It was hard for me to envision Hue as a regal imperial capital, or its wide streets during the 1960s filled with American GIs and the shudder of artillery, when the loudest sound on that still Tuesday morning was the wheels of my bike shushing over the road.

As we handed our bikes to the old parking attendant in front of #7 Truong Dinh Street, the few locals eating inside glanced up at us with brief surprise but little long-term interest. Huong and I squatted in anticipation on low red plastic stools at a low blue plastic table, and I thought how crazy this was. It was as if we hadn't eaten at all that day, when in fact this was our third meal; it was scarcely noon, and my appetite was raging for *com hen*'s tiniest of clams collected from Con Hen, a small island in the Perfume River.

Huong ordered a bowl of clam rice for me and some clam gruel for herself. Gruel, she told me, was one of her favorites. I was beginning to realize she had many, many favorite foods. As our dishes arrived, the staff watched us from behind the metal preparation counter that ran along the side of the wall. We were out of place, Huong in her spaghetti-strap white tank top and stylish knee-length orange shorts, me in a less-revealing tank top and the baggy linen capris that a former boyfriend once called my "Jane Bowles pants," a description that is romantic if you're into the literary scene, but certainly not flattering.

It was a safe bet to guess that nonlocals didn't frequent this nameless *com hen* place. There were no signs in English, there wasn't a menu, and to a passerby—particularly one from the West—the restaurant would no doubt seem grungy. The blackened vat of clam broth looked as it if has been simmering atop the makeshift charcoal stove for decades. Above it, over a shelf, there was a rust-colored stain on the wall, from the incense burned to honor ancestors.

The bits and pieces stored inside alcoves were haggard: a dented thermos, a scraped coal burner, a scale whose face had nearly faded away.

But if you looked closer, as becomes instinctive after living for a while in a country such as Vietnam, where health code inspectors do not circulate, you would see that the stainless steel bowls holding the ingredients were polished. Beneath the scraps of food on the floor, the tile had been scoured. There is a difference between a place that is unclean and one that has been scrubbed a thousand times over, growing gray—just as humans do—with time. It is a difference that sets one shop apart from the other ten on the same street that sell the same dish and look, on the surface, just like it.

Unlike *nem lui* and many other Vietnamese dishes, *com hen* is assembled in the kitchen—or in this case, on the metal table at one side of the restaurant—before it is served. Its foundation is a bed of rice, which is topped with what appears to be a scoop of minced clams. In fact, they are whole. The smallest clams I have ever seen, like little specks of mushroom. On top of this is a judicious scattering of *rau ma*, coriander, spearmint, basil, and marinated banana flower. For texture the greens are topped with wonton sticks, bean sprouts, roasted peanuts, toasted sesame seeds, and pork crackling. *Com hen* is accompanied by a bowl of the water that the clams were boiled in, to be consumed in place of a drink.

The staff was still watching, casually, as I prodded the ingredients with my chopsticks, lifting a strand of *rau ma* and examining it before dropping it back in, conferring with Huong, and scribbling in my notebook. The same process with each ingredient, all before taking my first bite …

"#@**!!!"

My throat burned. My eyes watered as I reached over the broth and grabbed my iced tea.

"Too much mouthwash herb?" Huong asked.

I shook my head and gasped, "Hot."

"Hot hot, or spicy hot?" she asked, languidly, despite the tears streaming down my face.

"Spicy hot."

This did not concern her. She had many foreign friends. She knew that my gulping and gasping would pass, and that I wouldn't die, despite all spasms to the contrary.

Through my tears, I glanced at the women and girls behind the counter. They were not laughing—the occasional local response to the collision between tourists and too much chili. Nor did they have *stupid foreigner* expressions on their faces. An older woman smiled at me, either with pity or with sympathy. I preferred to believe it was the latter.

As my mouth cooled and I geared up for my next bite, Huong ate her porridge. "It's okay," she said, "but it's not my style." Then she ordered another bowl.

I raised an eyebrow.

"It's just water," she informed me. "I'll pee it out. That's a Vietnamese saying, you know."

"Something's lost in the translation," I told her.

I sweated through the entire dish. I really wanted to like clam rice, and I thought that I did, but I couldn't be sure, because I was so distracted by the feeling that my entire body—from my eyebrows to my toenails—had been set on fire. I had been dreaming of clam rice for weeks prior to this trip, and between bites, I gasped, "I think we should come back." I took a gulp of iced tea. "To try it again." My glass of iced tea was refilled. "With less chili."

Our bill came to 12,000 dong for one bowl of *com hen*, two bowls of *chao hen*, and four iced teas. Less than a dollar. Even Huong was surprised by this bargain. As we paid, she chatted with the older woman who had smiled at me.

"What did she say?" I asked, as we climbed on our bikes, hoping they weren't having a conversation about what foreigners can and cannot eat. I hated being lumped in with the riffraff.

"I was asking her where to find the best *bun bo Hue*. She told me to come back. She says that theirs is very good."

Monica & Phoebe

On our way back to the hotel, we stopped at a roadside stall for guava and *coc*. I had never seen *coc* before, a fruit that looks a bit like a crabapple. The woman selected a dozen for us, as well as a bagful of hard little green guavas. She asked if we wanted salt and chili, which is commonly used as a condiment for fruits. Although I felt as if I'd had enough chili to last me a lifetime, I knew the fruit would be better with it.

The woman held out a paper bag, and Huong poked her finger in. "That's really good," she said with surprise. "You should try it."

Ignoring that our hands had been gripping the grubby handles of our bicycles, I dabbed my finger into the salt. It turned out that my scalding *com hen* experience had not destroyed my taste buds. The salt had the concentration of a crusty sea salt, but the texture of powdered sugar. Yes, Huong told the woman, we'd definitely have chili and salt. And if she didn't mind, a little extra salt, please.

Back in our hotel room, we woke Julie, who was feeling a little better, despite her unfortunate attempt to eat. She had ordered a grilled cheese sandwich and tomato soup from room service, seeking the restoration that comes from familiar, bland foods. "Not bland," she said, pointing at the unfinished bowl of soup. "Not bland at all. Who puts that much chili in tomato soup?"

I rolled my eyes. "The same person who puts it in clam rice, apparently."

Huong peeled the *coc* with a paring knife. I poured salt and chili into a saucer and took it out to the little table on the balcony, where we had sat the night before, drinking wine and gazing out at the deep purple shadow of the Perfume River. While I waited for Huong and Julie, I dragged my finger through the fine consistency of the salt. Had the ancient Romans, who used salt as money—hence the word *salary*—discovered Hue's fine-spun version, they would surely have reserved it for bonus paychecks, to reward the most loyal and diligent of employees.

It was nearly four when Sebastien called to cancel dinner on behalf of himself and his chain-smoking cohorts. He did not offer any kind of excuse, just a mumble about being suddenly "busy," as if it was possible for something to "come up" for all three of them at the same time in a town as sedentary as Hue. Although we were curious about their idea of a *bun bo Hue* joint that "isn't

and foodies who craved local dishes served in authentic settings. But Huong had been talking to me about food all day, and she would rather analyze our personalities based on the TV show *Friends*, which she watched on DVD.

After much discussion, she decided that she was a Monica. "I'm very, very clean," she said, relating herself to Monica's character, who had OCD housecleaning habits.

"She also likes to cook," I said.

"No more talking about food."

"I'm talking about you. You're not exactly a chef."

She grimaced. "Ha ha."

"Who am I?" I asked, hoping that she would liken me to sexy Rachel, but without the selfishness.

"Phoebe."

"Phoebe's a dingbat," I protested.

Huong backpedaled. "Sure, yeah, but she's so much fun."

We finished our drinks. Though the conversation was pleasant, the margaritas weren't, and we decided that one round was enough. As we left, the teenage boy who worked behind the bar called out in cheerfully truncated English, "Have a nice!"

We did.

—

Fit for Kings

The following morning, before we toured the imperial citadel, I insisted on having another bowl of clam rice. The women who ran the restaurant smiled approvingly as Huong, Julie, and I pedaled up, arriving today at the appropriate time, the breakfast hour, when the rice was supple, the herbs still tingling, and the clams just boiled from their shells. The sky was a pallid haze, refusing to release the heat that lay trapped beneath it. The air was motionless, on the streets and inside the café, which was full. We took a table, confidently. We were no longer novices.

Not fully recovered, Julie was armed with a paper fan and the determination to not miss seeing the Imperial City. She still wasn't ready for a bowl of clam rice, though, so she had also brought along a trusty baguette. Huong ordered her much-anticipated bowl of *bun bo Hue*, and she requested that my *com hen* not come ablaze with the standard dose of chili. The cook did not find this offensive or even unusual. This is something I have always appreciated from kitchens in Vietnam, an acceptance that not everyone enjoys the same degree of heat.

It had not rained in the night, and so this *com hen* was topped with thin slivers of star fruit. Their tartness sparked against the dry crunch of the wonton sticks. The clams were light, and just a bit gritty from the alluvial bed of the Perfume River. The chili pinched through, roguish but painless, and then there was that cheeky spearmint, fighting for attention among the distinctive flavors. The pork crackling was clean and crunchy, unlike the greasy bagged specimens sold at 7-Elevens back home. I was not disappointed. This bowl of clam rice was everything I had hoped it would be.

There are rare and beautiful foods that I crave not only when I do not have them but also while I am in the process of eating them. My mother's raspberry pie. *Com hen.* Foods I want to both devour and save for later. I lingered over a spoonful of rice, clams, coriander, and marinated banana flower. Eating a dish and yearning for it at the same time. It is one of the most satisfying sensations I know.

The wide, flat streets were the same damp, ashen color of the Perfume River, which flowed through the city beneath the opaque sky. From the clam rice restaurant, we pedaled along the tree-lined boulevard that ran between the quiet shorefront park and the front wall of the fortress. We biked through a tunnel and into the compound, which is like a Russian stacking doll, with the Forbidden

Purple City fitted inside the Imperial City, which is fitted inside the Citadel.

The world enclosed within these walls once served as headquarters for the Nguyen dynasty, which united the country for the first time under a single rule. In 1802, Nguyen Anh (Emperor Gia Long) consolidated the fragmented, serpentine region south of China, and his descendents reigned until 1945, although for much of that time their authority was token, since Vietnam became a French protectorate in 1833.

Despite attempted coups and ongoing Franco-Viet tensions, the dynasty managed to produce an elaborate cuisine. One does not speak of Hue without acknowledging its culinary glory days. I parked my bike in front of a high mildewed wall whose surface had crumbled to reveal the ochre brick beneath it. On the other side were the palaces where Hue's apocryphal gastronomy originated. We were here to get in the mood for the imperial meal we would eat that night.

As we walked the hushed grounds, I tried to envision the emperors' concubines, courtiers, physicians, eunuchs, and scholars scurrying along these dirt paths, all employed to do one thing: his majesty's bidding. I also tried to picture 1968 and the Tet Offensive, when the North Vietnamese seized control of the Citadel for nearly a month, and the United States bombed the irreplaceable treasures of the Forbidden Purple City. But the grounds were too calm. The history of this stronghold had abandoned it, fleeing to dwell in more appropriate locales, such as Pulitzer Prize–winning history books and compelling PBS documentaries. What remained was quiet and humble, the ghost of the geomancy that had inspired it.

The Citadel was filled surprisingly with open spaces. Gazebos drifted like islands in the middle of a field. It was early, and there were few tourists. An old Vietnamese woman, wearing a cotton blouse and trousers, meandered along a ridge of raised earth with a basket under one arm, as if she were in the middle of the countryside. Dreaming of afternoon naps, Julie, Huong, and I talked about where we would like to hang hammocks. We wandered through crumbling gates. We crouched and grazed our fingers along the leaves of the *hoa mac co*, the "shy plant," which closed bashfully beneath our touch, with the exception of one.

"He's old, so he's not that ticklish," Huong explained, her voice as soft as the balmy air.

The halls, palaces, and red-lacquered throne room were handsome. Their details finely wrought. Delicately carved beams were painted the color of ivory. Pillars were traced in gold. Enameled tile work—pale pink lotus adrift in a yellow sea—reminded me of a cloisonné ring I had bought at Nordstrom for twenty dollars when I was twelve years old. My first adult purchase with my own money. A gesture of affinity with the Orient my grandfather loved when he was a sailor in the 1930s. The details of the buildings reflected what I like best about Vietnamese food. The purity of individual ingredients that make up the exceptional whole. Rice, river clams, star fruit, spearmint, and wonton sticks. But *com hen* is commoners' food, and I was here to get a sense of the complex cuisine that included, at its most overwrought, according to *Life in the Forbidden Purple City*, swallow's nest, grilled chopped phoenix meat, and sour peacock hash.

We admired the gilded canopy above the throne in the Palace of Supreme Harmony. I dutifully read through descriptions of extravagance in the books I purchased at the gift shop. But when we left, I was no closer to envisioning banquets of orangutan's lips and elephant feet than when we first arrived. After touring the royal grounds, the only meal that seemed suitable was a quiet picnic of *banh mi* sandwiches purchased from a street stall outside the gates, with some *coc* fruit dipped in a bed of downy salt for dessert.

Although the first Nguyen emperor came to power in 1802, the royals' real culinary revolution did not begin until the appointing of Tu Duc, who ruled from 1848 to 1883. From his reign on, food became a way for emperors "to express their social rank and artistic sensibilities," according to an essay in *The Cuisine of Viet Nam*. The essay also claims that of Vietnam's 1,700 unique dishes, 1,400 originated in Hue. This may seem like an exaggeration, but under most of the emperors who followed Tu Duc, the royal chefs were not permitted to serve the same menu twice in a one-year period. As explained in *Life in the Forbidden Purple City,* "Every day, His Majesty has three meals ... Each meal consists of fifty different dishes prepared by fifty royal cooks [because] he found it boring to have the same food for a long time."

This means 150 dishes a day, served in different combinations, which were no doubt compounded with variations and new dishes throughout the year. Given the nine emperors who came after Tu Duc—particularly the playboy Bao Dai, and even excluding the modest Duy Tan, who cared about the royal budget and requested only three dishes per meal—1,400 is probably a reasonable estimate.

Imported delicacies and unusual ingredients such as rhinoceros skin and deer sinew aside, the question of how so many different dishes could realistically be conceived is in part answered with Hue's four seasons, which provide the variety necessary for such a labyrinthine cuisine, despite arguments to the contrary on the part of our hotel's management. Spring brings vegetables such as eggplant and pumpkin, as well as prawns, crab, cuttlefish, and in May, succulent duck meat. Oysters, my beloved clams, many of spring's holdover veggies, and a cornucopia of fruit—mangoes, pineapples, longan, jackfruit, papaya—are the main harvests of the summer months. In the fall, vegetable crops dwindle, and fruit becomes as dignified as the season: tangerine, persimmon, grapefruit. With winter come salted fish and hearty vegetables such as beets, green peas, cabbage, and mushrooms.

Vietnam is said to have taken its imperial cues from the excesses of China, with its elaborate, banquetlike feasts, and possibly some of its methods from Vietnam's ethnic Cham minority, who once ruled its southern region, and whose meals included many small dishes rather than a few large ones. Like under the old French monarchy, chefs were conscripted with the goal of achieving culinary perfection. As well, food was used to separate rulers from their subjects, both symbolically and physically.

In Vietnam's imperial dining realm, according to *Life in the Forbidden Purple City*, "Each cook made a different dish and gave it to the eunuchs through the royal guards' hands. The eunuchs handed the dishes over to five royal maid-servants who themselves served the King with them." This extravagance all took place within the unpretentious Citadel complex we had toured. That evening, we set out to experience what remained of this decadent legacy.

In Hue, there were a few well-known kitchens practicing the traditions of the imperial chefs. The last time Huong visited, she and her rugby team whooped it up in a famous restaurant where diners dress up in lavish robes. "How was the food?" I asked. She shrugged. She thought it was okay, but they'd had a lot of beer, so she wasn't sure. In search of authenticity over kitsch, we chose a quieter restaurant recommended by a few locals.

The night rain that is common in autumn was falling hard when we arrived at the old villa. We were dressed up mostly in black, and all in skirts, for a night out on the town. Women with umbrellas scurried out to shelter us as we dashed from the taxi to the porch. We were taken out back, where rain enclosed the covered, L-shaped terrace and served as a sheer backdrop for a bouquet of pretty yellow lanterns.

With rain pattering into the courtyard, the setting was romantic. The clientele was decidedly not: a budget-travel couple in khaki shorts, and two belching Australians in T-shirts and blue jeans, their table scattered with Huda beer cans. Apparently, when an empire capitulates to the proletariat, it's hard to uphold a dress code. I was annoyed. Back when I was a flat-broke backpacker, even in remote jungles, I carried one below-the-knee dress in a Ziploc bag for occasions such as this, out of respect for my hosts.

Because we had learned that many royal chefs based their recipes on ordinary dishes from their home villages, our expectations were high. We had spent the past forty-eight hours swooning over the ordinary dishes of Hue. We could only imagine how much better they would be, taken to imperial heights.

Huong had ordered our meal in advance, a standard imperial set menu for two and an imperial vegetarian set menu for one. Although the choices offered to diners did not include a vegetarian prix fixe meal, when asked, the kitchen was happy to oblige, as most Vietnamese kitchens are when it comes to guests who don't eat meat. Because of this, before we had even tasted a bite, the restaurant endeared itself to Julie, who was always grateful when anyone went out of the way to accommodate her dining habits.

The first dish in our imperial feast was just as it was described on the menu: *Spring roll decorated on formed peacock*. The peacock was carved from a pineapple and carrots; the crunchy little bulbs of minced pork and vegetable spring rolls represented the feathers, sprouting from skewers on the bird's humped back. Taking a bite with Vietnam's imperial rulers in mind, I was at a loss. The spring rolls were fine, but they were deep-fried spring rolls. Nothing special. I would certainly not dream about them the way I dreamed about clam rice.

Next came vegetable soup, which was followed by a cluster of steamed pink shrimp draped over the edge of a cocktail glass. The glass sat on a plate adorned with three red chilies, which had been snipped and given tiny black seed eyes so they resembled koi fish swimming among cilantro seaweed on a ceramic sea of blue. Cute, but again, the shrimp was nothing special. Nothing to strike an emperor's fancy.

And so the meal continued.

Banh khoai—Hue's specialty crepe. Fine. A salad of sliced green figs, peanuts, and sesame seeds, scooped onto little shrimp crisps. Fine. Mixed steamed lotus rice, served with an elegant lotus flower at the side of the plate. Fine. Fried fish in tomato sauce. Fine. At no point during the meal did any of us stop the conversation and declare a longing to have been born into the imperial family.

We had a menu listing the English name of each dish. Studying it, Julie said, "I wish it explained how boiled shrimp and lotus rice fits into imperial cooking. Maybe that would help."

"What do you think of the food?" I asked Huong.

She was silent for a moment and then said, politely, "These chopsticks are really nice."

"I feel mean not liking it," I said.

"They're so nice," Julie said, glancing guiltily toward the kitchen.

The women who ran the restaurant were lovely, and the setting peaceful and shabbily refined, but the food just wasn't spectacular. "I think I'm expecting too much," I said. "You know, because of everything I've read." If this had been just any old Vietnamese restaurant—without the weight of the emperors on its shoulders—perhaps we would have enjoyed our meal. I wondered if this wasn't revisionist history's fault, and if imperial cuisine was ever spectacular, or if this was a case of the emperors' chefs wearing no aprons.

During the course of my research, I had read, "After so many years of not having enough food, the Vietnamese are hankering for more, looking with nostalgia at food they remembered from the countryside, childhood or even the war." Was it possible that sentimentality was responsible for the revival of imperial cuisine? After all, it was not *pho*, which was born in the north. It was not *banh xeo*, which was born in the south. It was an amalgamation of specialties that chefs had brought from all regions of the country. It represented the original unification of Vietnam. It represented pride in the country as a whole.

We sipped our wine, the agreeable Bordeaux that was ubiquitous throughout Vietnam. Lightning flashed in the distance, and the rain flared like shattered glass. For a moment, the courtyard was iridescent. A buoyant Muzak version of *West Side Story* played over the stereo. With longing, I remembered the gossamer melodies of the imperial court, which I once heard during a concert at the Opera House in Saigon.

"I wish Hoang Anh was here," I said. I was speaking of the woman whose grandfather had been chef to the last emperor of Vietnam. She was an expert on imperial cuisine, and she had become a kind of invisible chaperone, accompanying us throughout our meals in Hue. It was not uncommon for one of us to take a bite of a dish or examine an herb and then say, "I wonder what Hoang Anh knows about this one."

I wanted to ask her what kind of imperial dishes she was dedicated to preserving. These dishes we ate tonight? If so, why? They didn't taste any different from foods I'd eaten around Vietnam. But our meeting with Hoang Anh, who lived in Saigon, was still a few weeks away, so we added these questions to the growing list we already had for her, which included the origins of clam rice and *bun bo Hue*, and why salt in Hue was so soft.

We ate our dessert. Tapped our toes to "Let's get physical, physical. I wanna get physical." Played with the litter of puppies that tumbled into the dining room—contrary to stereotypes, most dogs are pets in Vietnam. The women who ran the restaurant were delighted as Julie held and cuddled each one in turn. We finished our wine and let our conversation trail away from the food. Huong, as usual at the end of each day, was happy to change the subject, and she announced that she couldn't remember which character she wanted to be from *Sex and the City*, Samantha or Miranda.

"Samantha's the sex fiend," I said, looking at Julie, who looked back at me, concerned.

"The one with the short hair," Huong said, "and the baby."

"Miranda," Julie said, relieved.

"Yeah, that's right," Huong said, happily, "Miranda."

Somewhere up the Perfume River, Emperor Tu Duc—once the arbiter of Vietnamese culture, just as Carrie Bradshaw had become the arbiter for twenty-first-century women—was surely rolling over in his imperial grave.

Little Sisters

Between our morning spent at the Citadel and our evening at the restaurant serving imperial cuisine, Julie slept. Wandering around in the dense heat had wiped her out. Huong and I bought tickets for the next day's boat trip to the imperial tombs and then headed for the snack restaurant. But as we pedaled past the market, beneath the graying sky, she suggested that we swing in for a quick *bun bo Hue*, as if *bun bo Hue* were a modest veggie spring roll and not a tub of beef soup. She wanted to know how the market's version compared to Lac Thien's, which was still her favorite, with the *com hen* café coming in a close second.

"You'll ruin your appetite," I said, foolishly, as if such a thing were possible. Not only was Huong never full but she had also become single-minded in her determination to find the city's best *bun bo Hue*.

"Snacks really are just snacks," she protested, and she steered her bike into the little parking area in front of the market.

We wound our way past stalls selling metal saucepans, plastic colanders, soccer balls, twine, coffee filters, and baseball caps with the names of American corporations misspelled on their crowns, until we reached the food stalls clustered beneath a patchwork of corrugated tin and plastic tarp. Each shop consisted of a low, open preparation area, which also served as a display area. Squatting on low red plastic stools, diners used their laps as tables.

Huong studied the tapestry of vendors, which all looked the same to me, and made her choice: a cluster of pots and bowls presided over by a woman wearing a long-sleeved silk blouse and brown corduroy fedora festooned with a floppy velvet poinsettia. Huong ordered her *bun bo Hue*, and because I couldn't just sit there and not eat, I ordered *bun thit heo nuong*, one of my all-time favorite dishes, grilled pork on a bed of fresh rice noodles, whose flavor is tinted with the grassiness of the banana leaf bowl that it's served in. The pork was a little too fatty, but an even charring made up for it. Just the right degree of crispiness to set off the pliant texture of the noodles. Huong was growing authoritative on the subject of *bun bo Hue*, and she informed me that the broth in the market was better than Lac Thien's, and if the beef had been fresher, this might have been the best soup so far.

Her bowl was nearly empty when the sky collapsed. Water bore down on the tarps, flowed over the rims of the metal roofs, and irrigated the open lanes. The air, saturated within the walls of water, turned to steam, and the market brewed in the early afternoon monsoon.

through the world of snacks—collectively known as *banh Hue*—by sampling the *banh beo*. Many travelers are familiar with this dish. It is one of Hue's most popular, perhaps because it demonstrates how wonderfully simple—and in its simplicity, complex—Vietnamese food can be.

Essentially, *banh beo* is a medallion of steamed rice batter topped with shredded shrimp and a modest pork crackling. But this description, while accurate, is inadequate. *Banh beo* is often called a small pancake, but it's not a pancake, and it's certainly not the thin buttermilk pancake my father makes from my Grandpa Clarence's recipe every Christmas morning. It is gelatinous, though not really, because gelatin implies a limp jellyfish quality, and there is a chewiness to *banh beo*, not gum chewy, but a firm chewy that is offset by the shrimp, which is crunchy, although crunchy makes it sound too brittle. Nor will crispy do, and while crumbly gets a bit closer, it's not a pretty enough word, because *banh beo* is such a pretty tidbit of food.

Banh beo defies the English language. It is like love or sorrow, understandable only through the experience of it. Here in this spare little café, served in tiny saucers, it tasted fresher than any I'd had before. I drizzled the rich brown fish sauce spiked with slivers of red and green chilies over the shrimp before scooping out the "pancake" with a spoon and eating it in a single bite.

Next came *banh loc*, another hard-to-describe dish. It was served in small banana leaf parcels, and when I opened one, there was a moment of delight, as if I had discovered a prehistoric creature preserved inside a lozenge of translucent resin. But the creature was a fresh little shrimp, its vivid pink shell still on, curled up as if sleeping. The resin was steamed manioc batter. Because of the manioc and the banana leaf, the batter of *banh loc* tastes different from that of *banh beo*. It tastes of summer. It also has a stickier quality. And it is creamier.

I enjoyed the other two snacks well enough: *banh ram it*, a pork and shrimp cake, and *banh nam*, minced shrimp and pork on a bed of steamed rice batter. I was trying to decide which I liked best, *banh beo* or *banh loc*, when Huong, who was engrossed in a bundle of sour pressed pork that she had special ordered, said, "We should definitely come back tomorrow afternoon, after the boat trip."

Clam rice before the boat trip, snacks after. "Mmm," I said, settling on *banh loc* as my favorite and ordering another round, "definitely."

Happiness

I made sure we were up in time for clam rice before our river cruise. When I was done with my first bowl, I ordered another. After three days in a row, I might have grown tired of teeny-tiny clams and rice, but they continued to amaze me. Each bite had its own composition. A masterpiece to hang in the *com hen* gallery I was assembling in my mind.

Julie was feeling better, and she had her own bowl of clam rice, light on the chili, and without pork crackling. It was a daring dish to attempt while recovering from the flu, but not only did she try it, she also loved it and ate it all. Huong had *bun bo Hue*, mixing in herbs meant for the clam rice and adding more shrimp paste, which she said made it taste like the version at Lac Thien. She also had an order of clam rice, which she decided was pretty good.

Gazing out at the dusty, sun-stroked avenue, at the scruffy, less populated *com hen* shop across the way, she said, "This street is so nice. It's a cute little street. I'm happy." It was lovely, how often she declared her happiness.

"Me too," Julie murmured, her complexion wan but her expression peaceful, as she repelled the heat with the slow wagging of her paper fan.

"Agreed," I said. But I was sad, as well, at the thought of leaving Hue the next morning. I missed clam rice already, its eye-watering flare of spearmint beneath the star fruit and crispy rice sticks. I was tempted to order a third bowl, but I was so full I was afraid it would make me sick. Instead, I looked forward to my return, in a year's time, or maybe five, when I would come back to this "cute little street" to have this dish once again and remember, with the first bite, the happiness of being here now.

In *A Cook's Tour*, adventure-eater Anthony Bourdain asks, "When is food magic? When was the last time food transported you?" Not only to a higher plane, a deeper consciousness, primordial bliss, but to a time and a place—in the world, in your heart—where you have been before. Proust was certainly onto something. Food is the unrivaled trigger for memories, and from this point forward, *com hen* would join the cache of dishes that allow me to recall happy times.

Food not only provides a foundation for moments of happiness but it can also keep happiness alive, because flavors and aromas—the qualities needed to transport you into the past—can be re-created in the present. Give me a maple bar, and I am a fifth grader standing eagerly in the driveway of our house in Moses Lake, beside my grandpa's Toyota pickup as he arrives to visit,

With its simple lunch of star fruit soup, stir-fried beef with star fruit, and fried tuna filets, our leisurely day on the river was a perfect palate cleanser from the gluttonous behavior that had overtaken us in Hue. The reprieve, though, was short-lived. As the boat neared its moorage, our greedy appetites returned, and we willed it to go faster—we wanted Julie to try snacks before we left Hue. Sadly, we didn't make it back in time.

"It's okay," she assured us, hiding her disappointment. "At least I got to try clam rice."

Huong decided that she wanted to find Ba Rot, the "very best" *bun bo Hue* restaurant.

"We're having dinner at the hotel in an hour," I protested. "They're preparing several courses for us."

"I'm pretty hungry," she said, cheerfully.

Because our train for Hoi An would leave early in the morning, she feared she wouldn't have enough time to track the restaurant down before we left, so we rode our bikes up and down the riverside cafés, asking directions from people who seemed to know what they were talking about but didn't, as one dead end led to another until it was time to return to the hotel.

Sebastien, the loose-limbed resident manager, served as our host for a tasting meal prepared by Mike, whom we had secretly nicknamed The Hot Chef, and not just because of the spicy tomato soup Julie had gotten from room service. Given his criticisms of the local cuisine, and what we now believed to be our own expertise, we were curious to taste what he considered good food. Although it was not as dramatic as Didier Corlou's tasting menu in Hanoi, our dinner in the La Residence dining room was first rate—inspired by the flavors of Southeast Asia and creatively paired with a beautiful selection of wines. We were impressed, and at one point, as we were eating local snapper in a tangy caramel sauce, Huong muttered, "The Hot Chef can cook."

Our dinner also cleared up the question of the men's disdain for Hue food. A few times during the meal, Mike stopped by our table to check in on us, and I asked him, "Have you ever had clam rice?"

"I haven't heard of it," he said.

Astonished, I said, "How is that possible? How long have you been here?"

"Five months."

We were silent. Five months, and he hadn't even heard of *com hen*?

"But not really," he added, with a humble, boyish frankness that instantly bought our forgiveness, "because I've been depressed for three."

Julie, Huong, and I nodded sympathetically, drawn into the spell cast by The Hot Chef's deep, sad blue eyes. But the moment was quickly broken as Sebastien piped in. "Anyway, street food, well that's different. If that's what you were talking about, it is the restaurants in Hue that are no good. The street food here is great."

Fat, Full, & Happy

We woke early the following morning. The train for Hoi An was leaving in just a few hours, at nine, and we still needed to buy our tickets. We had been told that the railway allowed purchasing in advance only for Hanoi-to-Saigon passengers, and if on the day of travel there was space left over, we could buy our leg of the journey.

It was dumping rain, as if the sky had saved the water it didn't use the day before and added it to today's. We could not even see the river from our balcony. Julie was feeling sick again. I wanted clam rice. Huong was depressed over the thought of leaving without eating at Ba Rot. Our discussion was quick, our decision unanimous, and the phone call successful. A private car would take us to Hoi An for scarcely more than the price of three train tickets. Although sorry that she would not see Huong fulfill her *bun bo Hue* quest, Julie burrowed back under the covers. Huong and I headed for the front desk to ask the happy-to-practice-English receptionist directions to Ba Rot.

The young woman nodded thoughtfully at our request and then said, "If you want good *bun bo Hue*, you should go to the shop on Ly Thuong Kiet instead." This was the place where I had realized that I'm not the biggest fan of *bun bo Hue*. "It's in the Lonely Planet," she told us, as if that said it all.

We explained politely that the restaurant was more for tourists, and then told her what we had been eating. She was pleased with our choice of Ba Do. "Their quality of snacks is quite good," she said. She was amazed—laughing and clapping—when she learned that I had fallen in love with clam rice. "Foreigners can't eat that," she disclosed, as if I had pulled off a staggering feat, like starting my own Democratic party in Hanoi.

Huong assured the receptionist that we really wanted to go to Ba Rot, and the girl was nearly giddy as she gave us directions. Because of the monsoon rains, we took a cab, crossing over the river, whose gray flow we could scarcely make out from the bridge. We wound through the same muddy back streets that led to the snack shop, before the driver pulled up to a corner. We stared out.

In the space where there should have been a building, there was just a wet cement floor and a big tarp ceiling. The tarp was strung above three low plastic tables, a scattering of stools, bowls filled with raw meat, a steaming aluminum tureen, and a woman seated on five stacked stools beside the pot. She didn't seem the least bit surprised to see us hop out of a cab and splash through the puddles toward her café.

She was beautiful, with high cheekbones and bright eyes. Her slender figure was emphasized by a matching brown shirt and pants that blossomed with darker brown cabbage roses. Despite her rustic establishment, she wore diamond studs in her ears. As Huong hungrily watched her ladle out two bowls of what was reputed to be the city's best *bun bo Hue*, the woman explained why we had such a hard time finding her place. Decades ago, its original name was *O Rot*. *O* is the Central Vietnamese word for *Ba*, which means Mrs. in the north and south. O Rot (Mrs. Rot) was the woman's grandmother. Now that the woman ran the restaurant, it was named after her, Mrs. Roi, which could be O Roi or Ba Roi, depending on who you asked. Many older people, though, still called it by its old name of Ba Rot.

Huong was distracted as she translated this potential for confusion. She saved her concentration for stirring thin, glistening slices of raw beef into the broth. I could see the anticipation in her expression. Given our letdown at the imperial cuisine restaurant, I was as nervous as she was eager. I didn't want her to be disappointed.

Huong sipped the broth. Without making a final judgment, she said, "This one is really good. The flavoring, it's spicy." Another sip. "The shrimp paste, very good." And another sip. "It doesn't taste fatty."

I could tell by looking at it that the beef was fresh and lean, and although I was still not a fan of the pressed meat that is also a part of *bun bo Hue*, this was the best I'd had so far. The crab sausage was light, not salty and fishy. The broth tasted buttery rather than sweet.

"The chili paste is better. Moister," Huong commented. She conferred with Ba Roi. After a short discussion, she told me, approvingly, "She makes it herself."

I adored Ba Roi. It wasn't just because she made her own chili paste, or that her *bun bo Hue* didn't taste like a bowl of candied meat. I liked her saucy expression, and that she was proud of her restaurant, even though it was made of nothing more than a tarp. I liked it that she took my presence for granted. And I especially liked her when she asked how old I was.

This much I could tell her in Vietnamese. "*Ba muoi chin.*" Thirty-nine.

She gasped and declared that I looked *hai muoi hai*. Twenty-two.

Starting in on her second bowl, Huong said, "Don't get excited. She doesn't meet many foreigners. She doesn't know any better."

Although there were no walls, Ba Roi's space was cozy. Its air smelled of the warm broth, whose steamy condensation coated our bare skin. As I took pictures of her, Ba Roi laughed dismissively at the idea of being in a book about Vietnamese food, but we could tell that she was pleased. She and Huong suddenly became serious as they instructed me to look at the tureen, whose round, traditional shape—different from the stout, cylindrical pots in the other restaurants we'd been to—was responsible for the superior flavor of the broth. I'm not versed in the science of the kitchen and was happy to take their word for it, because the soup was so much better than the others I'd tasted, keeping me warm as the rain flooded off the tarp, bounced off the cement, and splashed onto to the backs of my legs. When Huong told Ba Roi about our clam rice obsession, Ba Roi recommended the very shop we had discovered, and I felt pleased to be a part of the local dining community.

Huong scraped her spoon along the bottom of her empty bowl. I knew the look on her face. She was considering a third serving. I nudged her. We still had to hit the *com hen* shop before being back at the hotel to meet the car at eleven. Reluctantly, we pushed away from the table, said good-bye to Ba Roi, and plunged through the rain to the waiting taxi. In the back seat, dripping wet, Huong smiled, finally feeling the satisfaction that she had begun to doubt existed. She declared, "That really is the best *bun bo Hue* in Hue."

In the 1800s Jean Anthelme Brillat-Savarin wrote, "The discovery of a new dish contributes more to human happiness than that of a new star." I first read this not in the author's own book, *The Physiology of Taste*, but in an essay in *The Cuisine of Viet Nam*, and I thought of it as the taxi pulled up to our clam rice shop. The entire staff gathered at the front, cheering as we ran toward them through the pouring rain. Huong told them that we were leaving town that morning and I needed one last bowl of clam rice before I went. I'd already had a whole bowl of meaty *bun bo Hue*, but anxious at the thought of soon leaving *com hen* behind, I had two bowls of clam rice for the road.

On our way back to La Residence, through a downpour that would have gotten on Noah's last nerve, we directed our taxi driver to our lady who sold *coc* fruit on the side of the road. Weighed down by water, the tarp over her cart drooped dangerously. She was cocooned in a blue rain poncho, and as we popped our heads out of the taxi window, she sloshed toward us, laughing as if we were the funniest things she had ever seen. Like our taxi driver, she thought we were crazy, cruising around in a cab that cost ten times more than the food we were eating. She packed an extra bag of salt and chili for us. Water ran down her face and over my arms as we exchanged fruit and money.

As we pulled away, I declared, "*Toi map, toi no, toi vui.*" I'm fat, I'm full, I'm happy.

Huong smiled and said, "I want to hug you now."

She wrapped her arms around me and held on tight as we returned to the hotel to pack our bags, rouse Julie, and leave Hue.

Hoi An

Central Vietnam

" Cooking is like love. It should be entered into with abandon or not at all. "

Harriet Van Horne

Entertaining the Barbarians

Outside the window of our van on the way to Hoi An, the sky was murky and the air bleak with drizzle. Still, we held out hope for Hai Van Pass, which is considered one of the most beautiful routes in the world. Perhaps the weather would show a well-timed clemency, as it did on the day of our boat trip up the Perfume River.

Suddenly, though, our van entered a hyper-lit, suspiciously long, and very dry tunnel. When Huong asked, our driver told her that we were going through the mountain rather than along its hazardous, hairpin rim. Sheryl Crow sang in the background, a plastic helicopter bobbed on the dashboard, and our driver smiled, understandably pleased with this new, 6.3-kilometer bypass that would make the trip much safer and quicker.

If I weren't preoccupied, I probably would have been upset at missing out on one of the planet's greatest views, but as I nibbled on *coc* fruit and stared at the fluorescent glow on the cement arc of the tunnel's wall, my thoughts—and appetite—were shifting from Hue to Hoi An. When I lived in Vietnam, I came to Hoi An with my then boyfriend, Sam, on one of my first holidays from teaching. We stayed three tranquil days, after living for nearly a year in Saigon, with its population of six very noisy million. Hue is sleepy in a poetic, dreamlike way; Hoi An is sleepy in a congenial, small-town way. I remembered sitting in the morning quiet of the Hoi An Market, having one of my first real conversations in Vietnamese, putting my lessons to use with the vendors, weathered women who were happy to include me in everyday gossip about fish and family. I remembered how the calm of the days flowed into the calm of the nights, and the hush of the main street where I sat with a shop owner who told me her poignant life story over the sale of a blue and white ceramic teapot.

Mostly, though, I remembered the meals. We protected fresh grilled crab and icy beer from tornadoes of sand on desolate, wind-blown Cua Dai Beach. We loitered for hours on the balcony of a waterfront restaurant with the owner's adolescent son, who spoke fluent French and cooked our meal. We sat one night amid the waxen glow of oil lamps in a timbered café eating the *hoanh thanh* (wonton) soup that the town is famous for.

There had been other travelers in Hoi An at that time, and I recalled them well, since there were so few of us, browsing the tailor shops whose showcase item that season was a bright, sunflower-patterned sundress; perusing the art galleries, all of which sold wispy watercolors of Hoi An's UNESCO World Heritage–protected shop houses; and sitting in cafés eating wonton soup. We the riverfront Bach Dang Streets. Although enticingly lantern-lit and prettily decorated, making the most of their historic Chinese architecture, they were filled with backpackers and tour groups. There were no street stalls in this area, and the night market looked damp and cold, despite the steam rising off the soup pots.

Huong scouted for signs of *mi quang*, another local specialty. This egg noodle soup was recommended by her friend Thong in Hanoi, who had spent a great deal of time in Hoi An while working as a liaison for the film production crew on *The Quiet American*. The rain felt as if it were going to last forever. There were no streetlights, and the night was dark and melancholy. Although we were not depressed, just chilly, tired, and coming down from our Hue high, we were hungry in the way that depressed people are hungry, craving food for comfort. I was leaning toward the warmth of wonton soup when Huong declared that she wanted a steak at the Tam Tam Café.

Although I had not been thinking about Western food, it was the right choice. I didn't want to leap directly from clam rice to *cao lau* without a buffer. In a noisy, foreigner-filled restaurant, Huong attacked a bloody steak while Julie and I surrendered to the familiar flavors of artisanal cheese, crusty bread, and red wine.

As the storm wrapped around the night, we climbed into our uncomfortable beds in a room that smelled like damp tea leaves and felt like the cabin of an old wooden sailing ship. Its walls, floor, and ceiling were made of dark timber planks, and the lamplight out in the hall seeped beneath the door, creating a brothel glow. Whenever anyone walked in the room across the hall, we felt the quiver of each footstep. But the heavy rains sang a sedative lullaby. Protected inside mosquito netting, we slept. I would like to say that I dreamed of the clam rice we had left behind, or the *mi quang* to come, but full of good cheese and red wine, I crashed beneath the waves and did not dream at all.

Family Traditions

When we woke, it was to a gray gloom lurking around the edges of the curtains. We wandered sleepily to the Hai Café, to rendezvous with twenty other foreigners who were also taking the Red Bridge class. Finally, we were going to cook. I was nervous.

I love being in the kitchen. I subscribe to *Gourmet*, *Food & Wine*, *Bon Appetit*, *Saveur*, and *Gastronomica* magazines. I've even been known to whip up an original dish for dinner with friends. But I'm not a natural. I have to work at it. Occasionally I have to make too many mistakes before I get something right. And when I do get it right, it isn't always the prettiest dish on the table. My cakes especially are known for their lack of beauty. With only one shot at each class we took, I couldn't afford my usual method of trial and error.

The students were divided into three groups, and as our clique of seven took the lead, I affixed myself to our guide, a gangly eighteen-year-old named Dong. Heading toward the market, I asked questions about his childhood. It was clear that he was not often asked about his own life. Eagerly, he told me that when he was a kid, he never set foot in the market, other than to buy snacks. "When I got this job," he said with a grin, "I had to ask my mother to give me a tour and explain everything."

"Ladies and gentlemens!"

Dong began each of his enthusiastic commentaries as if we were at the circus, introducing custard apples and lemongrass as if they were lion tamers and tightrope walkers. With the enthusiasm of a ringmaster, he described how to soften sheets of dried rice paper. "Ladies and gentlemens! Wrap a stack of ten to fifteen in banana leaves and leave them for three hours." He showed us the line of demarcation between the women selling fish from the river and those selling fish from the sea. He grasped a catfish, checking the body for firmness, the eyes for black color, and the gills to make sure they were dark red inside. He was a scrawny, theatrical, up-and-coming Vietnamese version of Didier Corlou. He was also incredibly sweet.

I scribbled everything he said in my little black notebook, because I was interested, and because like many kids when they are insecure, I had once sought confidence in being teacher's pet. Occasionally, Dong would pick up a kitchen gadget or piece of fruit and say, "Miss Kim, four years in Vietnam, do you know this one?" Happy to display the knowledge I possessed—to counterbalance any lack of expertise I might later reveal in the kitchen—I would say, "coconut shredder" or "banana flower," and then smile with false modesty.

The market's serious predawn fish trade had come and gone, and bargaining was less fevered now, taking place among housewives shopping for the day's meals. The others in our group—a couple from England and two pals from Germany—were awed by the sensory overload. As Dong moved from stall to stall, breezily describing longan fruit, stainless steel papaya peelers, and the roaming tax man, I marveled as I often did at how looking closely at a Vietnamese market is to peer intimately into the daily lives of the people who shopped there. The world may have been rocketing into the industrialized future, but people in Hoi An still got their vitamins as they had for centuries, according to Dong, showing us a nubby, vitamin-A-rich bitter melon. Spending so much time in these markets was also making me understand that I could tell as much about my own community by looking at where it shopped. My friends and I frequent Whole Foods and Trader Joe's, whose vitamin and nutritional supplement sections are as large as their organic fruit departments, and whose omega-3-, vitamin-C-, and calcium-fortified packaged foods reveal both determination and desperation when it comes to health.

The market also showed me how the people of Hoi An still lived on a human scale: laundry detergent was sold in dainty packets, toilet paper by the single roll, and cooking oil in eight-ounce bottles that fit into plastic carry bags tied to the ends of motorcycle handlebars. There were no shopping trolleys that could transport gallons of Coke and end-of-the-world-size cases of canned tomato sauce—or my grandma, who liked to ride through Costco waving to fellow shoppers as if she were on a float.

Looking around, I realized how the market represented something different for each person in our group. For me, it offered a greater understanding of the entwined relationship between food and culture. For the natives of Hoi An, it was life, just daily life, going about its business. For Dong, it was part of an exciting new job that brought relative prosperity for him and his family. For my fellow students, it was a journey into the new and exotic. For Julie, it was a mosaic of images influenced by aperture, exposure, and ambient light. For Huong, it was a beacon, signaling her place in Vietnam's future. As Dong picked up a bag of Trung Nguyen whole beans and informed us that the best Vietnamese coffee comes from the center of the country, and that this was the best brand, Huong leaned toward me and whispered, "We were just hired to help Trung Nguyen rebrand." And while Dong explained how to use a metal filter to make traditional drip coffee, Huong leaned her head on my shoulder. "We're going to change their packaging. It's very exciting," she said of the creative challenge that had been inaccessible to an energetic, ambitious young Vietnamese woman just a few years before.

We were all adrift in our own unique views of the market, until Dong picked up a bumpy green custard apple and reminded us just how small the world can be. "When I was a little boy," he said, "my mom warned me, never swallow the seed. If you do, a tree will grow inside of you."

Huong nodded in agreement. "My mom said that, too."

The girl from England murmured that her mother told her the same thing about regular apple seeds.

Julie smiled. "For us, it was watermelon seeds."

Reuniting with the other two groups of students at a boat landing near the market, we took a scenic river ride to the Red Bridge Cooking School. Hemmed by a picturesque stand of bamboo, the classroom was prettily situated on a bank of the river, in an open-air pavilion whose wooden tables held individual gas burners that gazed over the quiet water. The steep roof was made of thatch, and the rustic pots of clay.

Before we were taken to the cooking area, Dong led us on a tour of the grounds, where we met the au naturel form of many of the ingredients we had just seen in the market. Grinning slyly, he pointed to a branch and said, "This is a betel nut tree. You see this one, the nut, maybe you see old women chewing on it in the market. It makes your lips red, your teeth black, and … your head high."

His timing was great, and everyone laughed.

Dong was irresistible as he continued, "This is the seed from the papaya tree. Only the female trees give fruit. The male does not." Another sly smile. "If you have a male tree, throw it away. The male does nothing."

The Australian wives got a big chuckle out of this, and the husbands rolled their eyes. I laughed, too, although my mind was shooting ahead, to the individual stoves in the cooking area. My nervousness was holding steady, a stomach-tingling combination of excitement and a nagging fear of failure, goaded by the memory of my first attempt to cook in the third grade, when an accidental cup of water instead of a tablespoon turned peanut butter cookies into dense peanut butter cake. Despite my mom's reassurances that it could happen to anyone, my culinary self-doubt was born.

"Ladies and gentlemens …"

From our front row seats, Julie, Huong, and I looked up to see not Dong, but Chef Hai, the head of the school, and we instantly knew where Dong picked up his catchphrases, cadence, and rhythmic bonhomie. With the authority of a practiced comedian, Chef Hai declared, "You do a good job, you have a good lunch. You do a bad job, think about dinner. Now, we'll start with a demonstration. Later, we'll try hands on. More fun, but more dangerous. Good luck with that."

And we were off.

Decorative tomato roses and cucumber foliage. Warm squid salad and eggplant in clay pot. Nothing too complex. The prep work was done for us, and we were assigned stirring and simmering. Throughout the process, we learned tricks for modifying recipes with ingredients found back home. Huong thought the class was terrific: straightforward and practical. Julie was unable to participate, because that would mean putting her camera down.

I began to relax, as I inevitably do once I am actually in the kitchen, focusing on the steps, bringing crushed lemongrass and salt to boil in the clay pot. The overcast sky kept the debilitating weight of the sunlight at bay, and the temperature was comfortable. We were far enough from town for the quiet to enfold us. We could hear the breeze stir the bamboo, the river brush against the cement foundation, and the oil simmer in the clay pots. Around the perimeter of the classroom, students manned their burners, and there was a collective mood of modest achievement as the rich smell of deep-fried eggplant filled the air. As I was stir-frying the garlic and ginger for the squid salad, I felt a satisfying calm.

It didn't last.

Eventually, each of us was given a large aluminum kettle with a piece of cheesecloth stretched taut over its top like the skin of a drum. I checked my recipe handouts. *Fresh Rice Paper.* My anxiety returned.

I came to a passion for cooking when I was in my twenties, because of my love of reading. Working at the Elliott Bay Book Company in Seattle after university, I discovered food writers such as M. F. K. Fisher and Laurie Colwin. I was smitten with their fearless approach to cooking. I got a subscription to *Gourmet* magazine and purchased Greek and Indian cookbooks with my employee discount. I bought a springform pan. I learned how to make herbed olive oil from *Martha Stewart Living.* I mastered Colwin's tomato pie and shortbread. I read, therefore I can cook.

Or so I presumed. It always stung when I was reminded that there is something words can't teach you: instinct. This is the aspect of cooking that is God-given, and it is why recipes such as fresh rice paper intimidate me. They are reminders that for me, cooking is not a heaven-sent talent. I am fine when it comes to measuring and mixing the ingredients. For fresh rice paper, combine one cup of old white rice (rinsed, after being soaked in fresh water overnight) with two cups water and a pinch of salt. Mix it in the blender for seven to ten minutes, and then let it sit for an hour. Although this part had already been done for us, I would have no problem replicating the process at home. It was what came next that would trip me up, because the next step involved technique.

During my last year of living in Vietnam, while waiting to catch a morning bus to my short-lived marketing job at a water park, I discovered a *banh cuon* stall where I ate at least three times a week. Fresh rice paper is a main ingredient in *banh cuon,* the minced pork crepe that is one of my favorite breakfast dishes, and as I sat across from my bus stop, I would watch the cook whisking rice batter into a soft, round sheet. Talking with her customers, she didn't bother to look at what she was doing. I was often reminded of my dad and his sister, my aunt Janice, both expert pancake makers—so much so that my aunt Janice carries her cast-iron skillet in the trunk of her car and my dad travels with his electric griddle.

Every Christmas morning, my dad makes his moist buttermilk pancakes from the recipe he inherited from my grandpa Clarence. My aunt Janice makes her Swedish pancakes any time one of us cousins asks, which is nearly every time we see her. I can't count how often I have watched her glance nonchalantly at paper-thin pancake batter sizzling in her skillet as she told one of her never-ending stories. The last time I saw her make pancakes, the story had been about losing her phone and finally finding it in her shoe. "Can you imagine! How on earth did it get in my shoe!" she exclaimed, as she added more flour, or melted butter, or half-and-half to the bowl of batter. Never once did I see her measure it, as she sought just the right consistency.

"What does that mean?" I once asked her. "The right consistency?"

I could tell from the look on her face that it was as if I were asking her to define love, or God.

Some things just ... are.

Like the scoop of the spoon into the batter, the dollop of the batter in the cast-iron pan, the agile swirl of the wrist, the whirling of that dollop from the center outward into a circle that is just the right thickness.

But what is the right thickness?

The meaning of love, the definition of God, and the perfect thickness of pancakes and rice paper. Life's great mysteries. All requiring faith. The latter also requiring trust that your gut will tell you just when to lift, and how, so the fragile crepe does not tear.

I had been observing and admiring these acts of making pancakes since childhood, but always from a distance. After all, these weren't any old out-of-the-box pancakes. They had a history. If I attempted them, there would surely be plenty of mistakes, and worse, comparisons. How could I expect to compete with instinct and decades' worth of experience? But now, on a riverbank in Vietnam, my family's long-standing pancake traditions were confronting me in the guise of fresh rice paper. The water boiled. Steam seeped through the cheesecloth wrapped tight over the vat. There was no escape.

I gripped my spoon and dunked it into the bowl of batter. With the weight of my pancake-making ancestors on my shoulders, I spread the batter on the cheesecloth. I could feel the self-conscious stiffness of my wrist as I eased it into a circle that covered nearly the entire surface of the fabric. An assistant chef instructed me to swirl faster, but I feared that moving too fast would cause a reckless tear. The result, instead, was translucent at the center and gloppy around the edges. With the back of the spoon, I tried to smooth out the thick sections, but the batter was already gelling.

To my right, Huong had created a halo of batter. "This is easy," she said. Her smile was innocent, but there was smugness to the way her paper steamed so evenly on the cheesecloth. To my left, Julie had been convinced to set down her camera. She was struggling with the same issues I was, and when her paper tore, her smart-aleck assistant chef raised an eyebrow and said, "You're still single?" At least he let her start over. Her second attempt was level and smooth.

Then, on my own steaming vat, a strange and miraculous thing happened. As I was morosely prodding my gloppy circle of rice, trying to figure out how to fix it, somehow, on its own, it achieved symmetry. It became full and even, like the midautumn moon that children in Vietnam celebrate by carrying lanterns through the streets. I was afraid to touch it. I was afraid to ruin it with the flat bamboo skewers everyone else was using to lift their sheets from the cheesecloth and onto plates.

I eased a skewer beneath the paper to loosen it, catching my breath when the skewer snagged on a pucker, exhaling when it slipped free. Gently, I lifted the soft paper. For a moment it hung over the skewer, like the folded wings of a crane, before I set it flat on the plate. It was intact. It was stunning. It was a sheet of fresh rice paper. I felt the overwhelming urge to cry, just as I had the first time I made homemade pasta and it came out of the cutter looking just like ... pasta.

Huong and Julie looked at me. We were all beaming. "I've never made this one before," Huong whispered, reverently. We lined our supple rice papers with shrimp, shredded green papaya, shallots, coriander, Vietnamese basil, and mint. Bursting with confidence, we tucked and folded. Julie's sassy assistant chef cut the fresh spring rolls in half, and we arranged them around tiny bowls of chili dipping sauce on simple white plates.

Finally, when all of the students were ready, we ate the rolls that we had made. The rice paper was soft, and slightly chewy, a perfect match for the perky pink shrimp. I marveled that I had done this. I may never possess the coveted Jamie Oliver sixth sense, but I didn't embarrass myself by being the only student to produce a gelatinous blob of ground rice and water—a good-natured husband took that honor. At the age of thirty-nine, my time had come. It never would have occurred to me that the next recipe I would be inspired to make in Vietnam would be from my own family repertoire. When I returned to America, I was going to ask my father to teach me how to make buttermilk pancakes.

Someone Else's Favorites

It was Saturday afternoon, and we were free until Monday, when Huong would be back in her office in Saigon and Julie and I would finish up our stay in Hoi An with another cooking class. This gave us time to take advantage of the tailor shops and try the local dishes.

Because *mi quang* was the local specialty that Huong's friend Thong had singled out as "so good, I mean it, it's really excellent," Huong had her heart set on finding the best bowl in town. She was determined, the way she had been with *bun bo Hue*, and although she was not as frenzied, she managed to ask everyone we met for a recommendation. Dong, our Red Bridge Cooking School guide, suggested the morning stalls on Tran Cao Van Street and evening stalls on Phan Chu Trinh Street, adding, "To get the really good one, you have to go to a Vietnamese one. The best food is real Vietnamese."

As we whirled through town like Tasmanian devils in search of skirts, purses, and custom-made flip-flops, Huong prodded seamstresses for their top *mi quang* pick; she also checked in with a trio of motorcycle taxi guys loitering outside the shops. All recommended Minh Mi Quang on Huong Vuong Street. Because we couldn't get hold of Thong in Hanoi to find out the exact location of her favorite stall, and because it was no longer morning and not yet evening, thereby eliminating Dong's suggestions, we opted for the consensus, which was outside the center of the city and meant that we needed to hire the moto drivers.

We were not enthusiastic about using them, because the sky looked as if it were about to dump rain, but they were persuasive, and finally we hopped on the backs of their motorcycles. We headed out of town, too speedily as far as I was concerned. I had seen too many accidents in Vietnam, and I beat on the back of my driver until he slowed down to a speed where I felt that I could survive with just a few broken bones if we were to crash.

We cruised alongside the drab brown flow of the river to a shack that looked just like the rest of the simple shacks that lined the waterfront road, with the exception of a jaunty, hand-painted sign announcing *Mi Quang*. Separated from the street by a low chain-link fence, the covered, cement-floor verandah served as the dining area. It was attached to the front of an open-faced building, which was spliced down the middle, one side serving as a living room/bedroom and the other as the kitchen.

The sky was darkening quickly, and our drivers vanished. Before leaving, they had promised to return, but once it started to rain, we knew they wouldn't come back. The verandah was lit by a tube of fluorescent light, tied to the corrugated metal ceiling with a rusty wire. There was no electricity in the kitchen, and a middle-aged woman prepared our food by the light of a taper candle. She was accompanied by a black cat that sat at her feet, waiting for bits of shrimp to fall. The only thing setting this place apart as a café, as opposed to a private home with a few extra tables, was the wooden shelf holding neatly organized bottles of water, Coke, and Tiger beer.

Because it is pork-based, Julie passed on the *mi quang*. The woman brought a plastic bowl each for Huong and me. Containing a small amount of mild, salty broth, *mi quang* is more like a rice noodle stew than a soup. Coils of wide, chewy noodles serve as a bed for fresh, electric-orange shrimp and grilled pork, peanuts, bean sprouts, snips of sautéed spring onions, the fishy *rau dap ca* herb, and bitter *rau dang* herb. A light soy sauce is drizzled on top, along with a squeeze of lime juice, and we were given a disc of roasted rice paper to crumble over everything. In its composition, *mi quang* reminded me of *com hen*. Rather than blended together to create something new, ingredients were layered to emphasize the spirit of each one.

I liked *mi quang*, but as with *bun bo Hue*, didn't fall in love with it. As Huong ate, she admitted that although she was enjoying it, it wasn't at the top of her hit parade. But she conceded, "I don't know that much about it, so I need to ask around." To be fair, she had another bowl.

We were in the middle of our lunch when the rain turned from dribble to downpour. It was as if a dam had broken. The water was so thick that we couldn't see the individual drops, and the metal roof sounded as if it were going to cave in. The afternoon grew cold. Huong dug through her bags for a skirt she had purchased earlier, and she used it as a poncho, draping the clingy black fabric over her shoulders so that she looked chic and Parisian. Suddenly, the warm, heavy *mi quang* rose to the occasion. The café, which felt a bit seedy when we arrived, turned cozy, with its steamy air and sweet little cat curled up in the kitchen. Stranded within the storm, we hunkered down with a new appreciation for the hearty aspects of *mi quang*: the density of the noodles, the richness of the pork.

Eyeing our soup hungrily, Julie said, "Why not? I'm positive some of those vegetarian soups I've eaten had meat in their broth." She shrugged, philosophically, as if to say, *What can you do?* In the end, though, she decided that she wasn't prepared to deliberately give up her quasi-vegetarian ways.

Huong chatted with the owner of the café, seeking a *cao lau* recommendation. The woman mentioned the same restaurant in town as everyone else Huong had asked, including the motorcycle drivers and our Red Bridge guide. The woman wandered off, and the conversation turned, as it inevitably did by that point in our trip, to the food we had eaten, were eating, or were going to eat.

Huong told us, "One time in Saigon, I remember, I had to have *bun bo Hue*. My favorite place was closed, so I drove all over the city just looking for a place that served it. Finally, I found one, but while I was eating, I remembered another place I like, so I finished my *bun bo Hue* and raced to the other one to buy a bowl to take home. You see," she declared, "when I get something in my head, I must have it."

Julie and I smiled. "We know."

"When I'm hungry, I'm crumpy," she said, using one of my favorite mispronunciations. "But when I'm full, I'm happy." She laughed, as if this were all that needed to be said about her cravings. Then she finished her second bowl of *mi quang* and most likely would have had a third, were it not for the arrival of a taxi.

The following morning I woke at dawn and left Huong and Julie to sleep. I wandered a few doors down quiet Tran Phu Street to the small patio restaurant on the corner that served our hotel's complimentary breakfast. Although it was a buffet for travelers, it contained three of my favorite Vietnamese treats: traditional drip coffee, rambutan, and homemade yogurt.

I took a table by the street and watched the town, not yet flooded with tourists. The air was limpid from the rains that fell overnight, and the yellow walls of the old Chinese buildings shone in the morning light. I took my time with each piece of rambutan, piercing the thick, spiky Dr. Seuss skin with my thumbnail and peeling it back. Such a deceptive fruit. It looks thorny and sharp, but its spines are yielding, like the thick hair on the forehead of an elephant I once rode in Thailand. "*Chom chom*," I murmured. It is one of my favorite Vietnamese words, and perhaps this was why it became my favorite Vietnamese fruit, so I could have the satisfaction of asking for it at the market. The glistening bulb of flesh is tart and sweet.

I sipped my coffee, which I drink black, unlike many Westerners I know who are hooked on *ca phe sua da*, in which the coffee is flavored with sweet condensed milk. The yogurt was creamy, but with a racy tang; it tasted just like the yogurt from the park where I power-walked in the early morning hours when I lived in Saigon. That yogurt came in tiny glass jars, not a greedy amount, not an amount that filled me up, but an amount that kept me coming back for more. There were nights when I fell asleep dreaming about that yogurt, and I woke happily knowing I was about to have it.

Julie and Huong eventually meandered in from the hotel for croissants, caffeine, and people watching. The city was waking, its streets filling with sleepy foreigners. For the next few hours, we plundered purse shops and got fitted for more clothing. Then we went in search of #92 Tran Phu, the restaurant everyone had recommended for *cao lau*. But when we found the space where #92 should have been, the numbers skipped. We asked around, but no one knew what we were talking about.

Thwarted, we walked down the street to #27. Wan Lu was a pleasant but unassuming restaurant that sat across from the much prettier Yellow River, which had a restored timber porch and fluttering silk lanterns. Both restaurants advertised the same dishes—*cao lau*, *hoanh thanh*, and *banh vac*—but Yellow

River was occupied by tourists, and when we had walked past Wan Lu on Saturday night, it was filled with Vietnamese. We chose Wan Lu, and there was a part of me that was disappointed. I like pretty places.

Unfortunately, our *cao lau* was mediocre. Even generous Huong gave it a "so-so" rating and said that if she must compare, she liked *mi quang* better. The yellow noodles reminded me of the only foreign food I had eaten when I was a kid, aside from Mexican. When my family lived in Eastern Washington, we would drive over the Cascade Mountains to Seattle for Christmas, or in the summer to watch Jimmy Connors play Eli Nastase at the Seattle Center Coliseum. Occasionally, on these big trips to the city, we had a Chinese dinner at the Four Seas. It was as exotic as it got for our all-American family, with a lazy Susan swirling sweet-and-sour chicken, slices of pink-rimmed pork dipped in hot mustard and sesame seeds, and some kind of noodle that tasted starchy and saline, just like the noodles in this *cao lau*.

I also ordered wonton soup, which was fine, but it was not as I remembered from my first time in Hoi An: a simple, light broth dappled with slivers of spring onion and a few plump wontons. This version was heavy and had those yellow noodles in it.

Idly, Huong gazed around the restaurant, studying the dishes on each table. Finally, she said, "I wonder what's in that." She asked the waitress for a few banana leaf packets. Her passion for funky pressed meats knew no bounds.

Huong's flight left early in the evening, so a shopping frenzy followed lunch. As we ravaged shoe racks and purse displays, Huong asked each shopkeeper where to find the best wonton soup—she was determined to salvage my fond memories. Despite its contrived prettiness, Yellow River kept coming up. Huong made it clear that we didn't want watered-down tourist pap, we wanted the real deal, but we were continually assured that Yellow River was the place. As we took a table on the front porch, I was hit with a feeling of déjà vu, and I realized I had been there before. It was the restaurant where my former boyfriend Sam and I had sat in the evenings; it was where I'd first had wonton soup. Things were looking up.

Next to our table, a young Western couple was eating spring rolls, that ubiquitous, deep-fried Southeast Asian food. How many spring rolls, I wondered, had they eaten back home, wherever they were from? The criticism rose in me instantly: couldn't they be more creative? Then I considered the unique pleasure of eating the familiar in an exotic place. How, when you return from your trip, it adds exoticism to the routine of daily life. For this couple, spring rolls would now be couched in a memory of their trip to Vietnam, and from that moment on, every time they ate a spring roll within the confines of their regular old humdrum everyday lives, they could slip away for a moment and recall, *Remember the day we ate spring rolls in Hoi An? Wasn't that a great day? Yeah, that was a really great day.*

Not that this inspired me to have fried spring rolls myself, but that was only because I didn't care for them. They were too greasy, especially in the heat. Besides, I was on a mission to taste dishes that were exclusive to Hoi An. Along with wonton soup, we ordered *banh vac* (white rose), a simple, dumpling-style dish of minced shrimp in steamed rice paper, topped with crispy shallots. As much as we wanted to like it, the rice paper was too thick and chewy, and the *nuoc mam* too salty. Strangely, the wonton soup had tomatoes in it, as well as cilantro and white onion.

Despite the deviations from a classic wonton soup, this version tasted fresher, probably because Huong had ordered it without yellow noodles. It was the noodles, we decided, that made Wan Lu's soup so unappealing. Still, I wasn't crazy about any of it. "I wish I liked Hoi An food more," I said.

"At least my salad's good," Julie announced. Along with her standard, a baguette and Laughing Cow cheese, she had ordered green papaya salad. She took another bite. "How weird. I'd forgotten all about it. How could I forget about it? It's one of my favorite dishes."

Four years earlier, she had fallen in love with green papaya salad at the Jim Thompson House in Bangkok. As that trip progressed, she ate it in Laos and Vietnam, as well. When she returned home, she taught herself to make it. Now, as she finished a plateful, she was happier than any recently sick person should have been over a dish made with unripe fruit, chili, and fish sauce. How different her Hoi An food memories were going to be from mine.

Huong glanced at Julie's salad before returning her attention to her wonton soup. She poked it with her spoon. "This isn't my favorite, either," she admitted. She looked at the couple next to us, content with their plate of spring rolls. Then she turned her attention to me, the way a mother looks at a spoiled child, and reminded me, "But it might be someone else's."

At five, after a last dash to our favorite tailor, Julie and I accompanied Huong out to the main road, where we told one another not to feel sad. We would be back together in just over a week in Saigon. Huong left in a taxi to the airport. As Julie and I returned to the hotel without her, Hoi An felt quieter, despite all the people laughing and chatting in the shops and on the streets. We changed for dinner and walked down along the river, past cafés that shimmered with twinkle lights and silk lanterns. We were on our way to have dinner at a restaurant that lingered fondly in my memories. Of it I had once written:

> We are led up to the second story balcony by a young gentleman who appears to be no older than nine. We realize, though, that he is probably in his teens. Like many children in this country, his expression is world-weary and world-wise. Inside the café a stereo plays gritty New Orleans blues. There is a small side table covered with laminated reviews, praising the restaurant as

one of the best in the country. Instead of a menu we are given a choice: vegetarian or seafood. The prix fixe is 35,000 dong, a little under three USD. The plates continue to arrive long after we are full. We roll our eyes at the surplus of shrimp and fish prepared with rice pancakes, papers, and pastes.

My expectations were high, and when we arrived, the restaurant was full of travelers, laughing and eating, drinking and talking. The atmosphere was festive. This seemed like a good sign. I wanted to sit upstairs on the balcony, like the last time I was there, but was brusquely informed, "Upstairs are reservations only." This did not seem like a good sign. A Vietnamese restaurant that required reservations? Since when? Julie and I took a table outside, at the edge of the street, but the moment our wine arrived, it started to rain. Rather than offer us a new table, two waiters carried our damp table indoors, to a cozy corner at the back of the restaurant.

The menu had expanded. The prix fixe choices now included meat. My partner in pork-eating crime was probably already back in Saigon; Julie and I opted for seafood and vegetable selections. Drying off, we relaxed. Music from an ancient stereo inspired visions of a Parisian bistro. The mood was convivial as the owner dashed about in his black beret, explaining how to eat certain dishes, passing out notebooks in which previous diners had scrawled praise, and breaking toasted rice crackers into customers' soups. But soon his rushing from table to table took on the hollowness of a performance that had not been freshened up recently. Our food was sped to us: white rose, seafood soup, squid sautéed with veggies on a rumpled rice crisp, rice dumpling, another soup, noodles. One dish came right after the other, piled haphazardly onto our table with a speed that matched the pace of the goateed owner. It was unnerving. We were eating as fast as we could; we felt obligated to, even though we had nowhere else to be that night.

Ten years earlier, Sam and I had the place to ourselves. We lingered on the balcony for hours, served by the owner's son, who kept us company between dishes with easy, unobtrusive conversation. The boy was still there. He was now twenty-three, and with no time for a chat. The restaurant was packed, and there were people on the street waiting for tables. The food continued to arrive at the speed of light, as if haste and quantity could make up for the quality, which was fair. The squid tasted fresh and complemented the texture of the rice crisp, but it was lost in its heavy sauce. Although the white rose wrapping was more delicate than any others we had tried, it was the only dish that stood out. The crème caramel was mushy.

I wondered if these diners tonight would recall this place with the same degree of fondness I had for my first time there. Maybe the food was just okay then. Maybe I had been caught up in the quaintness of the setting. Or I was being a spoilsport, or was simply spoiled, because I felt that my territory had been invaded. Perhaps these people loved the theatricality and would have found my experience dull. Perhaps this restaurant now fell into the category

Huong had newly created: someone else's favorites.

I wanted to be generous, especially since I was beginning to feel like a curmudgeon toward the dining scene in Hoi An, a town I still hold dear. But I didn't like the restaurant anymore. An acquaintance who writes a major guidebook told me she removed it from her listings because it became too touristy. It's a Catch-22. Obviously, if Sam and I were among the only customers back then, the place wasn't making much money. But why did it have to become like this for it to be a success?

If this were just about playfulness, I wouldn't have minded. What bothered me was the feeling of being forced to have a certain kind of time. Rather than simply enjoy myself in the cheerful atmosphere, I felt manipulated by the owner, who posed in group photographs, paused to take dramatic puffs of his cigar, and dropped his notebooks onto our table, unsolicited, making it clear that if we were not enjoying ourselves, there was something wrong with us. After all, according to the pages in the notebooks, this was "the best restaurant in Vietnam," and in more than one case, "in the whole wide world."

We returned to the hotel early, to get a good night's sleep for our next cooking class the following morning. The rain was so loud that I put in my earplugs, and I was sound asleep when the night, which was already puttering along on the wrong track, "took a bad turn," as Julie wrote in her diary.

The room was pitch black, and a tapping on my shoulder woke me, sending my pulse into a tailspin. I removed an earplug just as Julie turned on the lamp beside my bed and said, "There's something scratching in the cupboard."

"Mmm," I said, half-asleep, "gecko," and I began to put my earplug back in.

She considered this, skeptically.

"My house in Saigon was full of them," I assured her. One time, digging into a bag of chocolate chip cookies, I discovered two fat geckos staring up at me with looks of dazed satisfaction. Another time, forgetting a cake on a counter, I woke to find it patterned from the ecstatic dance of tiny gecko feet, with a trail of frosting footsteps up and down the walls. "They're just looking for something to nibble on."

A very loud scratching came from the cupboard beneath the fridge. Julie frowned. "That is not a gecko."

"Yes, it is."

"No, it isn't. I'm getting someone."

I nodded and rolled over.

Downstairs, she woke the night attendant, a young man who slept on a cot next to the front door. She told him there was something in our room, and he told her, cheerfully, "Rat." Her suspicion was confirmed, and she wasn't happy that he was so matter-of-fact about it. She dragged him upstairs to search for the beast. He rummaged around, unenthusiastically, but didn't find anything. He pointed to the cabinet. "Candy?"

"Nope, no candy," we told him, shaking our heads. We gave him our fruit and cheese from the fridge, just in case.

After he left, I said, "He doesn't know what he's talking about. It was just a gecko."

Julie climbed back into bed, but didn't turn off the light. "Really?"

"Really," I promised.

I was lying. It was definitely a rat. In the house in Saigon, along with my sweet little geckos, I'd also had visitations from the local rodents, uprooted when the house next door was torn down. They'd found their way through the only hole in my kitchen wall. Here in Hoi An, the rain was pounding down. The town's waterfront critters needed to take shelter. Where better than a hotel more than one hundred years old, with plenty of cracks and gaps for sneaking in? I was almost back to sleep when Julie woke me again.

"Listen," she said, urgently. Added to the scratching was the sound of something being dragged. "That. Is. Not. A. Gecko."

"You're probably right," I agreed.

Again, she put on a robe, and again, she went downstairs. This time, in the back of our cabinet, inside a bag, the guy discovered a Luna Bar. The wrapper was gnawed away, and a large chunk of the bar was missing. He scowled at us. "Candy," he declared, quite crumpily, as Huong might say. We surrendered all of the offending bars, and he took them downstairs to throw away. Julie insisted that we were going to leave the light on all night, and as she closed her eyes, I looked across the room to see the rat scurrying away from the cabinet and out a small, chewed hole at the base of the wall.

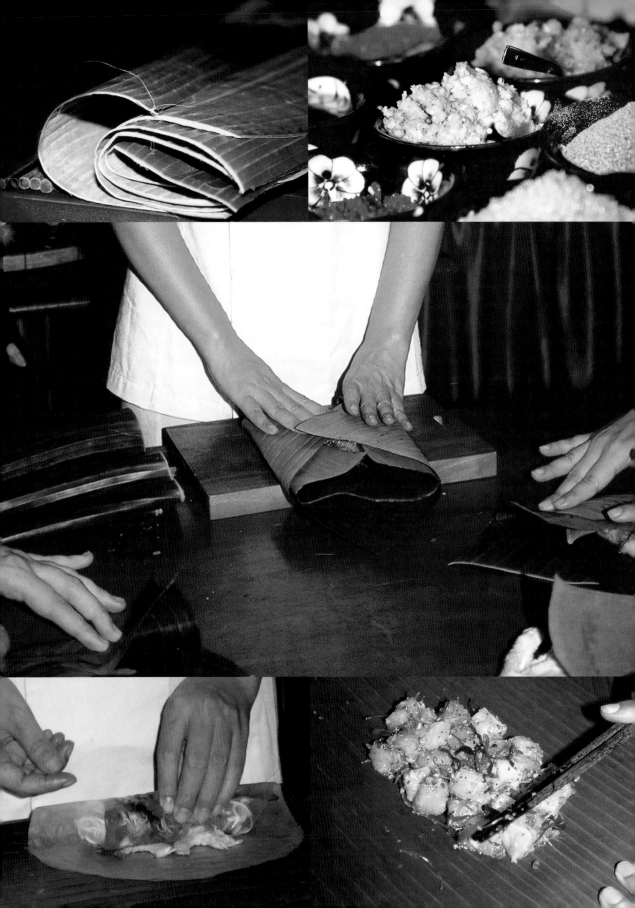

Individuality

We woke to a compassionless deluge. With a sandal, I prodded around behind the cabinet, but there was no sign of our protein-bar-craving rat, which Julie named Willard, in an attempt to turn her sleepless night into an amusing travel anecdote. As we sloshed our way to the Morning Glory restaurant, home to the Cargo Club Cooking School, the town was abandoned, and the street running along the river was on the verge of flooding. In the restaurant, a few people lounged with glasses of drip coffee and fruit shakes, listless in exile from their plans for the day. Although the ceiling was high and the louvered shutters open to the storm, the room felt like a cocoon, steamy and warm. The walls and furniture were dull in the absence of the sunlight that, when shining, makes Hoi An feel like the inside of a honeycomb.

There was just enough time for a dose of get-your-motor-running caffeine before we were rounded up with six others and escorted upstairs to an airy hall in which three wooden tables had been lined up as if for a banquet. Petite dishes at each setting contained prechopped raw ingredients. At one end of the room, behind a cooking and demonstration station draped in a ruby-colored satin cloth, were three large windows, their shutters pulled open. Outside, the storm whipped the cool air. I felt positive. My success with making fresh rice paper had boosted my confidence.

Unlike Chef Hai the day before, the chef/owner of this restaurant and school did not dazzle us with her practiced flair. Miss Vy did not open the class with witty one-liners or an attention-grabbing joke. In her soft voice she told us, "This is my third restaurant. I am a third-generation cook. I am going to teach you my family's recipes." She had the slight physique of a preteen. Her hair was cut into a pixie shag, her white pants chicly boot cut. How could I be anything but enamored?

Standing at the front of the room with her hands folded behind her back, she leaped into our lesson. Behind her the wind blew gray rain at an angle nearly parallel with the street. "In Vietnam," she explained without prelude, in heavily accented but fluent English, "there are two types of dishes. Daily dishes, like rice, vegetables, and seafood, and special occasion dishes, which usually have meat. At parties, special dishes are served one at a time. And there is no rice. Instead, there are baguettes. From this you can tell a strong French influence. In a daily meal, all the dishes are served together at the same time, usually on a round tray or table. It's a communal experience," she explained, and then informed us that a common meal also includes broth, which is customary to drink instead of a beverage, "for digestion." I thought of clam rice, and the bowl of water from the boiled clams that was always served on the side.

Her dark eyes shining, Miss Vy held the gaze of a point just above our heads. It was almost as if she were talking to herself as she now clasped her hands in front of her, and moved on to the significance of food as medicine, informing us that ingredients such as duck embryo should be eaten after an illness, when the body is weak, to restore balance. "You know, yin and yang." She revealed that herbal shops sell "special drinks for men," elixirs of gecko or snake in rice wine, which she bashfully called "Vietnamese Viagra." As for the seahorse a traveler might see brewing in a jar of alcohol, that's for the kidney. "For Oriental doctors, the most important organ is the kidney." She gazed into the back of the room, unblinking, as she waited for us to absorb this fact. Then she gave us more.

Lemon basil with honey and salt can be used in a tisane for a sore throat. Rice paddy herbs are an antidote for snakebite. Chinese coriander prevents high blood pressure. Wild watercress is for women, to which she added, with another shy smile to our mixed-gender class, "But I'm not brave enough to tell why in front of everyone." Quickly, she added, "It's also used for heart disease and cholesterol, because it thins the blood." With the storm tangled in the curtains behind her, she politely pointed out to us foreigners wealthy enough to travel all the way to Hoi An and take a cooking class, "Poor people cannot afford to be sick, so they must prevent it with the food they eat."

Miss Vy also took great care in explaining the ingredients that give Central Vietnam its culinary distinction. Its food is spicier. Women make special chili sauces to give as gifts, and there is a saying, "How hot is the chili, how jealous is the woman." Because there is often only one crop each year—the second is usually lost to flooding—salt is essential for preservation. It is also crucial for digestion, since people who live in the central region eat mainly veggies. Even if they do have the chance to eat beef, the cows feed on vegetables. As she talked, I remembered the salt lick for our horses in our corral in Moses Lake. Once, out of curiosity, when I was in the sixth grade, I licked it. It was salty, as to be expected, and a little slimy, because the horses had been licking it, too. It never occurred to me to wonder what it was for. I always assumed it was just a tasty treat for my old mare, Dusty.

The rain thinned, and watery sunlight spread a film over the yellowing facade of the French colonial building across the street. Miss Vy's musings on ingredients merged with reflections on the local economy, and we learned that 85 percent of the income in the Hoi An area was generated by tourism. Still, living conditions were poor. Outside the town's few main streets, which were where all the money went, life was hard. "Thirty years in a Communist country should have meant change," Miss Vy said. "We won, but no jobs, no skills, no money, no choice. We are still a feudalist society."

Miss Vy's voice remained sweet and melodious as she announced, "Because our background is feudalist, this means women very low and men very high. Boys are still treated like kings in Vietnam. After marriage, a woman belongs to her husband's family. Someone to work for free. Women here become tough because they have no choice." Her fingers were laced, and her hands fretted rhythmically. It was as if she were saying, *I became tough because I had no choice.*

It felt as if Miss Vy had opened the library of her mind and invited us to join her on a rambling perusal of its contents. She plucked a bit of information from this shelf, and some more from that; occasionally she opened a door marked *Private*, and we were given a glimpse before she gently drew it shut. I wondered what the rest of the class thought of this particular glimpse—Communism, feudalism, and a clear irritation with women's relegated roles.

In private conversations in Vietnam, I had often heard what Miss Vy was saying, about the disappointments of Communism and the sexist, ideologically condoned treatment of women, but these issues were not generally part of a public forum, especially one involving foreigners. Some of the students were listening intently, while others' attention wandered out the windows, toward the gleaming promise of a sunny day wafting through the air. Probably, they were plotting a trip up the river or to the beach, once our class was done. There was a couple from Holland, a couple from America, and two stylish young women from Hong Kong. Free speech is taken for granted in all of these places, and no one appeared to find Miss Vy's soft-spoken rant a source of fascination.

Suddenly, Miss Vy blinked, as if waking from a dream. She stared at us, seeming surprised to see us sitting there. She blinked again. "And that," she said, laughing, as if she had been joking with us all along, "is why the women in Vietnam are very jealous." Then she told us that most of the fruit in Central Vietnam comes from the south.

Born in 1970, Miss Vy came of age during Vietnam's homogenized, post-1975 Communist era. Hers was a generation comprising hundreds of thousands. But she was an individual. I cannot emphasize enough how uncommon certain types of individuality are in Vietnam. Huong and her outspoken, halter-top-wearing, globe-trotting girlfriends were a growing breed, but as yet they were a minority. They also lived surrounded by the cosmopolitan attitude that was infiltrating Hanoi and Saigon. Although Miss Vy's business relied on tourism, hers was still a provincial world, and to hear her tell her life story candidly, and express herself in ways not hampered by the ideological language she was raised on, was exciting.

At the end of the American War, Miss Vy's parents were a young couple with five children, and during the first lean years that followed "liberation," they spent much of their time arguing about food. This was not an uncommon situation among families in Vietnam. My own eldest Vietnamese sister has described how she and her usually peaceful parents and sisters often fought because of constant hunger.

While the government was punishing many former capitalists by sending them to the New Economic Zone to work for the country, Miss Vy's father dreamed of opening a restaurant, because he wanted his children to "grow up with good food." Because of his prewar role in the South Vietnamese military, her parents could not get a license for a new business, but her grandmother had permission to run a food stall at the market. "You know, we lived together, three generations in the family, so we shared everything. She allowed us to use her license and run the business in her name. I went to school half the day and worked the other half in the kitchen. I loved this job." Miss Vy's voice lifted, as if buoyed on a current of fragrant lemongrass-infused memory. Her eyes shone even brighter. "Helping my mom in the kitchen, I was able to find a lot of passion. I enjoyed being with her, and I realized, this is what I would love to do."

When *doi moi*, or reform, came in the mid-1980s, business in the market collapsed because business out on the street—out in the open!—became legal. Miss Vy's parents decided it was time to set their children free to do whatever they wanted, but what Miss Vy wanted was to run a restaurant. A real restaurant. She found a space. Drawing her clasped hands up to her chest, she said, "Oh, my passion, all I could think about was this room. The rent was 330,000 dong [twenty dollars] a month. I needed a deposit, more than 50 percent, so much, but I knew I must have this location. I had my gold wedding ring, and I sold it for 225,000 dong. Now I had a 200,000-dong deposit and 25,000 dong in capital. I was the banker for the old market stall, so I knew how to make money. At first I shopped on credit, which I would pay back at the end of each day, and I sold only breakfast and lunch, because there was no electricity at night. But I was happy, because I had a job after marriage. And after six months, I made 1,800,000 dong. I can't believe I have this much money."

As Miss Vy talked, she slipped into the present tense, and she was right there, or there came here. She was not recalling. She was not transported back in time, but rather transporting time forward so that today was the day that she counted her earnings. Today was the day she was "stunned and thrilled" to have paid back her debt and still have 1,500,000 dong left.

She was breathing heavily as she continued, "I want to scream, I want to yell, I want to shout out I have this much money. After cleanup, it's around nine or ten, and I can't wait until tomorrow to tell my parents. I go out at night in the dark, and my mom answers the door. 'What's wrong?' she asks. She thinks something has happened between my husband and me. We go into the kitchen, and I show her the money. When she counts it, she says, 'Are you sure you paid all your suppliers?' I just sit in silence, smiling."

Despite the tremble of emotion in her gentle voice, Miss Vy was losing the attention of some of her students. They didn't get it. They didn't understand the big deal about making a hundred dollars in six months. Why was she breathless?

Because, I wanted to shout, feeling protective, as I often did toward Vietnam, *in impoverished, postwar Vietnam, where hope and opportunity were virtually nonexistent, she was hopeful. She had an opportunity.*

"At the end of 1992," Miss Vy persisted, indifferent to those whose thoughts were straying, "I see four foreigners pass by my restaurant. It is about four o'clock in the afternoon, so it is a little late, and they come in and look at the food we have out on tables at the front. They talk with each other, and after a while one man comes up to me and says, 'We want to have dinner here at seven for four people.' I am so panicked, I just look at him, this very weird person with blond hair and blue eyes and such a big nose. And very hairy. We have no TV, no news at this time, so I don't know what foreigners look like. And I learned English in school for seven years, but to communicate with it I was very bad, because we had no chance to practice. To see a foreigner in real person." Her hands fluttered. Her cheeks flushed. "I can't speak any words. But after a while, I realize he wants to come back for dinner.

"I call to my father to come over to help me. He was so angry. He says, 'I'm tired, it's four people, you can do it.'

"I tell him, 'No, they're not Vietnamese.'

"He says, 'Where are they from?'

"'I don't know, but they're looking pretty hairy.'

"He says straightaway, 'Don't you know that I don't speak any Russian!'

"You see, the only white people in the country at this time are Russian, like Big Brother, because it's a Communist country, you know. I say, 'No, no, they speak English.' Then everyone in my family is keen to see them, to see some English-speaking people and be involved with a capitalist country. Oh, I can't forget about that day, because it's a landmark for my career. But how panicked we are. We all get together, and we have an argument, not a big argument, but we do not agree with each other about what kind of food we should serve. We have no idea.

"My father worked for the army for South Vietnam. He lived on an American base, and he cooked for them, but to be the chef for their restaurant, he has no idea about that kind of food. So he just keeps telling me, you know, they love to eat food in the tins. The only thing he saw was the canned food. 'They *love* food in a can.' And my mom says, 'No, I saw them eat turkey, the Christmas thing, for the soldiers, they had turkey that came from America.' So, these are the only things we know about Western people.

"In the end, we decide we won't prepare anything. We wait for them to come, and we show them what we have in the kitchen. I ask my father to ask them what they want. They have no idea about stir-fry, what is the difference between stir-fry, steamed, or fried. So they say to me, 'Whatever you want to do.' I think about what we usually serve for Vietnamese people, and I make it, and they love it. And that," she concluded, modestly, her voice even-keeled once again, "is the story about my restaurant and the first restaurant in town for tourists."

At the end of 1995, Miss Vy began offering cooking classes for tourists at her Mermaid Restaurant. They were simple, focused on preparing family dishes. But in 1998, she traveled to Australia, where she observed the country's first

Vietnamese restaurants. Despite the sizable immigrant Vietnamese population, the restaurants used Chinese and Thai cuisine to attract "white people." More than twenty years of economic détentes and emotional reconciliations had passed, but the stigma of the war lingered. This is a subject that Susan Brownmiller wrote about in her book *Seeing Vietnam*. In the United States, she noted, Vietnam had to be romanticized in restaurants with names such as Indochine and Cuisine de Saigon in order for the food to first be accepted.

When Miss Vy returned to Vietnam, she decided to incorporate history and philosophy into her lessons. The lessons, as well as the dishes she teaches, had been honed over the years, but one thing remained constant: the food she shares with her students is personal. Following her lecture, our class spent the remainder of the morning preparing grilled mackerel with turmeric in banana leaf, prawns in tamarind sauce, crispy eggplant, banana flower salad, fresh spring rolls, and even the town's famous white rose.

We were spoiled as we had been at the Red Bridge school, since the time-consuming prep work had been done for us. Round wicker trays held eight small bowls each, containing fundamental ingredients, already chopped, measured, and minced: shallot, garlic, chili, brown sugar, salt, pepper, vegetable oil, and *nuoc mam*. There were also portions of galangal, lemongrass, and turmeric that had been peeled, sliced thin, mashed in a mortar and pestle, and soaked in oil for three weeks at room temperature to make a paste. Ancillary dishes held star anise and cinnamon.

As we shredded pliant wood ear mushrooms for the grilled mackerel, Miss Vy enlightened us with the healing properties of each ingredient. A parasite of the mulberry tree, the mushrooms were rich in calcium and used for drug detox, since calcium reduces cramping. One teaspoon of turmeric, which we mixed with the cubed fish, could be combined with one teaspoon of honey in a tisane to prevent cancer. The Spanish mackerel, which had long been served to show wealth and respect for guests, was high in omega 3.

As we continued to prepare our feast, we learned, "Never cook food too spicy. Always put the spicy on the side." We were instructed to flavor the oil we were heating with lemongrass, and to choose small squid, so it doesn't have to cook too long, which will make it tough. When making the mango salad, we tasted the fruit first to determine its sweetness, so we could know how much *nuoc mam* to use for balance. Best of all we learned to assemble white rose, Hoi An's signature shrimp dumpling, from a young woman named Ba, who had been making this specialty since she was fifteen. She was taught by her uncle, a member of the Tran family, whose third-generation business supplied all of the local restaurants.

The Trans' enterprise employed eight workers making one thousand to two thousand white rose dumplings every day, and because the Trans had the monopoly on white rose, it seemed that it would be consistently good throughout town. But they did not make the same quality for every restaurant—different restaurants could afford different grades. Then there was the freshness factor. If a restaurant was popular, it quickly used up its daily order of white rose, but if it wasn't busy, it might freeze some and serve them over the course of a few days.

Although she looked thirteen, Ba was probably in her early twenties. She was a pro, oiling her fingertips and expertly twirling small pats of dough into translucent coins. Watching her was deceiving, because white rose is not easy to make. Shaping the dough required an adept, delicate touch that none of us had. The day before, this would have made me anxious, but now it just seemed to be part of the fun, as we laughed and fumbled our way through the process. Each student, including myself, produced amoeba shapes that the Trans would surely distribute around town in their low-quality category, but it didn't matter. I joined in the communal sense of pride, perhaps not for our technical achievement, but for having the chance to participate in one of the town's culinary traditions.

As I ate around a small table with Julie and our fellow students, I was busy trying to decide which dishes I would re-create back home. Other than the fresh spring rolls and banana flower salad, they were not familiar to me. Tucked inside a banana leaf packet, the grilled white mackerel nestled in a soothing paste of turmeric, and the squid stuffed with pork and wood ear mushrooms would sit well on any dinner party plate. But in the end, the eggplant won a place at my anticipated dinner party.

The eggplant started off fresh and firm, a pure white globe the size of a tennis ball. To begin I made a series of parallel slices into one side, then flipped it over, turned it ninety degrees, and made another set of slices, so that after soaking and boiling it, I could press it flat. The remaining steps and ingredients were wonderfully simple. Sauté the eggplant until it turned golden brown. Then drizzle it with sautéed green onion with a hint of fish sauce, a blend of soy sauce and sugar, and fresh minced garlic and chili. The crunch of the eggplant's lightly fried skin played off the meatiness of its flesh. The soy sauce marinade would have been too sweet were it not for the chili; the chili would have been too hot were it not for the marinade. The result was balanced. It was unique. It was as delicate and flavorful as Miss Vy. Just as Julie appropriated banana flower salad, I claimed crispy fried eggplant for my own.

Miss Vy's Crispy Fried Eggplant

The trick to this dish is finding the right eggplant. In our class, we used the hybrid white ball variety of the Thai eggplant, which is pure white, round, and about the size of a tennis ball. I couldn't find these in the United States, even in Asian grocery stores. One suggestion is to grow your own, as seeds are sold online. (Try evergreenseeds.com.) For acceptable substitutes, use the rosa bianca or prosperosa heirloom. No matter what type you choose, make sure it's round and not too small. Otherwise you will have difficulty preparing the dish.

INGREDIENTS:

1 hybrid white ball eggplant
2 tbsp. vegetable oil
2 tsp. light soy sauce
1 tsp. brown sugar
1 tbsp. green end of a green (spring) onion, chopped

4 tbsp. fish sauce
1 tsp. garlic, chopped fine
1 tsp. chili, chopped fine

DIRECTIONS:

1. Thinly slice grooves into eggplant halfway down. Flip over and turn 90 degrees, repeating the slicing on the other side.
2. Soak eggplant in cold salted water for 30 minutes.
3. Mix soy sauce and sugar, and set aside.
4. Mix garlic and chili, and set aside.
5. Place eggplant in boiling water for 7 minutes. So that the eggplant is completely covered with water, put a plate on top of it to weigh it down. Do not overcook, or the eggplant will get soggy.
6. Remove eggplant from water and place between the bottom of two plates and squeeze flat, draining excess water from the inside of the eggplant.
7. In a sauté pan, heat 1 tbsp. vegetable oil until hot. Place eggplant in pan. Cook for 2 to 3 minutes on each side. When done, it should be golden brown and crispy on the outside.
8. In sauté pan heat 1 tbsp. vegetable oil until hot. Add green onion, and fry for 2 to 3 minutes, adding fish sauce at the end of cooking time. Then cook a tiny bit longer until there is a caramelized smell.
9. Arrange eggplant on a small plate. Top with fried green onions, and drizzle with the soy sauce mixture and the leftover liquid from the onions.
10. Scatter garlic and chili on top, and serve.

Serving: 1 as a side dish.

One Hundred Bites

After lunch, the sun came out, and it was no longer necessary to roll up our pants and wade through the streets. We were lounging on our beds in the hotel, deep into our siesta, when Huong called. She wanted another skirt. Would we please run out and order it for her? She had also talked to a former coworker who was from Hoi An and found out that the town's famous well was not down an alley, as many guidebooks claimed, but in front of the market. If we went there we would find an old woman selling *mi quang*. "She's the one, the famous one, the one Thong loves!"

Early in the evening, Julie and I tracked down the well. It was a coarse, ugly cement thing. Nothing about it inspired visions of casting pennies and making wishes. Surrounding it were crude stalls comprising cooking pots heating atop sawed-off oil drums, low tables that could be folded away at the end of the day, and squat plastic stools. It was hard to tell where one stall stopped and another began. Only one of the stalls was run by a woman. She wasn't old and she wasn't selling *mi quang*.

Julie and I stood there, stymied. When I finally found a woman who claimed to speak English, my inquiry was met with a confident: "Come back afternoon." I was pretty sure she had no idea what I'd just asked, and as we attempted a discussion with her dubious handful of English words and my Vietnamese that did not include "Do you know where the town's famous *mi quang* maker sets up shop?" I was reminded of a passage in Monique Truong's novel, *The Book of Salt*. The main character is a fictitious Vietnamese chef working for Gertrude Stein and Alice B. Toklas in Paris in the 1920s. At one point he muses:

> I wanted that afternoon to ask Miss Toklas whether the household budget would allow for the purchase of two pineapples for a dinner to which my Mesdames had invited two guests. I wanted to tell her that I would cut the first pineapple into paper thin rounds and sauté them with shallots and slices of beef; that the sugar in the pineapple would caramelize during cooking, imparting a faint smokiness that is addictive; that the dish is a refined variation on my mother's favorite.
>
> I wanted to tell her that I would cut the second pineapple into bite-sized pieces, soak them in kirsch, make them into a drunken bed for spoonfuls of tangerine sorbet; that I would pipe

unsweetened cream around the edges, a ring of ivory-colored rosettes. And because I am vain and want nothing more than to hear the eruption of praises that I can provoke, I wanted to tell her that I would scatter on top the petals of candied violets, their sugar crystals sparkling.

Then, he told Miss Toklas that he wanted to buy a pear.

Language failed him. Not only could he not communicate the intricacy of the dishes he knew so well, but he also could not even communicate the word for pineapple, which he, to his shame, had suddenly forgotten. As for me, I could not communicate that all I wanted to do was find the famous old woman who made famous *mi quang* by the famous well.

"*Ba*," I said, using the Vietnamese word for an older woman.

"Afternoon," said the woman, still confident.

"*Mi quang*," I said, still certain somehow that we were not talking about the same thing.

"Afternoon," she said, pleasantly.

Smiling at the woman, who smiled in return, I wondered how many culinary delights we miss as travelers, without the words to ask for what we want. Without the words to ask, "Please tell me, what am I missing?" Without even knowing that there is something to miss in the first place.

We went to sleep early and passed the night peacefully, without storms or visitations from Willard the rat. When we woke, Hoi An was luminous. The rain had passed, of course it had, since we were leaving town that afternoon. I had a couple of hours before I was to interview Miss Vy, who had agreed to spend the morning talking with me. Bypassing the lower river street, which was flooded knee-deep, Julie and I wandered to the market so she could take photos.

She had already been out shooting a few times in Hoi An, and although the traditional Chinese buildings that lined the main streets were picturesque, she liked the market best, especially its outer perimeter, occupied by old women and vegetables. Everything a person could want to learn about composition and presentation was found in a single basket cascading with tendrils of morning glory. Stalks of lemongrass the color of pale buttercups were tied into bundles with green, grassy strands, and chilies lay like fiery petals on round woven trays. "The only problem," Julie said, as she scanned the scene with her camera, "is trying to avoid clichés. It's impossible. The women really *do* wear conical hats. And they *do* carry veggies in baskets on bamboo poles, just like in the postcards."

The women who peddled on the periphery of the Hoi An Market, squatting on a pedestrian street that flanked the main building, brought produce directly from their homes. Early every morning, while travelers were still sleeping, these women walked or rode motorbikes, often for miles, toting plastic bags of morning glory, spring onion, string beans, and squash. "In the market," Miss

Vy explained, later, when I joined her at her restaurant, "there are two parts. One is official, inside, for retail buying and selling. But the other, you can see, the women are sitting everywhere, selling a bit of everything. It's free trade. That means they don't have to pay taxes. Their produce comes from the farms, which are really just their backyards."

I had left Julie to her photography, and Miss Vy and I were sitting next to a window whose louvered shutters had been clipped open to let in the warmth of the day. Our table overlooked a quiet patio. We sipped iced tea, its condensation pooling at the base of the tall glasses. She wore a black T-shirt and silver necklace, just as pretty in her casual clothes as she was in her chef's whites.

In one-on-one conversation, unlike in class, Miss Vy did not shy away from eye contact. She looked at me intently as we talked about how long the little, independent market sellers could last in the face of industrialization, the importance of the proximity of the producer to the buyer, and how she got all of her seafood and produce from the market, which had a fluctuating effect on her menus. Seasonal or "market fresh" cuisine is the doctrine du jour of the American restaurant scene, but in Vietnam, seasonal cooking just is, as it always has been.

"If I invite you to come for a meal at my house," Miss Vy explained, "I'm the one to go to the market. I'm the one to choose the ingredients. I'm the one who makes the menu, you know. I never promise you that I'm going to cook anything specific, because you never know what's available at the market. And then, for example, you decide to cook this fish, but this fish needs special ingredients to go with it. You have to walk around to see what is available, what is fresh that day, and what can go together. That is what you are going to cook for lunch or dinner. Things aren't available all the time here the way they are in the West in the supermarkets."

She looked out the window, beyond the small patio, to the street still soggy from yesterday's downpour. "With this type of rain, it's time to eat pork, and time to eat catfish, because the pork, it is a lot more tender, and the catfish tastes better. You have to go to the market to see if there are some baby shrimp available, because that means it's time to eat this kind of fish. If the fish have enough shrimp to eat, then they have more flavor." She paused and cast her eyes down at her iced tea. "This kind of shopping, it takes a long time. That is why, before, a woman's only job was cooking. She spent her time shopping all morning and afternoon for lunch and dinner for her family."

Now, because women were working and had less time to spend in the kitchen, Miss Vy wanted to open a restaurant that focused on the medicinal aspects of food. She also wanted to open a cooking academy. It would cater to professional chefs and tourists, as well as locals. The latter she would teach the basic principles of Vietnamese food. "How to help your family for living in a healthy way. How to prepare good, economical meals for your children. Knowledge about tradition. I think this is why there are many problems with disease. Because we have lost our traditions. And because we have lost our patience."

I considered Vietnam an incredibly patient country. I asked her how this fit into the country's changing food traditions.

"For food to work for your health, for it to work as medicine, you must be patient," she explained, "But now, the young generation, they say, okay, I'll just take this tablet. One pill can cure many things. It can cure all your problems. So, do you see how difficult it is, to convince them to go in another direction? They need to learn this from their parents, but this is a big problem starting with my generation. They could not learn this because their parents were too busy just surviving.

"I think we have lost our morality, because we were raised in very bad times for so long, so now that we have the chance to make money, we're very aggressive. We cannot wait anymore. It is the same for food. We had the coupons, after 1975, nearly sixteen years with the ration coupons. We have to get on line at the end of every month. We start from two o'clock in the morning, and maybe you go home without anything in your hands because we run out of grain, so they only give it out to half the people, and the rest, we have to wait some more. But you never know how long you have to wait. Maybe a couple of days. Your family has been waiting for a month already. That's why now, in their minds, they must hurry for everything. That is one of the problems with traffic. Even if they don't have anywhere to go, even if they have nothing to do at home, they still must try to get everywhere as fast as possible."

"They're still thinking about getting to the food before it's gone?"

She nodded and said something that is difficult to reconcile, given the wealth of restaurants on Hoi An's main streets, their menus brimming with *cao lau*, white rose, and wonton soup. "It takes so long for people to forget hunger." She sat in silence, contemplating the collective memory that still gripped her country. "I think I am lucky because my parents started a restaurant when I was little. I had a chance to eat good food, you know, to know what the real Vietnamese food tastes like. But a lot of people of my generation, they didn't have any chance to do this, so how do they know what to expect? This is a big problem now. Being a chef, I was a bit disappointed when I traveled from north to south recently. I wanted to keep saying that Vietnamese food is very delicate, but to be honest ..."

I was surprised that she was hesitant to criticize. She had been so frank in the classroom. But she was diplomatic as she continued, "This is the result of the hungry times. You just need something to feed yourself. That is good enough. You don't have to make it look nice, you don't have to make the details perfectly. Even now, with people who are still hungry in my country, food is different for them. They eat more fat, to give them more energy. They eat more sweet, to give them more energy. The food must be very oily, so it has flavor. This is how most people ate during that time in Vietnam. I think because they had no experience with good food for so long, they don't expect anything more now. This is why the restaurants disappointed me."

I asked, "So you think there is an entire generation, your generation, without a culinary history? Without a culinary foundation?"

"Exactly," she said, "They don't have a foundation. It's worse up in Hanoi, because for us in Hoi An it was just from 1975 until 1990, but for Hanoi it was from 1945 with no flavor. They lost it. The previous generation had no chance to show the next generation. They didn't have ingredients to cook with, and the only thing they were concerned with was how to survive. And another problem," she added, "is that we don't write anything down. It's not our tradition. How it used to be, being a girl in the family, you go to the market with your mom and she shows you, okay, you see, this is the way to tell how fresh the fish is, and how to choose vegetables that aren't chewy. That's how we learn. That's why after thirty years it's so easy to lose everything."

Just as I had asked Didier and Mrs. Loc up in Hanoi, I wanted to know how serious Miss Vy thought the risks to culinary tradition were now, in the face of packaged and processed foods, farmed seafood, and globalization.

She looked around her restaurant, solemnly, at the travelers drinking fruit smoothies and reading newspapers and Lonely Planet guides. "I want to be clear about this, because it is one of my concerns." Her eyes rested on mine. "A very big concern. First, I think time is a problem. Life conditions have changed in Vietnam, and people spend less time shopping for food and cooking. Like I said before, about how women used to go to the market every day. This is changing. Second, there is the problem of globalization, it makes people forget what they want, so they just buy what people want to sell them. Packaged food looks so beautiful, especially to us because we have never seen anything like it. And even though it's not good inside, it is used to show that you are a higher level of society.

"I think this is the same problem like when the French came to Vietnam more than one hundred years ago. You know, when we eat the rice, they say, 'You have to polish it.' We say yes, because we think the French are a very high civilization and the Vietnamese very low, so they must know better than us. We believe that everything they do is right. And that's why even now, we know brown rice is very good for our health, but ... we say you can tell how wealthy a family is by how white their rice is. Because that means you had to spend money to polish it. Just like you have to spend money to buy packaged food.

"We have another story about a young woman who lives in the suburbs," she explained. "She takes her products from her farm to the market nearly every day, and one day she buys two cans of Coca-Cola. She sells all of her eggs and vegetables just to have enough money for these two cans. Is this woman stupid? Not really. If you ask her why she spends her money on just two cans of Coca-Cola, she says, 'I only do it sometimes.' She gives the cans to her children to drink, and it makes her look like a good mother, because it means they are not poor, they are not in too bad a position if they can afford these cans. And this helps their mentality. Sometimes, she needs to do this for herself to feel better, in her heart. To show that they don't have to sacrifice anymore. And so that her children will feel better. So they will feel the same as other children. This is about psychology, about being human. We have a proverb that says, "Eating a bite in the middle of the village is worth more than one hundred bites in the middle of your kitchen."

Nha Trang
Central Vietnam

Hanoi•

•Hue
•Hoi An

Nha Trang
•Dalat
•Phan Thiet
•Saigon

The Lobster Farms

Along with exploring Vietnam's culinary scene, I was checking out hotels for a guidebook company, and I had been invited to stay for three nights at Ana Mandara, a favorite of mine in the central Vietnamese beach town of Nha Trang. I was also offered one night at the new Evason Hideaway, a swanky resort in Nha Trang's scenic boonies. Due to availability issues, the bookings were flipped. Were I a leisure-loving supermodel, as many of Evason's guests turned out to be, I would have been over the moon at the extended stay in paradise. I may be skinny, but I am no model, and I am not leisure loving by nature. Also, I couldn't be in the middle of nowhere. I had come to Nha Trang to investigate the role the sea plays in Vietnamese cuisine, and I needed to be close to markets, docks, and boats. But because there was an Evason management shakeup a few days earlier, I was not informed of the switcheroo until after our van had passed through downtown Nha Trang and a boat had taken us out to the remote peninsula that Evason called home.

Julie and I were given an entire villa to ourselves. It was a striking, blond-wood structure whose al fresco bathroom was larger than my spacious bedroom back home, and whose entire upstairs was an open-air salon that looked over the sea. There was a small plunge pool, as well, but I didn't go near it. I'm afraid of snakes.

Sitting upstairs on the daybed, in the balmy afternoon breeze, I leaned back into the pillows. Julie opened a bottle of Chardonnay from our bar, and as I sipped wine, I stared at the calm blue waters of the bay and started to worry. After I had sent him a detailed list of requests, Evason's general manager had offered to introduce me to locals involved in the fishing industry. He said he knew just the right people to help me. "But it is probably best," he emailed, cryptically, "to wait and make all of the final arrangements once you have arrived." Thinking that everything was taken care of, I had relied on his plans and thought no more of it. It turned out that he left the company the week before my arrival, and the new GM, while a terrific guy, was given no information about my visit, let alone my needs. He could not help me, in any case, since he was new to the area and did not have local connections.

As for getting back to the fish market and fishing boats harbored in Nha Trang city, this required scheduling an hour-long boat and then van ride, and once I was there, I didn't know where to begin. I wasn't prepared. That night, while Julie organized her fifty-plus rolls of film and watched movies on satellite TV, I tried to figure out how to politely get out of our stay at the resort and get us back to the real world. Mindlessly, I thumbed through the resort's extensive activity brochure. Listed among a cultural excursion to a local village and a city shopping tour by cyclo, I found two outings that seemed promising: a visit to a lobster farm and a fishing trip. Although I was sure both would be sanitized for the moguls, models, and movie executives in the villas around us, I booked them. Until we extricated ourselves without offending the people who were generously hosting our stay, it was better than nothing.

The following afternoon, we were fetched from the serenity of our villa for our lobster farm excursion by our personal attendant, Mai. A sweet, unworldly nineteen-year-old from the countryside, she was always just a mobile phone call away. If we wanted aspirin or a bottle of water, even at three in the morning, all we had to do was call. And if we did call (which we never would, unless one of us were dying), her cell phone would chirp like a bird in the staff dorms, since ringing cell phones were forbidden, even among guests.

Mai escorted us through the maze of wooded pathways to the water sports center. Waiting for our guide, I asked her if she knew much about the fishermen in the area. Standing attentively next to a pair of water skis that were propped against the trunk of a palm tree, she told us that there was a fishing village about twenty minutes away by speedboat. A few times a year, the staff was taken there to play games with the children. "So poor," Mai muttered, "and so dirty, the garbage. The children go through secondary school, but not high school, there is no opportunity ..." She paused and squinted, as if the sun were in her eyes. Then, quickly, she covered her eyes with one hand. "Sorry," she whispered.

It took Julie and me a moment to realize that she was crying. Silent tears for the poor children of the nearby fishing village.

Back in her rural hometown, Mai had a family and a dog named Astaire, but she lived isolated from everyone she loved in a dormitory on this peninsula in order to make a living. She did not take days off, because she was saving her money for a trip to Cambodia, where, she had heard, "the temples are beautiful." From dawn until as late as the job required, she waited for us in the trees outside our door, or in a hidden corner of the dining room while we ate. And she cried for the children of men who put fresh seafood on the tables here, where a room cost more for a single night than many fishermen made in a year—and certainly more than she made each month. Her compassion was humbling. This was something that always caught me off guard in Vietnam, that people who had so little could feel such tenderness toward those who had even less.

We assured Mai that it was okay to cry, but she shook her head. She was embarrassed. She wiped her face with the back of her thin wrist. She was probably afraid we would report her, and that she would be fired. She looked grateful when our guide finally arrived. Just a little older than Mai, Son had a handsome, toothy smile, and he was everything Mai was not: self-confident and professional. Chatting away, he walked us to a boat that the resort rented from a local fisherman. It was the kind of turquoise blue and jade green vessel that made Nha Trang Bay so scenic. It was authentic and rustic, with the exception of two narrow mattresses on the roof of the cabin for lounging, a silver ice bucket containing a bottle of sparkling wine, and a tray of sushi. As the boat pulled away, Mai stood on the end of the dock, waving solemnly, as if we were leaving on a long journey.

The afternoon was warm and brushed lightly by the wind. Away from the shoreline, the bay was a rippled well of indigo ink. The light was transparent on the surrounding rocky hills. Unlike Mai, Son did not grow emotional as he answered my questions, beginning with those about our pilot, who turned out to be a former fisherman. Resting in the stern, wheel in one hand and rudder in the other, he was just seventeen, and Son told us that this was a great job for the kid. If he had stayed in his village, he would not have finished secondary school, would already be married, and would make just enough money fishing each day to get himself to the next. "He would live a very hard life," Son said. "His family is happy that he has a regular income."

As our adolescent pilot guided the boat unhurriedly through the shadowy waters, I told Son how much Nha Trang had changed since Julie and I first visited ten years earlier. "It was so quiet then," I said. I was recalling a serene night that Julie and I had spent riding in cyclos along the untrafficked promenade, the cool sea breeze slipping over our skin as we searched for a café famous for its honey-beef cooked on clay braziers. "We drove through it in the van yesterday. It's ugly. That strip along the waterfront. All those cheap hotels."

"No," said Son, gently correcting me. "It's okay. Without the tourists, the government would not clean up the natural areas."

Although I was more like Mai, prone to crying in the face of injustice, I admired Son's pragmatism, his acceptance of lesser evils. He was referring to Nha Trang's conservation efforts, and specifically the Hon Mun Protected Area pilot project. This area, made up of nine islands and their surrounding waters, was said to have the highest marine biodiversity in the country. Among its habitats and ecosystems were mangroves, sea grass, and more than 350 species of hard coral, representing approximately 40 percent of all hard corals on the planet, according to the International Union for Conservation of Nature.

Because of the damage done by dynamiting, trawling, dredging, and other destructive fishing practices, it was feared that the area would be ravaged, and tourists—who had turned Nha Trang into Vietnam's first popular beach destination—would steer clear. Along with ecological preservation, the goal of the protected area was to create favorable conditions for sustainable tourism, which in turn could bring much-needed income to locals from all of the lesser-evil hotels, as well as restaurants, scuba diving and boat tour companies, handicraft sales, and so forth. Hon Mun was also intended as a "breeding ground for fish species to reproduce and to repopulate the area, creating more fish and marine life in the 'no fishing' areas as well as outside them," according to Bernard O'Callaghan, the project's chief adviser.

As Son and I talked, Julie sat in the bow, her lens exploring the landscape. A floating shantytown approached. One-room shacks were built on islands made of wooden trestles kept buoyant by oil drums painted the same bright blue as our boat. The shacks were patchworks of wood, tin, and woven matting. In a region known for its monsoon season, they looked as if they could be knocked down with less effort than it would take to collapse a house of cards. Everything in sight was either bleached or rusted from sunshine and salt. Traditional, round, bamboo *thung chai* boats and small, blue rowboats were yoked to the pontoons. Men with sun-baked skin, wearing old shorts, sweatpants, and T-shirts, or no shirts at all, lounged outside doorways, smoking. There were lots of dogs. As we passed by one of the shacks, the men waved and the dogs barked. Son pointed out that there were no toilets, which meant, he explained with a grin, "No ladies live there."

This was not what I expected. This was not some EPCOT Center, made-for-tourists cultural development. It was not the sort of place I imagined the Evason Hideaway sending its guests, since the reason for staying there was to be sheltered from the ugliness of reality—even the garbage cans at the resort were prettily disguised. I knew the object of this excursion was to nab a local color experience and be able to say that you helped catch your own dinner, but all I could think about was what it must feel like to be stranded on one of the flimsy outposts during a storm. I could imagine no way in which this could be seen as quaint.

We tied up at one of the man-made islands, which Son informed us was owned by a kind of lobster farm kingpin, but had been run by the family that lived on it since 2000. Our young captain emerged from his indifference and leaped out. Agile on the narrow beams, he trotted around the lobster beds, grinning and chatting amiably with the occupants of the farm, two bare-chested men and a boy of about ten. He looked as if he would much rather be on the ramshackle island than at the helm of his boat, despite what Son told us about the resort being a better, more reliable job.

This was poverty in its least charitable form. I asked Son, "Do they ever leave?"

"Not really."

I caught sight of an antenna on the roof of the shack. "What do they do here? Besides fish?"

"They drink every night."

"They don't get bored?"

He shrugged. "They have no choice."

I considered what Mai had told us when I asked her why people didn't just give up fishing and head for dry ground. She explained that for a kid who was raised in a fishing community, life on dry land is also hard. For the first time in his life, he has to pay rent, for which he has no money, and get a job, for which he is not qualified. Plus, he is completely out of his element, having grown up far from a diversity of lifestyles, so even having a social life is difficult.

With no realistic alternatives, these men were beholden, drifting at the bottom of the lobster industry's trickle-down organization, an industry that mutated in 2000, according to Son, because there were so many farms that pollution was out of control. Now, farming was limited, and there were only three areas in which a farm could be set up. As for the profits of each farm, the cost of a baby lobster was approximately seven dollars. When grown, it would sell for around thirty. This seemed like a decent return until I took into account that it took up to fifteen months to raise a one-kilo lobster. For every hundred lobsters a farm raised, it would make a gross profit of about $2,300 every year and three months, most of which went to the farm's owner, the rest of which must be divided between expenses and the men who worked on the farm.

We wandered barefoot around the crosshatch of netted lobster pens. The surrounding hills were layered in leafy shades of green, and the late afternoon sun rimmed the low, distant clouds with glowing crescents of liquid mercury. Julie and I examined the beds swarming with lobsters. "I wouldn't want to meet one of those in a dark alley," she said, scowling. They were prehistoric-looking, blue-bodied creatures with writhing, scorpionlike legs. Son pointed out a pen of less-dangerous-looking snapper and some squid traps, which the men maintained as a side business, and we talked about daily life on the water, the supply boat that came twice a week, and the long periods without cash flow while waiting for lobsters to grow.

Sucking on an acrid cigarette that looked as if it were embedded between his lips, the farm's head fisherman snagged a lobster in a long, white net. We were being entertained by his efforts to grapple it out of the water when our attention was diverted by a shaggy yellow dog leaping onto our boat and shoveling its snout into the plate of uneaten sushi. The net stilled. The men looked at us, uncertainly. There's nothing like an angry tourist to take the fun out of a day. Self-conscious when it comes to the ambassadorial obligations of being a traveler, I quickly smiled and shouted, "Bad *cho*!"—"Bad dog!"—which made the men laugh.

Swiftly, the fisherman seized the lobster from the net. He lifted it up by its antennae for our inspection. "It's a female," Son declared, and I pronounced it "*dep trai*"—"beautiful girl"—and everyone laughed again. It is one of my favorite things about Vietnam, how readily people appreciate even the most meager attempt by a foreigner to speak the language.

Knowing nothing about lobster, we approved this one, even though it looked wicked, arachnid, and not the least bit palatable. It was three times as large as our Chihuahua back home. Son showed Julie how to hold it, one hand clenching its sharp antenna, the other clamped around the calloused body, which reminded me of an armadillo's. Quickly, I took her photo, and even more quickly, grinning and wincing as the lobster fought her grip, she thrust it back at the fisherman, who stuffed it into a plastic bag so that we could take it to the resort.

Later that night, back at Evason, the lobster was prepared by the executive chef for our dinner with the general manager and his wife. He used a small portion for a spicy seafood soup. As for the rest, the billows of sweet, alkaline flesh in thin-as-porcelain coral casings, he charred it lightly over the grill and served it with just a trace of melted butter. As I drank good wine, talked of books and travel, and ate lobster fresh from the sea, I thought of the fishermen drinking cheap rice whiskey in the dampness of their dark island, and I experienced a greater appreciation for this meal than any other I had eaten before.

Fishing Like La Vong

Julie and I embarked on our fishing excursion at seven the next morning, Evason Time, which was a universal adjustment of the resort's clocks to ensure prime sunset viewing during the dinner hour. This meant that it was actually six in the rest of Vietnam. Like a loyal fishwife, our attendant Mai saw us off, waving sleepily from the end of the dock. We had a different guide this morning. Hoanh was less suave than Son, but chummier. He had a second thumb on his right hand, which for some reason made him immediately interesting. Our boat was the same one from the day before, as was our nonchalant teenage pilot, whose name we finally learned was Hoa.

A clear blue light spread chiffon ripples over the water, whose deep, brooding blue played against the waking blue of the hills, white-blue of the clouds, and hyacinth-blue of the sky. Heat was already pushing at the air, but the layers of blue kept it at a distance. In deference to the hour, a tray of coffee and tea, rather than wine and sushi, had been prepared. Julie and I savored the mocha-tinged flavor of good Vietnamese coffee as Hoa guided the boat along the shore.

I had prepared my usual zillion questions for Hoanh, but before I started I wanted to enjoy the cool, not-quite-awake feeling of being out on the water. Sitting on a cushioned bench in the stern, I leaned back and dozed in the breeze. I was in the mood for a leisurely rest, but less than five minutes after leaving the dock, Hoa cut the motor, and the boat sputtered to a stop. He dropped anchor. We could still see the curving expanse of the resort.

"That's it?" I grumbled, my morning mood clearly not yet uplifted by the caffeine. "Can't we go out a little farther?"

"We can't fish in open waters," Hoanh explained. "Government regulations."

While this made sense, I still felt grouchy about it. But Hoanh's genial attitude made moping seem ungracious. I drank more coffee and adjusted my attitude while he showed us our fishing gear: a choice of poles or Vietnamese-style plastic wheels with nylon lines, both using bits of prawn for bait.

Having grown up nearby, Hoanh loved and knew much about life on the water. As he talked enthusiastically about living so close to the sea, it began to sink in that even though our coffee was served in fancy cups, and our overpriced resort was within view, this boat was real. It was the exact kind that local fishermen lived on. Our pilot, despite his blue Evason T-shirt and baseball cap, was the real deal. And the stories Hoanh spent the morning telling us were very real. Just as the visit to the lobster farm had opened my eyes to the hardships of

me a chance to think. Like La Vong, the Chinese fisherman. Have you heard of him?"

"We saw a statue of La Vong in front of Cha Ca La Vong restaurant in Hanoi."

"You know him. Foreigners don't know him." He smiled. "La Vong fished without a hook or bait. He just used a weight. He wasn't interested in catching fish. He liked coming out on the water to meditate."

I thought about my grandpa. He would have been happy with us that day. A Navy sailor in the South China Sea by the time he was twenty, he was a quiet man who was most at home on the water. While mystery and majesty certainly influenced his love for the sea, I think his passion had more to do with the spirit of La Vong inside of him. An appreciation for the water when it was mute and motionless, when it invited the mind to slow down, as it did that morning around our boat. Hoanh closed his eyes. Hoa gazed sleepily at the distant hills. Julie was leaning back on one elbow, her pole abandoned at her side. My skin was warm and dusted with salt. I too closed my eyes. Despite its hardships, I could imagine that there was also an incomparable solace that came with life at sea.

Kim's Caramelized Clay Pot Fish

We made variations of this dish in Nha Trang, Dalat, and Saigon. After much experimentation, I came up with a recipe that is a crowd pleaser. When multiplying it, cut back on the oil and fish sauce in both the marinade and the sauce. And don't forget to remove the chilies before serving. The clay pot I usually use for this recipe and its doubled portion is the equivalent to a two-quart saucepan. If you can't find a clay pot, a heavy-bottom saucepan will do.

FISH:
1/2 lb. firm white fish such as halibut cut into 1-inch chunks (chicken or shrimp can also be used)
1 tbsp. fish sauce
Up to 1 tbsp. peanut oil

SAUCE:
2 tbsp. peanut oil
4 tbsp. sugar
2 tbsp. shallots, minced
1 clove garlic, minced
2 1-inch chunks ginger, peeled
1/2 cup coconut juice, not coconut milk, warmed (for a less sweet version, you can substitute water)
2 whole red Thai chilies
1 tbsp. fish sauce
pinch black pepper

PREPARING THE FISH:

1. Marinate the fish in fish sauce with a little oil for half an hour at room temperature.
2. Once it has marinated and the sauce below has been prepared, warm your clay pot with a cup or so of hot water, to keep it from cracking as it heats up on the stove. This is especially important for a new pot.
3. Remove water and put fish in clay pot. Pour the remainder of the marinade over the top of the fish.

PREPARING THE SAUCE WHILE THE FISH MARINATES:

1. Heat oil in a heavy-bottom saucepan. Add sugar, and stir until sugar dissolves. The mixture may seem too dry at first, or the sugar may crystallize a bit. Be patient, and keep stirring. Make sure the heat is high enough. Eventually, the sugar will dissolve.
2. Add minced shallots, garlic, and ginger.
3. Add coconut juice or water. Make sure it's warm before you add it. If not, the cold liquid hitting the hot oil/sugar will cause an instant case of hard candy. If this happens, just keep stirring until the "candy" dissolves.

4. Stir in chilies, stir in fish sauce, and add a pinch of black pepper.
5. Bring the sauce to a boil and then down to a simmer.
6. Put clay pot with fish on a burner and heat. Don't brown the fish, but simply warm it up a bit. (Now that I've used my clay pot a few times, it produces the most mouth-watering smell when I heat it up.)
7. Add caramel sauce to clay pot.
8. Simmer, covered, for 20 minutes.
9. Remove chilies and ginger before serving. Serve over rice.

PREPARING THE RICE:

This dish is good over white or brown rice. Prepare the rice according to the instructions on the package so that it is ready by the time the clay pot fish is done.

Serving: 1 as a large main dish over rice.

Dalat

Southern Vietnam

Hanoi•

•Hue
•Hoi An

•Nha Trang
•Dalat

•Phan Thiet
•Saigon

Into the Highlands

After Julie and I left Evason Hideaway, we spent a night at the Ana Mandara resort in Nha Trang city. Our stay included a cooking class and a tour of the fish market, a smelly, silvery place filled with colorful plastic crates; muddy, slushy ice; and every type of sea creature imaginable, including swordfish, stingray, and one dopey-looking shark. Early the next morning, we were loaded into a van and headed out of town. A few hours earlier, we had woken to the kind of rain that made it feel as if the world were coming to an end. Now, it was an opaque gray film that clung to the clefts and shadows of the landscape. I pressed my cheek to the window and peered down over the abrupt shelf that marked the rim of the road, at the inlets of water and their loose clusters of fishing boats. The boats looked tiny, wet, and cold.

On the bench in front of me was a French couple just coming from their honeymoon at Evason Hideaway. The husband worked for the Sofitel Dalat Palace, the hotel that sent the van. Behind me, Julie was curled up cozily in one corner of her seat.

"Banana flower," she murmured. "Definitely a favorite. And green papaya salad. I need to start making that again."

"Clam rice," I whispered. "I know it sounds crazy, but I really do miss it. Do you think I'll ever have it again?"

"Of course," she said, reassuringly. "Are you going to try making clay pot fish when we get back?" she asked.

"Definitely."

"Good." She smiled.

The day before, we had taken a cooking class at Ana Mandara. It wasn't the most inspiring lesson, but as I was beginning to learn, even disappointing experiences yielded gems. In this case, a new favorite dish: *ca kho* (clay pot fish). With its addictive caramelized sauce of sugar, chili, fish sauce, and coconut juice, we could easily see it center stage at a dinner party back home. Its sweet flavors would be set off by the freshness of banana flower salad, enhanced by the richness of crispy fried eggplant. I was looking forward to scouring my Bangkok Market and the shops of Chinatown for a clay pot.

As if we had eaten a great meal, rather than just talked about one, we grew drowsy. Conversation evaporated. I snuggled into the anticipation washing over me. We were on our way to Dalat. It was my favorite city in Vietnam. It was one of my favorite cities in the world. It was graceful and cool, a beautiful isolation of pine trees and flower gardens five thousand feet above sea level. It appealed to the recluse that resides within me.

On the drive between Nha Trang and Dalat, the road was flat for the first few hours. It was a new road, the only thing that looked new, aside from the police checkpoint, for hundreds of miles. Shacks balanced on the perimeters of rice fields, patchwork structures constructed over time with scraps of tin and sheets of Styrofoam for insulation. Occasionally, there was a house made of concrete. No doubt the owner was prosperous, and this was the reward for prosperity in rural Vietnam: a squat cinder block that wouldn't blow away in the next monsoon. But for the most part, the homes looked like works in stunted progress.

Bougainvillea crested a montage of wall panels that had been lashed together with chicken wire. A young man secured a swathe of blue plastic to the side of a house that looked as if it had been abandoned for half a century. An old man wearing a pink shirt and a white fedora crouched in a field of green, knees bent up, back hunched, his body adapted to his labor. Plastic bags flourished in ditches, like well-tended crops.

The landscape swayed with the motion of the ashy clouds across the sky. The horizon melted and glided. Colors brightened and faded. A grungy white dog trotted knee-deep through the soupy water of a rice paddy. A man slept in a collapsed haystack, and a boy herded a goat. Fields of dry, brown corn alternated with fields containing a plant I didn't recognize. A kite was caught in a power line. Another boy sprayed the ground with a substance from a pack strapped to his back.

I have always been fascinated by the diversity of images that create the Vietnamese countryside, and my mind buzzed with questions. I wanted to know what the boy was spraying and more about the weird Catholic influences that sprouted among the crops. An enormous plastic Jesus balanced on top of a mint green house, his arms outstretched to the sky. Art Deco hands folded in prayer, more than two stories high.

Julie was sleeping. The couple in front of me dozed, and besides, I didn't know them. I couldn't just tap their shoulders and bombard them with inquiries about the Cham and plastic Jesus, especially since technically they were still on their honeymoon. The driver didn't speak English. Silently, I contemplated a field that was subdivided into a grid of mud-walled pools of water. As a Trung Nguyen coffee billboard flashed past, I wondered if Huong's company had begun its rebranding campaign yet.

We navigated through a town, and I looked out at women crouched over baskets of purple grapes. Pedal sewing machines were displayed like museum curios in a tall glass shop case. *Banh mi* sandwich and sugar cane juice carts reflected the dull steel of the overcast sky. On sheets of woven reed on the shoulders of the road, translucent discs of rice paper dried in the intermittent sunlight. As we passed a street market, I searched for produce I recognized. Melons and custard apples, a tableful of tomatoes. In front of another market, tin bowls were arranged on a plank tabletop. The bowls overflowed with rice. Hard and sticky, broken and whole, long and short, each used for a different purpose. I wished I had someone to talk to about all the different kinds of rice.

An hour into the drive, in one of the small towns that populated the rural landscape, the van pulled to the side of the road, where a Vietnamese woman stood, holding a satchel. At first glance, she looked young, as many middle-aged Vietnamese women do. She was wearing a white sleeveless blouse and white pants, the kind of outfit I admire in a country where dust and dirt prevail. She climbed into the front seat, said hello to the couple, and as the van took off, introduced herself. Her name was Linh. We chatted for a few minutes before I realized that she was the guest services manager for the Dalat Palace, the woman I had been exchanging emails with for two months, planning this trip.

Unable to censor myself, I blurted the questions I had been storing up, dumping them over the shoulders of the polite but uninterested French couple. Finally, Linh asked the driver to pull over again so she could switch seats. As she settled beside me, I pointed to the grassy crop I had not been able to identify, and she said, "Sugar cane. Most of the farmers in this area cultivate tobacco, cotton, and sugar cane. And they have been growing grapes here since 1985." It turned out that Phan Rang, the town where we picked her up, was the heart of wine country. The Bordeaux of Vietnam, in its own humble Vietnamese way.

With Linh seated beside me, a large, anonymous-looking warehouse became a cotton research center, surrounded by three hundred acres. "This one is really interesting. It is farmed in rotation, six months of cotton, three months of rice, and sometimes peanuts, you know, to put nitrogen back into the soil."

"What about that?" I asked of a plastic-coated greenhouse.

She squinted out at the passing landscape. "Oh, that one. It's interesting, too. They're experimenting with seedless grapes."

"And that?" I asked, in regard to two rustic stone towers.

She leaned over me to get a better look. "The ethnic Cham still live in this area. Mostly they stay in their own communities, although some are leaving their traditional rice production to grow grapes."

"How do you know so much?"

She smiled. "I grew up here. My mother brought me down from the north when my parents were divorced. My husband is the dean of horticulture at Dalat University. Right now he's working to replicate the wild orchids of the highlands for export to Korea." She said this with great pride.

As the van climbed Ngoan Muc Pass, the air grew chilly. A fine, smoky mist floated through the late afternoon air. Linh was talking about various projects at the university, such as how the school had signed a contract with a French dairy research facility to import cows and technology. "Everyone wants milk for their kids, so they will grow tall, you know. Now, people can afford milk. It is not like after the war. Even if people had the money for it, there wasn't any milk for them to buy. I remember, food was especially scarce between 1977 to 1979. So much was needed in Cambodia to support Vietnam's fight against the Khmer Rouge. We got some aid relief from Bulgaria. Mostly rations of wheat, but it couldn't be used for bread because there wasn't any yeast, or oil or eggs. There wasn't any charcoal, either, for baking. Instead, I would boil the wheat to make porridge." She looked at me apologetically, as if I were the one who had suffered, and said, "I ate that for breakfast every day when I was in college."

She did not sound bitter, just matter-of-fact, like most people of a certain age I had met when they recalled the lean decade that followed the war. I could not help thinking: *So, this is what happens to the children of the winners of a war.* I imagined how Linh's delicate frame must have turned gaunt and brittle after years without protein and vitamins. I saw her as a teenage girl, her body craving the milk I drank every day during the same decade that she had lived without. Me, a child of the losers of war, drinking milk with graham crackers, drinking milk with spaghetti, drinking milk any old time I wanted to, or not drinking it, because I wanted a Shasta with my pizza instead.

Despite the serpentine road, and the joy-driving locals who used it like a Formula 1 racetrack, the steep climb into the highlands of Dalat was soothing. Salmon-colored hibiscus flashed between the trunks of pine trees. Poinsettia and sunflowers flared like lanterns in the darkening green foliage. Persimmon trees staked a claim, and moss coated the roofs of tiny houses that reminded me, sweetly, of *Heidi*. In glens, plastic-wrapped frames cocooned their floral chrysalides from the astringent mountain air. Air that was beneficial to the lungs, but unforgiving to the gladioli, azaleas, peonies, and dahlias that the City of Flowers was known for. Despite its discreet mountain temperament, Dalat was a city lusty with flora, not only flowers, but also produce. Asparagus, melons, and avocados; basil, cardamom, cloves, sage, and saffron.

Perhaps the sense of sanctuary I felt came from the landscape's evergreen reminders of my childhood. Or perhaps it reflected my first association with Dalat, how tranquil it seemed to me after living in Saigon for nearly half a year. Dalat was the first place in Vietnam that I visited outside the city. It was cool after the crushing heat. Silent after the crushing noise. The air was a relief, clean, fresh, and tinged with wood smoke, just as it was on this trip, ten years later, nearly to the date of that first visit, reminding me what a joy it can be simply to breathe.

Far from major cities and cruise ships, Dalat has long been spared crushing foreign tourism. Because of its geography and Vietnam's still fledgling transportation infrastructure, it is secluded and has the wonderfully eccentric personality that goes with a hermetic lifestyle. In Dalat you will find the daughter of a high-ranking Communist official running a capitalist hotel out of a house in a fake tree. There is a lunatic monk painter, elderly men in berets conversing with one another in French, young "cowboys" offering taxi services on the backs of Hondas, and nearly every newlywed couple in the country touring nearby waterfalls on their honeymoons. There is romantic Xuan Huong Lake, named after an eighteenth-century poetess; a championship golf course, originally designed as a diversion for France's puppet emperor, Bao Dai; and almost one thousand villas, many built by the French to reflect the half-timbered architecture of Brittany and the Basque. There are countless produce farms and the country's top winery, and ... swoon ... there is the Dalat Palace.

As we approached the hotel in the fading dusk, the Palace was just as I remembered it. Over the years, it had always been as I remembered it, unlike other places I had known that collapsed beneath the weight of nostalgia. Its facade was still the color of cream tinged with cinnamon, its edges were still sharp as a knife, and it still sat poised at a summit of stone steps that rose, in tiers, from the main road above the lake. The steps were flanked by smooth, sloped lawns, and at their peak was a pair of sentinel evergreens that rose beyond the hotel's rooftop. Our van approached along the drive that runs between the top two banks of steps, and as I looked up at the louvered windows, my mind filled with their views. Of the mist that floats in the morning over the lake, like the hem of the phantom poetess's skirt. Of the sable silhouettes of frayed treetops against the indigo night sky.

Unlike the region's assiduously preserved grand dames, the Raffles in Singapore, for example, or the Metropole in Hanoi, the Palace does not feel like the victim of commercially driven restoration. For me, there is a hint of Disneyland about the lovely old Raffles, particularly when you order a savagely overpriced Singapore Sling in the Long Bar and it is served in the glass equivalent of a Big Gulp cup. And although the Metropole's historic wing is stunning, its colonial style is a sophisticated interpretation for designer-conscious, twenty-first-century travelers.

The Palace, on the other hand, is well-kept. It does not feel haunted by a need to safeguard its past, but rather feels comfortably inhabited by it. It has a quiet dignity that does not pander to the trend of romanticizing history. It is romantic because it does not try. Because it is the real thing.

Officially opened in 1922, the originally named Lang Bian Palace was "at once social club, de facto headquarters of French colonial high society ... the *domaine reserve* of a minute elite," according to Eric T. Jennings's *From Indochine to Indochic*. The ambition that conceived it is intertwined with the city it inhabits.

Before Dr. Alexandre Yersin scouted the Lang Bian highlands in 1893, the region was inhabited by a scattering of ethnic groups, including the Lat, from which the city gets the latter part of its name. The first part, *da*, means stream. Yersin determined the cool climate and fresh air to be ideal for the kind of hill-town sanitarium that was popular in colonial India at the time. Although initially chosen as a retreat from the heat of southern Vietnam, it was destined to become much more.

Dalat was proprietarily designated *le petit Paris* by civil servants, administrators, and military personnel in Saigon who could not afford to spend their holidays back in France and so settled into the Dalat Palace with the same aplomb as the French monarchy inhabiting Versailles. Sure, Dalat was also home to the summer palace of the Vietnamese emperor, but everyone knew where the real power slept at night.

The Palace's heyday, though brilliant, was brief. Conflicting French, Vietnamese, and ethnic minority interests, and then a massive devaluation in rubber that led to a depression, brought about the closing of the hotel, from 1934 to 1937. When the Palace reopened, it—like French colonialism—had passed its prime, and by the time the Japanese occupied Vietnam in 1945, its golden years were demoted to sentimental whispers of *Remember when?* When my boss from Saigon's Phu Dong Language School stayed there in the early 1990s, there was no running water, and he had to use a lantern to find his way to his room at night.

But oh what a difference a few years can make.

By the time I arrived for my first stay in the fall of 1995, the Dalat Palace had been expensively, but gently, nurtured back to health. Rather than defending its partisan past in the form of an aggressively nostalgic restoration, the hotel was radiant with humility, as if it had finally discovered—and graciously accepted—what it should have been from the start: a place where the best of East and West unite.

A chill alpine wind accompanied Julie and me into the hushed foyer. Although the hotel was fully booked with a bicycling tour from the Butterfield & Robinson travel company, it felt as if we were alone. This was another thing I remembered fondly about the Palace. No matter how big our group, milling wine-flushed in the lobby, or encountering one another in the quiet halls, I somehow always felt as if I had the place to myself. No matter how cold it was near the front door while we checked in, our room was warm in a mountain-estate-with-lots-of-fireplaces kind of way.

A three-story chandelier hung above the lobby, radiating liquid beads of light onto a quartet of cocoa brown leather armchairs. It descended through the landings of the first and second floors, whose railings encircled it. We were escorted upstairs by a bellboy, past reproductions of works by Renoir and Manet, to the first floor, where Julie and I had stayed once before. Our room had a terrace that overlooked the lawns and lake. Taking a peek outside, I saw that the terraces had been modified since I was last there. They were now separated by dividers, so that I would no longer step outside in the morning, cozy in my robe, warming my hands on a hot cup of coffee, and come face to face with my neighbors in their robes, greeting the day with the view and coffee as well.

Other than the terrace, nothing had changed. The ceilings still soared, and the tall paned doors were secured with locks that looked as if they had been installed during the days of French colonialism. The sheets smelled of spring cleaning, and the claw-foot tub called to me. During my first weekend there many years before, my friends spent the days golfing and skydiving while I, after six months of tepid showers in my cheap lodgings in Saigon, stayed in and took baths. At least four over the course of two days.

Julie and I changed into warmer clothes and made our way to the basement, where Larry's Bar was located. Unlike in the rest of the hotel, it had ceilings that were low and dark, like a cave. Larry's was not the kind of place you would expect to find in a hotel like this. It was a tavern rather than a bistro, and because of it, I adored the Palace even more. We ordered wine and pizza, played a few games of pool, and were asleep by nine o'clock.

Just for Fun

In response to my inquiries about farming in Dalat, Antoine Sirot, the general manager of the Dalat Palace, had written to me:

> The highlight of Dalat is mainly the vegetable produce and fruits grown in this area for some one hundred years. In the early days, Dalat was a perfect place to establish an experimental farm, due to its exceptional climate ... Mostly the early varieties of vegetables were basics, such as potatoes and other roots and cucurbitaceous vegetables (tomatoes, cucumbers, squash, zucchini, bell peppers, eggplant). In the late '30s, Mr. Borel, a French farmer, originating from the Savoie, introduced and developed not only new crops, such as the round-shaped "Brittany Artichoke" and the spiky-shaped "Artichoke of Provence," from the South Mediterranean shores of France, but also brought a special species of cows from his mountainous region in the Alps, the "Abondance" cows, famous to produce high-quality dairy. All of his work has brought the result of what you can see today at Dalat Market: a unique choice of Vietnamese and French cuisine ingredients, the basis of a real fusion of the two cultures.

With his detailed emails about the produce of Dalat, Antoine had piqued my interest. In person, waxing poetic about the turniplike vegetable kohlrabi, he was captivating. "Yesterday in the market I saw *le chou-rave*," he announced in lieu of hello upon meeting Julie and me. "This was quite popular in the European countryside in the 1930s, but not so today."

We were in the hotel's business center, waiting for Linh, the woman from the van, who was going to serve as our guide that day. As if describing a star that scientists thought had long ago burned out, Antoine proclaimed, "Amazing, really amazing, to find this here."

We gazed at him, fascinated not only by the intensity of his emotion in regard to a vegetable (it was possible that his fervor exceeded Didier Corlou's), but also by his appearance. He was just five years older than I, with wavy blond hair and a tan that validated his résumé: his stints before Dalat were in the Indonesian islands. His natty suit brought to mind Michael Caine circa *The Italian Job*, and his eyeglasses were Elvis Costello gone expat in Asia. In an article for *DestinAsian* magazine, my fellow writer James Sullivan wrote, "From the first, one suspects him of cufflinks."

Linh rushed into the room and declared, "We're late." Much to our disappointment,

Antoine checked his watch and said, "So sorry, but I must be going. I have an appointment with an old Daletite. We're putting together an architectural tour of the city for hotel guests. Let's meet up for a beer later at Larry's Bar."

"Dashing," Julie whispered, as he departed.

"Dapper," I agreed.

Linh brandished the itinerary that she had prepared from the list of places I told her I wanted to visit—along with various farms, which were my priority, I had requested a meeting with the head of Dalat Wine and a meal at a restaurant that served *ragu*, a local specialty. It was 9:35, and our first appointment was at 9:30. "Let's go, let's go," she said, clapping her hands, as if Julie and I had kept her waiting. As she hustled us to the car, I browsed through her schedule of assignations, each set an hour apart. An hour was scarcely enough time for most of the interviews, especially since some of the destinations were half an hour away from one another. I braced myself for the next three days of rush, rush, rushing and the very Vietnamese experience of always being late.

When it comes to the performance that is Vietnamese cuisine, rice is the headliner. It has been traced back to Mesolithic times in the area that is now northern Vietnam, and by the eighteenth century there were seventy recorded strains. Among Vietnam's food, it gets all the best aphorisms, folk songs, and legends. *An com*, which literally means "to eat rice," also means "to take a meal."

When I long for Vietnamese food, though, rice is rarely among my cravings. This is not because I am put off by its carb count the way many young Vietnamese women now are. Nor is it because I dislike rice. I enjoy a serving of rice with my meals. It's just that for me, Vietnamese food is what it is at heart—fresh and light—because of its produce. Diners will find bright green vegetables in nearly every dish, aromatic herbs on nearly every dish, and fruit, always a piece of dewy *vu sua* or tart-sweet mangosteen, for dessert at the end of a meal.

According to an article published by the PPD (Plant Protection Department), a state department established under Vietnam's Ministry of Agriculture and Rural Development, at the time of my visit the Vietnamese were consuming six million tons of fruits and vegetables each year. A report financed by the French Ministry of Foreign Affairs a few years earlier assigned this statistic solely to vegetable consumption, and excluded regular and sweet potatoes. In either case, in a country of eighty million people, this was a substantial annual serving per person, and it put produce second only to rice, which sat at thirteen million tons per year. Add to this the PPD claim that farm owners invested approximately $1.83 billion in "intensive farming and production expansion," an increase of more than 90 percent over their investments just four years previously, and it is clear that, despite rice's loyal following and the growing influx of fast and packaged foods, fresh produce is still essential to Vietnamese daily life.

Vietnam's flourishing farms include vast state-run enterprises, as well as small private gardens. The French report claims, "Forty-three percent of the fruits and vegetables consumed by Vietnamese households are produced at home."

And from Ngoc Ha in the north, producing its coveted water spinach, to Lai Thieu in the south, harvesting its pungent durian fruit, individual villages and areas are still known for what they grow. But there is no place in the country like Dalat.

Since its origins, Dalat has been a place of experimentation, and although its first gardening innovations were introduced by the French, they seem to me to fit in with the personality of Vietnam, a country I consider ingenious and adaptable, despite its Communist-applied veneer of intractability. The Vietnamese may have disliked French rule, but that wasn't going to stop them from futzing around with "Western bamboo," for example, and coming up with what is now the ubiquitous and distinctly Vietnamese *sup mang tay cua*, or crab and asparagus soup.

Now, in the twenty-first century, experimentation in Dalat was enjoying a renaissance. Among its farmers were two notable growers producing new vegetable varieties and promoting clean growing practices. While organic food was all the rage in the United States, it was still a gleam in most farmers' eyes in Vietnam. The country was heavily criticized for unsafe farming, and there was the loitering, controversial issue of the millions of gallons of defoliants dropped in the south during the American War. I was going to meet with both growers, one a Vietnamese and another an American, but before I got into the nitty-gritty of responsible farming, there was a little side trip I wanted to make.

While researching Dalat in preparation for my trip, I stumbled across an article about "master grafter and hybridist" Bui Van Loi and his Valley of the Peach Blossoms nursery. Mr. Bui, the article explained, had grafted a Japanese cherry tree with a Dalat cherry tree to create a tree with white and violet blossoms. His grafting of an Australian plum variety onto a Dalat cherry tree resulted in two kinds of fruit, one with white flesh and the other with yellow. He had also successfully grafted five kinds of pomelo onto a single tree.

As I sat at my desk in L.A., staring outside at my own tree that bore only lemons, Mr. Bui came to life in my imagination: the Willy Wonka of fruit farmers. I completely forgot the original intent of that day's research to find out more about pesticide use, as my mind filled with visions of growing my own fruit cocktail on a single tree. I emailed Linh and insisted that I *must* meet Mr. Bui.

Now, as Julie and I followed Linh past a small wood house and down a steep dirt path, she told us, "I just found that Mr. Bui is the father of one of my old college friends. Isn't that exciting?" Although we were scheduled for a day of visiting farms, she was dressed as if she were on her way to afternoon tea: trim black trousers, a white blouse, and a girlish black felt bowler with a tuft of feathers at the back. Making her way gingerly over the uneven ground and beneath low-hanging branches, she said, "When you wrote to me about him, I didn't realize he was the same man you wanted to meet, because he used to be a legume farmer."

I smiled at the use of "legume," which is a common word among Vietnamese of a certain generation, who learned their English from outdated schoolbooks.

The air smelled of the clods of earth that had been churned up with a nearby hoe. As I shook Mr. Bui's callused hand, I examined the small orchard, searching for a pineapple hanging on the same branch as a carrot—an ideal combination for the pineapple-and-carrot Jell-O salad that used to be a staple on our family's Thanksgiving dinner table. But the trees looked normal, and instead of a herd of Oompa-Loompas, he was trailed by only his nine-year-old granddaughter in an electric pink poncho. His cloth cap was the kind that my grandfather used to wear, and his leather bomber jacket, although stylish, was most likely for keeping him warm while working outdoors.

Mr. Bui learned to graft in high school, and for many years it was a hobby, nothing more. Now, it consumed all of his spare time, bringing in extra income. These days, he was heady from recent successes, and I could see in his face the pleasure that his life's work had given him. "You see that greenhouse over there," Linh said. "It contains succulents. Mr. Bui has trained them so they will bloom during Tet. Isn't that incredible? And he created a cherry tree to bloom during the December flower festival. The city has already ordered sixty trees. They are worth more than sixty million dong." She paused so we could absorb this figure, the equivalent of four thousand U.S. "He has also grafted avocado varieties from Australia and France."

My knowledge of grafting was still young, and I asked, "But why? Dalat already has avocados."

Linh conferred with Mr. Bui. "Quality. When the president of Vietnam's Southern Fruit Research Institute visited France a little while ago, he saw that the quality of the French avocado was much higher than the Vietnamese."

"That's strange," I said. "Isn't the Vietnamese variety originally from France?"

"Of course, but it has changed over the years. So the president brought back shoots for Mr. Bui to experiment with. Mr. Bui had to try three grafts before he produced a fruit that met international criteria. But he's only grafted onto one tree so far, so he can't make any official claims yet. First, he's going to send the results to Dac Lac province. The soil there is better for avocados. They'll be grown for domestic use. Over time, if the quality is high enough, France will consider importing them."

Linh and Mr. Bui were studying me, as if uncertain that I understood the significance of such an outcome, the prosperity this could bring to Mr. Bui and to other farmers in the country. I smiled and nodded in a way I hoped reflected the respect I felt for Mr. Bui's work. Although he was talking about the avocado—a fruit that I, as a resident of California, took for granted—I appreciated what he was doing, both as a farmer and as a man of passion. Over the years, I had encountered many people like him in Vietnam, small-time connoisseurs, painting in their living rooms or wood-carving on their patios or tending bonsai trees on their roofs. To their obsessions they had given their hearts away. I had a vision of him in this small orchard, alone during the day when his granddaughter was at school, while high above the quiet, plastic-covered garden beds the power lines hissed. His hands were cold and much stiffer now that he was no longer a young man, but I could still see how tenderly he would hold a willowy shoot as he eased it into a notch cut into the stock.

Many credit the Roman Empire for cultivating the world's earliest grafting techniques. It's true that there are many mentions of this, including in the book of Romans, where the apostle Paul writes, "If some of the branches have been broken off, and you, though a wild olive shoot, have been grafted in among the others and now share in the nourishing sap from the olive root, do not boast over those branches." In fact, Greece's Aristotle wrote knowledgably about grafting in the fourth century BC, and Adam Wheeler of the University of Vermont claims that it was "first documented by the Chinese as early as 5,000 BC, when Feng Li, a Chinese diplomat, began grafting peaches, almonds, persimmons, pears and apples as a commercial venture."

There are numerous reasons for grafting. To produce stronger plant varieties and plants that are immune to certain bugs, to repair damaged plants, and to create seedless fruits and ornamental plants, and yes, even my fruit cocktail tree. I thought I was being a smart aleck when I dreamed this up in L.A., but it turns out there is a single tree that produces nectarines, peaches, plums, and apricots. You can order one for $19.95 over the Internet ... that is if you don't live in Washington, California, or Arizona—which is the state I was born in, the state I relocated to, and the state my parents relocated to, respectively. Apparently, I'm not meant to have a fruit cocktail tree.

Mr. Bui grafted to create a peach with an enhanced flavor, and to produce fruit trees small enough to be tended inside Vietnamese homes. He grafted out of curiosity, to find out which foreign produce could thrive in local conditions. He also grafted to grow tangerines for his family's enjoyment. As a rooster crowed at one of the farms down the hill, he plucked a piece of plump pale-green fruit from a tree and peeled away its glossy rind. He shared the sections, bound in their filigree of pith. As we bit into the cold citrus flesh, he told us that the flavor would linger in our mouths for hours.

He had explained nearly everything in his garden, but there was one experiment he had yet to talk about. I asked, "Why did he graft five pomelos onto a single tree?"

He laughed as Linh translated my question. Up the hill, on the balcony of a house above us, a teenage boy broke into song. The off-key carol rained down on Mr. Bui's cactus and cherry trees. Linh explained, "Sometimes, Mr. Bui grafts just for fun."

Sadly, as in mainstream America, Vietnam's agricultural vision does not include the gentleman farmer. I had heard rumors that the government intended to take over Mr. Bui's land and use it for industry crops, such as tea or coffee. The city, apparently, was destined for an influx of casinos and new golf courses, and who wanted to look at plastic greenhouse roofs while teeing off? Mr. Bui could relocate, but that wasn't the point. The point was the dullness of uniformity, and an increasingly universal lack of appreciation for individual endeavor. The point was the satisfied look on Mr. Bui's face as he scraped his Honda key over the bark of a cinnamon tree, drawing out its downy scent. The cinnamon, too, was just for fun. But it was fun that he was having on his own modest, honestly worked, honestly earned plot of land.

Annabel Jackson's Fruit with Cinnamon-and-Lime Dressing Dessert

I wanted to include a dessert recipe, and this one is terrific. Because it consists of mixed fruit, I find it fitting to include it after Mr. Bui's chapter. I am grateful to Annabel Jackson for allowing me to offer this recipe from her cookbook, *Café Vietnam*. It is the perfect ending to any Vietnamese meal. *Café Vietnam* has gone out of print, but I recommend tracking down a used copy. It's a reliable primer for classic Vietnamese dishes.

INGREDIENTS:

A selection of peeled fruit such as mango, papaya, banana, dragon fruit, pineapple, star fruit, and even watermelon or honey-dew melon.

INGREDIENTS FOR DRESSING:

Grated zest and juice of 6 limes (about 2/3 cup)
3 tbsp. honey
1/2 tsp. sesame oil
1 tsp. ground cinnamon
Pinch of sea salt

DIRECTIONS:

1. Cut the fruit into chunks in a bowl.
2. Combine the lime zest and juice in a separate bowl. Gradually add the honey, stirring, to make a creamy mixture. Taste, and add a little more honey if the dressing is too sharp. Stir in the sesame oil, cinnamon, and salt.
3. Pour the dressing over the fruit, and stir gently to combine. Leave in a cool place for about 15 minutes, to allow the flavors to develop. Serve.

The Secret World of Ragu

"We're late," I commented, as we climbed into the van.

"Yes," Linh agreed, amiably.

"Does it matter?" I asked.

"I don't know," she said, in an offhand way that did not reassure someone like me, afflicted with an old-fashioned American sense of punctuality.

The radio's cool Parisian jazz provided a surreal soundtrack to the passing landscape of leafy terraces in steep descent, greenhouses caped in plastic, and shacks with yellow poinsettias like small wildfires in their yards. We gained on a motorcyclist, whose blue jacket stuttered violently in the wind. At one time in my life in Vietnam, I was obsessed with motorcycles and everything they transported: refrigerators, plate glass, half a dozen live hogs, and wire cages astir with venomous snakes. On this trip, motorcycles captured my attention only when they were transporting food. The back of this one was piled high with celery.

Our driver got lost on the winding back roads. Added to our overtime with Mr. Bui, this made us almost an hour late to Golden Garden Produce. "I'm sorry, so sorry," I called out as I strode across the dirt parking area, but Bob Allen, the farm's owner, did not seem to care. No doubt he had long ago adjusted to the Vietnamese clock. He was dressed for the day's work in clothing as laid-back as his attitude, baseball cap, jeans, and a fishing vest over a short-sleeved shirt. My guess was that he was in his fifties.

As Julie and I matched Bob's leisurely stride toward one of many massive greenhouses, he told us, "I came here in the mid-1990s. I started off with strawberries, with my old partner Hung, and with Rolf over there."

He introduced us to Rolf, a craggy Dutchman who throughout the morning interrupted our conversation to entertain us with stories, such as one about the time he shipped broccoli out of Vietnam and the customs inspectors wanted to know why he had painted his cauliflower green. I did not comment on Hung, even though I knew of him. Nguyen Ba Hung was a local farmer whom Didier bought specialty vegetables from. A few years earlier, Bob and Hung went their separate ways, a parting swathed in rumors, as if Dalat were a junior high school cafeteria. Hung now owned Organiks, the site of my next interview later in the day, and Bob's farm was the force behind Veggy's, a produce shop in Saigon that was causing a stir that at first seemed strange in a country known for its fresh fruits and vegetables.

In her blog *EatingAsia*, Robyn Eckhardt wrote, "Right now Veggy's is the only place in Saigon to nab a bit of rocket or a bulb of fennel." Herein lay the cause for my interest in Bob's farm, not to mention joy on the part of expatriate housewives and locals with disposable incomes. Bob's four-hectare Golden Garden produced seventeen varieties of lettuce, as well as fifty to sixty vegetables and herbs, many of which could not be found in traditional Vietnamese markets.

Like Mr. Bui's farm, but on a larger, more utilitarian, masterminded, and fully-staffed scale, Golden Garden was an agricultural laboratory where Bob experimented with delicate flowers for garnishes and stir fries, and with lettuces such as chicory frissée, cultivating the yellow, frilly leaves that chefs in Vietnam's luxury hotels loved so much. He had created his own Oriental salad mix, whose greens—raised in tidy rows in tidy beds—were harvested one by one, with scissors.

"It's incredibly labor intensive," Bob told us, as we studied a tray filled with soft newborn leaves. "But it makes such a beautiful salad. You just can't afford to grow like this in the U.S., where produce is grown in the ground and machine-harvested." This method meant that his baby squash mix could contain five or six types, rather than just one or two, and that he was able to send chefs a new surprise every week.

I chose not to ask him how much, or how little, he paid his workers for this intensive labor. I knew the amount would not be enough, in my opinion, but I also knew from years of experience that arguing this issue was futile. And that people on the opposite side of the fence weren't always "bad guys."

The day was overcast, and the light inside the greenhouse diluted and gray. The air was murky with moisture. A woman wearing rubber boots and a conical hat tended a row so meticulously that it looked as if she were watering each tiny plant individually. Watching her, I asked, "What does all this mean? What does a farm like Golden Garden mean for Vietnamese cuisine?"

"I've been raising iceberg lettuce, zucchini squash, and broccoli for about seven years here in Vietnam," Bob said. "Gradually, I've watched these vegetables ease into local dishes. I'm also working on a Vietnamese-style salad blend. I plan to introduce it for *pho*. In general, though, the majority of my produce, particularly the highest quality, goes to foreign markets. For the domestic market, we usually introduce second-quality crops."

My knee-jerk reaction was to shout "Unfair!" and then mutter crankily about the disadvantages of being born in a developing country. But as with wages, it wasn't as easy as that. Nothing in Vietnam ever is. It wasn't just that locals couldn't afford the prices it took to raise high-quality vegetables. Unlike foreigners, they weren't familiar with produce such as rocket and fennel, nor was the general public accustomed to trying new things. Even if these obstacles were surpassed, there was the problem of regulation. Poorly enforced regulations, due to lack of experience and a lingering culture of corruption, could have a detrimental effect on the local food-buying scene.

One example of this came when I asked Bob why corn was so lousy in Vietnam. He explained that once upon a time the local company Dalat Hasfarm grew high-quality sweet corn for export. To see how the Vietnamese public might respond, they introduced the second quality for domestic use. The response was positive because the flavor was outstanding compared to the old feed corn that everyone was used to. But the next year local seed companies tried to capitalize on Hasfarm's success and dumped what Bob called "crap seeds" on the market. The result sank prices, destroyed Hasfarm's sales, and most damaging, destroyed the public's trust in the sweet corn market.

In a country like Vietnam, where public awareness was limited, government oversight minimal (despite a lingering Big Brother mentality), and annual incomes ridiculously low, a farmer couldn't just grow kale, Swiss chard, or broccoli rabe and send it out to the masses. The sweet corn story was proof, but this was also a lesson that Bob learned personally, the hard way. When he introduced his Golden Garden produce in Vietnam, people were excited about it. While his was not a fully organic farm, it was founded on a clean philosophy. Word quickly got out. In a country known for its pesticide use, Golden Garden produce was safe to eat. But, as Eckhardt wrote in her blog, "Almost immediately problems arose. The stores where their products were sold, like Citimart, began copying the Golden Garden trademark sticker and attaching it to every fruit and vegetable on their shelves. Employees in Dalat walked off with seeds and seedlings and even produce, selling them on the black market."

When most people think about bootlegging, copyright infringement, and pirating, they think about CDs, movies, and hideous Louis Vuitton handbags. But in Vietnam, the ripped-off product can be anything. When I lived there, I bought cooking oil that promised to be "cholesterol free." A local friend learned that those two simple words had influenced my buying decision, and she set me straight, laughing hysterically at my American gullibility. "Anyone can print that on a label, Kim." Apparently, no one monitored this sort of thing, or if someone did, he was open to bribes. Most likely, the cooking oil producer didn't even know what it meant, other than that it boosted his sales.

Most Vietnamese I talked to about this issue were skeptical shoppers, and for good reason. Golden Garden could not afford to become the object of this kind of collective mistrust, and so Bob opened Veggy's market, where only Golden Garden or imported produce was sold. Sadly, such an approach excluded most of Vietnam's consumers, but it was necessary, for the time being, to safeguard quality and good faith.

As for the future, as Vietnam advances with the development and enforcement of trademark and health/safety regulations; as enterprises such as Golden Garden introduce the benefits of clean farming to their communities by working with contract farmers and holding them to a higher standard; as it becomes more cost effective to use clean farming methods; as more new foods are introduced and a sense of adventure among the eating public grows; and as incomes rise, there is hope that one day the average Vietnamese will be able to walk into a neighborhood market and both afford *and* trust a safe and tasty little bundle of chicory frissée, mesculin mix, or whatever else Bob happened to have conjured up in his greenhouses in the hills of Dalat.

Although I had been to Dalat many times and enjoyed many meals there, I could not think of a single dish that I associated with all my visits. In advance of my arrival, I asked Antoine to name a typical Dalat specialty. In his wonderfully epistolary way, he replied:

> Dalat being the favorite domestic vacation destination, the city attracts the Vietnamese seeking "Exoticism": The cool climate, vegetation of pines, the French architecture and city plan around the lake are what they are looking for. They wear their "winter clothes" only in Dalat, giving them the opportunity to hang around with overcoats, sweaters and woolen scarves. This search for "something different" is also reflected in their choice of food in the Dalat restaurants. A popular delicacy, much appreciated in Dalat, is the Ragu, spelled "Ragout" in French. It is basically a long-cooking stew, mixing meat and vegetables, and flavored with herbs. This dish is traditionally served with French bread in a local restaurant and people would dip slices in the stew, just like French peasants used to do in their countryside. This dish is very suitable to Dalat's cool temperatures, quite affordable and kind of flexible in its container: potatoes, white beans, peas, carrots, mushroom mixed with beef or sometimes pork. My guess is that it was a favored meal of the French Army, as it can be prepared for large numbers. The Vietnamese, forming a good 80 percent of the troops, would have later brought the recipe back home from all over the country.

The moment I read this email, I craved *ragu*, and when making all arrangements with Linh, I asked her to choose a restaurant where we could try it. As we drove from Bob's farm to Doan Doan, we were two hours late for our reservation. Linh was concerned, and I found this odd, since reservations are not common in Vietnam, and since her itinerary made running two hours late to everything we did inevitable. When I questioned her scheduling prowess, she made it clear that our tardiness was my fault. "You talk too much," she chided. She then dropped Julie and me off and told us to call her when we were done.

The lunch crowd had come and gone in the small café, located off the town's main square. It was simple and clean, in the way the best Vietnamese restaurants are. We were given a table at the front picture window, and beyond Julie, across the street, were two slender buildings separated by an alley. Down the alley, crowning an upslope of tile roofs like a coronet, was the Eiffel Tower. For some crazy reason, the local powers that be had the telecommunications tower built as a facsimile of Gustave's Parisian original. The theme song from *Love Story* played softly, providing a sense of continuity, since we had heard versions of it—on a harp, a piano, a xylophone, and by a Filipino band— throughout the trip.

It was tranquil inside the café. The staff was attentive but unobtrusive. As happens in dreams, when events occur out of sequence but still make sense, two bowls of *ragu* were brought to our table before we placed our order. One was beef, and the other vegetarian. Both smelled warm, not just in temperature but also in the promise of snug comfort, antidotal to the overcast day. A plate with thick slices of a fresh baguette was set on the table between us. We asked for Tiger beer. Nirvana was within reach.

"Onion," I said as I took a bite. "And peas."

"Potatoes, and mushrooms," Julie added. "It's kind of like a stew. But lighter."

I thought about the surrounding farms, the wonderfully short distance these vegetables had to travel to reach my bowl. "They're definitely fresh. I wasn't sure if I'd be able to tell the difference, but I can." I took another bite. The broth was lustrous, a satiny consommé rather than a thick gravy. "Mine's so buttery," I said.

"Mine too. It's probably beef broth, isn't it?"

"Probably."

Julie studied the bowl, filled her spoon, considered the implications. She took the bite. "It's too good. I can't help myself."

A few days later, cooking with the head chef of the Dalat Palace, we would learn that the irresistible flavor was a combination of fish sauce and tomatoes, the former used sparingly, the latter completely reduced so not a trace of their flesh remained. I bit into a peppercorn and felt a thrill, as I had with the spearmint in Hue. The bread in Dalat was different from bread in the rest of the country. Lighter, as if to better absorb the broth. Julie finished all of her soup, despite her misgivings.

I requested a menu, to see how Doan Doan described this specialty. I found steamed porcupine, wild boar, grilled anteater, and fried deer, but no *ragu*. Back in the van, I asked Linh about this. She told me that *ragu* is rarely on menus. It takes too much time to prepare. You can't saunter into a restaurant and ask for a bowl. You must order ahead, as she had done for us. This explained her earlier concern about our being late.

I considered her revelation: the secret world of *ragu*.

It was a world that the average traveler did not know about. A world I now knew about because one insider, Antoine, gave me the password, and another, Linh, showed me where to use it. As we drove to our next appointment, I savored my initiation into this exclusive club.

The distinction between Bob, of Veggy's farm, and Nguyen Ba Hung, the owner of Organiks, was evident immediately. Whereas Bob was low-key, Hung bounded around his office in his socked feet, talking rapidly about exporting romaine lettuce to Japan, his agricultural training in France, and a vacuum cooling system that takes only forty minutes. "Just forty minutes," he repeated, emphatically, shaking his head, as if he was still getting used to this miracle of technology. He spoke enthusiastically about his company's pioneering home delivery of three- or six-kilogram bags of organic vegetables in Saigon, and of his recent Swiss IMO certification, which made his produce acceptable in the EU. Pointing to his certificate framed and hanging on the wall, he grinned like a varsity quarterback showing off his MVP trophy.

A fifty-two-year-old with the energy of a kid of eighteen, Hung had welcomed Julie and me into a modest office with cups of hot tea. Drowsy from our *ragu* lunch, we removed our shoes and took seats in front of a display of vegetables and flowers that had been prepared on a low coffee table. The plastic containers looked like a painter's palette. Mounds of Windsor violet fashioned into the shape of plump radishes. Lit-from-within streaks of cadmium yellow in the form of miniature tomatoes. A Fauvist splash of edible flowers for garnishing sorbet. This was the kind of elevated, elegant produce I might covet at high-end farmers' markets in America, but some of it was new to more than just Vietnam. When I had been with Didier in his kitchen in Hanoi, a package arrived from Hung. Examining the dark purple butter beans inside the box, the expert, well-traveled chef said, "This is the first time in my life I have seen this one."

Hung was eager to talk about the subject that had occupied much of my conversation with Bob: quality control. "Organiks has guidelines for sowing, harvesting, processing, and delivery. All of our contract farmers are required to comply with them. We provide them with seeds, technical advice, and technical control support. We even have a detailed tracking system. We can trace a bag of spinach sold in Saigon to the exact farm, plot, row, and date of its origins. It's very rigorous. Since 1996, we've gone from working with sixty-five family farms to just six." We were putting our shoes back on for a tour of his facilities, and he frowned as he tied his laces. "I don't like that we have to let them go, of course, but it could ruin my business."

We left his office and walked to the open-air processing area, where young women wearing turtlenecks and trendy athletic jackets were packaging zucchini and cucumber by hand. Thoughtfully, he said, "Some farmers comply, and some don't. Some panic and use pesticides because they are afraid of losing their crops. " It is easy to criticize the farmers in Vietnam for abusing pesticides, but Hung was sympathetic. "From 1975 to 1989, people were unfamiliar with quality," he explained. "We don't blame the farmers, because they don't know better. The government's agricultural department will give you a clean certificate if you declare that your produce is clean. But the responsibility for making sure it's clean falls solely on the farmer." He examined a blue plastic basket filled with purple, scarlet, and white baubles: radishes that would have looked as at home in a jewelry case as they did on a farm. He said, "A farmer washes his hands and thinks he is being clean, but he doesn't understand that the water he is using is dirty, or that the soil he is growing his crop in is dirty. Because of the history of Dalat, the area's soil is not clean. We have to test for lead, arsenic, copper, chemicals ..."

It is no secret that pesticides have been a long-standing problem in Vietnam. Their use began in the 1950s, when little was known about their hazards. Under the direction of the country's Plant Protection Department, they were applied to crops in cooperatives and collective- and state-run farms. Post-1975 brought embargoes and shortages, but a resurgence came in 1988, with decollectivization. Able to work their own plots of land, individual farmers needed ways to keep their crops, and incomes, alive.

As Hung saw it, there were two main barriers to responsible farming. As well as the fear of lost income, he pinpointed lack of education. To combat the latter, he was creating a pilot farm where he could grow produce on land that had not been heavily abused or affected by neighboring spray. "It will be a living supermarket," he declared. "We will use it to educate tourists and locals."

Dalat is the perfect city for such a venture. Already adored by the Vietnamese for its fruits, vegetables, and flower festivals, it is one of the country's top domestic tourist destinations and its number one honeymoon destination. This meant that a farm such as Hung described had the potential to attract a significant number of people, particularly those under the age of twenty-five, who made up more than half the country's population, and who would soon be responsible for the majority of its food purchases. If effective, the result would be an educated consumer and a subsequent insistence on quality. It was still impossible to say which direction the Vietnamese might take in regard to their food sources as they moved forward, but it was reassuring to know that there were farmers like Hung and Bob. One an insider and one an outsider. One sympathetic to his countrymen's mistakes. One highly practical about what needed to be done. Despite their personal differences, and their personal approaches, both were working to put Vietnam on a healthy path.

The night was cold and black, and the air so crisp that Julie and I could feel its blade grazing our faces as we walked down the slope of the Dalat Palace grounds and around the end of Xuan Huong Lake. As we huffed our way up the hill toward the main square, we could see the white effort of our breathing. Behind us, the ember of the Eiffel Tower smoldered in the sky. We were layered, T-shirts beneath long-sleeve shirts beneath second long-sleeve shirts, all beneath shawls we bought in Hoi An. We wished we had brought close-toed shoes. People passed on foot and motorcycles, warm in their jackets, boots, and knit caps.

I left all thoughts of grafting and trademarking and cultivating baby vegetables in my notebook back in our room, and we made our way to Maison Long Hoa. After the disappointment of my once favorite café in Hoi An, I was a little worried. Maison Long Hoa was the keeper of even fonder memories. Cherished conversations. Reassuring food. I had been there many times, and whenever I ate there, it was always the kind of place that made me feel, if only for a few hours, that all was right with the world.

The restaurant was located on a side street, and the tawny glow of its front window had a folktale quality about it, the promise of rest to a weary traveler on a lonely night. Steam blurred the rims of the window pane, assuring us of warmth within. As we stepped inside, we could feel the heat from the kitchen in the back. The room was prettily decorated, in a way that brought to mind an alpine village. With the exception of a large Vietnamese family eating steaks and fries—the daughter wearing a knockoff Gap Girl T-shirt and the son in a Brooklyn Industries jacket—the diners were Western, as they had been at the café of dashed hopes in Hoi An. But that was where the similarity ended.

There was no carnival atmosphere. There were no bursts of showmanship, no madcap routines to distract from mediocre food. We were escorted to a small table off to one side. Just as I remembered, the atmosphere was quiet and welcoming. It invited the kind companionability that can only be found between people who have known one another for a very long time. It suited my relationship with my sister. More than anything, we just liked to spend time together, from a journey through Vietnam to a trip to Target or IKEA to waste time wandering up and down the aisles. A restaurant such as this brought out the best in our effortless enjoyment of one another.

The first time I came to Maison Long Hoa, ten years earlier with my former boyfriend Sam, we bought two bottles of the house strawberry wine, which was made by the wife of the owner, Mr. Pham. We drank one bottle with dinner, and one bottle later that evening, at the Stop 'n Go Café during a blackout, while candles flickered and the café's proprietor played flamenco guitar. Mr. Pham's wife still made strawberry wine, which was served to Julie and me in a more modest quantity, in two rustic cordial glasses.

As we were served sautéed spinach, beef in *la lot* leaves, and clay pot fish made from fresh Phan Rang tuna, Mr. Pham sat at the table behind us. He was a small man, wearing a black cardigan. While he worked over a ledger, he smoked and sipped from a glass of local Vang Dalat wine. He glanced up occasionally, looking around the room to make sure that all was well in his small domain. His son took care of the diners. A piano soundtrack played "Fur Elise," "Auld Lang Syne," and "Windmills of Your Mind" from the original *Thomas Crown Affair*.

The food was not imaginative, but it was very good. I had planned on informally interviewing Mr. Pham, but now I didn't feel like it. I just wanted to sit with my sister and be warm and fed. I wanted to talk lazily about the denser flavor of tuna compared to the snakefish we'd had in the clay pot fish we made in Nha Trang. I wanted to sip the wine that was now more than Mr. Pham's family tradition—I felt that a decade of ordering it had made it mine, as well. I wanted to savor the feeling of good will as we walked back through town in the chill to our hotel room, where we left the balcony door open and slept beneath heavy blankets with the cold fresh air on our faces.

Linh's Strawberry Wine

Linh told me that most women in Dalat make strawberry wine. This is probably the least sophisticated strawberry wine recipe in the world. It is based on Linh's recipe, and although some of the procedures may sound crude, it did produce two 750-milliliter bottles of strawberry wine. This is one of those recipes you will make more for fun than anything else. But it's satisfying to serve it in little cordial glasses as a digestif after a Vietnamese meal.

INGREDIENTS:
1/2-gallon jar with a lid
10 lbs. strawberries
2 lbs. sugar
5-gram packet of wine yeast if you live in a
  cold environment

DIRECTIONS, PART ONE:

1. In the jar, put one layer of strawberries, one thin coating of sugar, one layer of strawberries, one thin coating of sugar, and so on until all the strawberries and sugar are used up.
2. If you live in a cold place and don't get much sun, mix half a 5-gram packet of wine yeast according to the instructions, and dribble this into the jar.
3. Put the lid on the jar, and keep it in a warm place (75–80 F) for two months. I kept mine in a window where it could get direct sunlight in the afternoons.

DIRECTIONS, PART TWO:

1. *"Manually filter the liquid using a plastic screen, Vietnamese style"*—these are Linh's instructions, and I love them, although I don't quite know what they mean. I filtered my wine by first pouring it through a strainer to get the liquid. Then, I poured this liquid through coffee filters. The filtered liquid was clear and deep ruby pink in color.
2. Pour filtered liquid into a clean jar, and let it sit for another week or two, to let the final sediment sink to the bottom.

DIRECTIONS, PART THREE:

1. Strain this liquid from the sediment.
2. Bottle wine, and make beautiful labels.
3. Let wine sit in bottles for at least another month in the fridge before drinking.

Recipe

NOTES ON THE PROCESS:

Oxidization:

When putting the strawberries into the jar, don't leave a lot of air at the top. The jar should be full with just an inch or so of space at the top, to keep the liquid from turning brown.

Fermentation:

Fermentation begins after about five days. It's fun to watch the concoction start to fizz and bubble. Mine did this for about a month before becoming a weird-looking science project in the kitchen. I have seen jars of wine in the making in my Vietnamese friends' houses. In every case, the fruit rises to the top of the liquid and stays there. In my case, the fruit rose during the first month and then sank during the second. The strawberries began to look like mushy little sea anemones, sleeping on a thick bed of sediment. My advice: just be patient, and see what happens. I honestly thought the whole effort was going to be a waste of time, but I ended up with two yummy bottles of wine.

Potential Explosions:

Linh's instructions call for an airtight jar. Apparently, or so pros have told me, if the jar is truly airtight, it will explode. I didn't know this, and since I sealed my jar as best I could, I am going to assume that it wasn't completely airtight. You may want to do more research on this before blowing up a jar of strawberries in your kitchen.

Listening to History

"Now, living standards are rising," said Nguyen Van Viet, chief executive officer of LadoFoods, the state-run company under which Vang Dalat, also known as Dalat Wine, operated. "More Vietnamese people are traveling overseas, where they are tasting wine. When they return, they talk about it, but like me, most can't afford imported wines. Also, imported wines are not really suitable to Vietnamese tastes, since the Vietnamese palate hasn't adjusted to these types of wines. Because of our past, because of what we are accustomed to, the Vietnamese like strong wines. We are used to our strong rice liquors and vodka from the Russians."

It was ten in the morning, and our guide Linh, Julie, and I were seated on chrome-and-vinyl office chairs drawn around a nondescript coffee table. Though it was hardly the cocktail hour, we were passing around LadoFoods' latest experiment, a scrumptious peach wine cooler, which Linh was hogging just a little, because she had never had anything like it before, and she loved it. Mr. Nguyen stood between us and the window, framed by the filmy gray backdrop of the declining morning. Although Vang Dalat was arguably the country's primary wine producer, we would never know it from this office, whose gray metal desk and particle board shelves brought to mind an underpaid, inner-city high school principal. One wall was pasted over with a faded, sentimental photomural of cherry blossoms and a mountain peak. On another, above a laden bookshelf, was a large black-and-white photograph of Dalat from 1952. Born in the city around this same time, Mr. Nguyen pointed it out within minutes of our meeting. The view in the picture was not much different from the view out the windows, past tattered pine branches and the roof of a processing plant to farms in the distance.

While we three sipped, Mr. Nguyen held the floor, but it did not feel as if he was lecturing. Later, Julie would tell me that he was one of her favorite people to photograph: "The way he just stood there, so proud and humble at the same time. I thought he was going to burst when Linh told him how much she liked the cooler."

Hands tucked into his pockets, he was soft-spoken, compelling, and earnest as he explained, "I am thinking about how I can produce European-style wines that are similar to traditional Vietnamese wines, and that all families can afford. I know there is a market for fine red wines in Vietnam, but I also want to please Vietnamese tastes. In France, grapes are for wine, but in Vietnam, grapes are for eating. The Vietnamese are accustomed to the flavor of table grapes, and so we

can be elevated, as well as benefited, through a gradual transformation from the throat-scorching familiar to the ripe, full-bodied, with-just-a-hint-of-tannins unknown. Although this left him on the fringe of Vietnam's fine-wine big league for the time being, he was working to its advantage, eventually bringing the general population to a place where—though East may still be East, and West may still be West—the twain shall meet.

"I know that my wines don't meet international criteria," Mr. Nguyen told us without apology. "That is okay. For now my goal is gradual education."

Linh set the empty wine cooler bottle on the coffee table. As she let it go, she looked at it nostalgically, if not inappropriately, given the hour. I couldn't fault her, though. Julie and I felt the same way. It was dangerously good.

He continued, "I have signed contracts with producers in France to provide wine grapes, so in the future we will eventually upgrade our techniques and the quality. But because of our history, I think it is very important to adapt slowly. To understand the Vietnamese mentality as we try new things."

Given the satisfied look on Linh's face, his method was working. Middle class and middle-aged, she was his ideal audience, and with just one drink, he had already found a way to satisfy her Vietnamese tastes.

After a tour of the Vang Dalat facilities, where Julie was allowed to photograph the industrialized warehouse winery that processed eight thousand bottles a day, including red and white grape wines, mulberry and strawberry liquors, and artichoke wine "for liver function and uninterrupted sleep," we were—no surprise—late for lunch. The day before, after eating *ragu* at Doan Doan, I asked Linh how authentic our experience was. She admitted that the *ragu* at this restaurant was more refined than at local places without a steady foreign clientele—even though foreigners rarely ate *ragu* because they didn't know about it. I asked for a "real" local joint, and after she was absolutely, positively sure that that's what I wanted, she chose Hoan Kiet. "It's where I take my kids on the weekends."

As with at Doan Doan, we had just missed the lunch crowd, and the restaurant was empty. Before asking Julie and me if we could get back to the hotel on our own, Linh assured us that it was packed at dinnertime and weekends, then she took off to get some work done. Once again she had ordered ahead, vegetarian *ragu* for Julie and pork *ragu* this time for me, so I could compare it to the beef.

Hoan Kiet had the kind of kitsch appeal that shows up in a certain type of homegrown restaurant around the world, from diners in the American Midwest to taverns in small-town Germany. The outdoor dining room was protected by a permanent canopy, and suspended from thin metal rafters were clumps of strange, plastic, snowball-like lamps and twines of plastic grapes and vines. Plastic, red-checked cloths covered the tables, and the folding chairs were sturdy and comfortable enough. I was reminded of M. F. K. Fisher's description of a restaurant she once happened upon in northern Burgundy: "cheerful ugly."

I could guess at the clientele, locals who for the most part all knew one another. I could imagine Linh laughing with her children here. Although I would love to have seen Hoan Kiet when it was crowded, I was glad it wasn't. I was growing tired from the go go go of our trip, and the silence was nice.

Waiting for our *ragu*, Julie and I felt the need to show our respect for Mr. Nguyen, and we ordered a bottle of Vang Dalat Superior 2005 and then amused ourselves by reading the menu aloud to one another.

"Shredded frog. Yummy," she said. She raised an eyebrow. "After all, it swims, and it tastes like chicken."

"What's mountaineer style?" I asked, referring to the roasted pigeon.

"No idea." She shrugged and grimaced. "Cooked pig's legs as dogs?"

The wine arrived, along with a do-it-yourself corkscrew. We continued to rattle down the list: mixed crab nippers with ready fish and teal in more than a dozen different styles. A few days earlier in an email, our mom had written, "Have you eaten anything gross yet?" If we had been in the mood, this menu was certainly a good place to start.

I know there is an Anthony Bourdain school of travelers that feels the obligation of adventure dining. You can't say you've eaten in a country unless you've eaten "like a local." Why "local" is so often equated with weird or gross, I have never understood. Isn't *pho* local? Isn't *banh cuon* local? Not enough, apparently, for some. As for my participation in this rite of passage, I have eaten my own very small share of so-called "local" foods. One night, with one of my students, I discussed O. Henry's "The Last Leaf" over crispy fried whole sparrows and beer in a not-so-savory café. And one of my classes once took me out for pig uterus salad for my birthday. For the record, "special to the lady pig," as my students vaguely called it, tastes like stringy rubber. Then there was the night in Saigon when Julie and I joined a former coworker of mine for dinner, and I gagged down a bowl of eel simmered in milk before reluctantly nibbling on a chicken foot. It was the foot that brought home that "eating local" isn't always for everyone, not even the locals.

The offending poultry appendage looked as if a chicken had wandered off, leaving its fibrous, fetal-looking foot behind. It tasted just as I imagined it would when looking at it, like toe gristle. As I nibbled on the elastic membrane that encased the rubbery bones, I realized that my coworker had not touched any of the chicken feet on her plate. Casually, hoping she wouldn't think that I wanted her share, I had asked, "Are you going to eat it?"

She looked at me quizzically. "No, of course not. Disgusting."

"Then why did you order it?"

Blushing as she noticed the half-eaten foot that I held gingerly by my fingertips, she said, "I thought I was ordering chicken legs. The menu says chicken legs."

I stuffed the gnawed foot into my napkin while she and Julie howled with laughter.

As for Vietnam's most taboo-to-outsiders food, dog, the first thing to understand is that there is a misconception about how common it is as a dish.

When I once asked one of my English classes how many of the students had eaten dog, every single person looked at me as if I'd asked them about eating their mothers. One woman, a rich and generous housewife who often secretly paid poor students' tuition, brought her Maltese to class in her handbag, as if to prove to me that only a barbarian would eat a house pet. But some Vietnamese do eat dog, particularly in the north, where history stands behind them, and where the dog-as-taboo-food influence of the French era was followed by tough times, when a person had to learn to eat everything. By the twenty-first century, eating dog for some was a case of a necessity that had evolved into habit.

It is a habit that is hard for most Westerners to come to terms with—especially Westerners like Julie and me, whose Chihuahua is treated like a miniature member of a royal family. When we were in the market in Hanoi with Didier, we came to the dog section, where furless dead canines were displayed on tile counters, looking like wizened burn victims. Julie fled. I remained, pretending that each poor little pooch was a tofu sculpture dyed with soy sauce, while Didier told me how dogs had been eaten in Vietnam for thousands of years. "These were rice-fed and raised on farms." Equitably, he added, "I can respect it, but it's not a part of my culture."

The practice was best explained to me by Mr. Nguyen, the elderly leader of the UNESCO Gastronomy Club. During our rambling interview, he had playfully offered to cook dog for my publisher, Huong, and me, assuring us that if we ate it from his kitchen, we would love it. Politely, the three of us had declined, and Mr. Nguyen went on to explain the relevance of cultural context when it comes to eating dog meat. "People eat dog meat here," he had said, matter-of-factly, "but Westerners come and are disgusted by it. That's because they don't understand the culture. In Western countries, dogs helped people a lot in the past. When people had to move from place to place, dogs helped them with that. And dogs protected them. Dogs became their friends. That's why you love dogs and care about them. But in Vietnam, we started with fishing and planting rice. The dog didn't help with anything. It was useless. And so the dog was like the chicken or the duck, something that we grow to eat."

While Julie and I may never have felt obligated—or enticed—to try dog, or the braised beef penis cooked with Chinese medicines that was on the menu at the Hoan Kiet restaurant in Dalat, we did feel compelled to taste our Vang Dalat wine. Not just drink it, but sip it slowly and reflect on its qualities. We liked Mr. Nguyen, the head of the wine company, and we wanted to appreciate what he was doing. So we swirled and we sniffed, and although we weren't savvy enough to discuss structure and mouth-feel, we could distinguish the flavor of table grapes. The wine wasn't sugary, as we had expected a wine from such grapes to be, nor was it heavy, which made it a pleasant partner for the *ragu*, which was thicker and sweeter than the version we had the day before.

The amber broth had the consistency of syrup, denser most likely from the chunks of white potatoes and yams, and sweeter maybe from the onions, or maybe from the tomatoes, or maybe—in my case—from the pork, which was left on the bone, as most meat was in Vietnam. Though stronger in flavor, this *ragu* was less complex as well as more filling than Doan Doan's.

Later, I would learn from Linh that this rustic style was closer to what locals made at home for special occasions and on weekends; it takes too much time to prepare it for weeknight meals, she explained. As with *bun bo Hue*, I would never find two *ragu*, even homemade, that tasted exactly the same. This, it turned out, led to a kind of unofficial competition. "If you meet someone whose *ragu* is better than yours," Linh told me, "you must find out how she makes it, so that yours will be the best it can be."

Linh was not joking. On our last night in Dalat at Y Nhu Y restaurant behind the Dalat Palace, I asked our waitress if she liked *ragu*. Her demeanor instantly transformed from that of disinterested serving staff to dear friend. "Oh yes," she said, leaning chummily against the back of my chair. "My mother cooks *ragu*."

"Does she have a special recipe?" I asked.

"Everyone in Dalat uses the same beans and potatoes, but every family has a different way of cooking, so every *ragu* tastes different."

"And your mother's is the best?"

She laughed, and then said, quite seriously, "Of course."

That afternoon while I wrote, Julie rented a zippy blue moped from the hotel. After a quick lesson from Antoine on how to use it, she was off to photograph the farmlands. When she returned, shivering and pink-cheeked, I asked her how she'd liked driving around on her own.

"It was chilly," she said with a smile. "It felt good. I hate being hot. I really hate it."

"And yet you keep coming back to Vietnam?"

She sighed. "Someday I'm going to Prague."

Rested and recovered from lunch, we wandered down for dinner in the dining room on the ground floor of the hotel, where lofty French doors opened onto a view over the terrace and down to the lake. With high molded ceilings, pleated swag valances, and a tawny wood floor, Le Rabelais restaurant recalled an era when words like "salon" and "drawing room" were in common use. Outside, we could see the silhouettes of hydrangeas, the color of summer dusk.

This was a place I could imagine only in Dalat, and only under the tender direction of Antoine, who had written to me, "Cooking has always been a passion. I was born in a classic French bourgeois family, and here in Dalat all the archives I found were ringing bells of the time of my youth in my grandmother's property in Normandy. Once in the market here I found some artichoke stalks that could well be used as cardons, a specialty of the Lyon region that are braised in stock and wine with beef marrow. The result was quite stunning. At Le Rabelais, we play this card of the freshness and uniqueness of the Dalat produce, but also the remembrance of the period style."

After our rustic *ragu*, dinner at Le Rabelais felt especially indulgent. Since 1922, Le Rabelais had maintained a prix fixe tradition, and as Julie and I settled into the hush at a table near a window overlooking the amethyst dusk, we selected two different menus, to give us a chance to sample a variety of dishes. Only one other table was inhabited, and there was a solitary mood, as if we had come in and discovered that we were left behind after a coup. While in a way it added to the romance of the atmosphere, it was a shame, as Le Rabelais is one of the nicest dining rooms in the country.

Crafted by the hotel's Executive Chef Huong, whom we would be cooking with the following day, our meal was preceded with an amuse-bouche of smoked salmon and beets, whose surprising combination delivered satisfyingly on the Vietnamese principle of salty and sweet. I began with a starter of grilled shrimp with creamy fresh leek-and-vanilla sauce, which was followed by grilled beef sirloin with butter "maître d'hotel." Julie has never met a lobster she can resist (much to the dismay of our dad and many of her dates over the years), and she chose the steamed lobster with chili orange sauce. With its citrus, spice, and hint of the sea, it was one of the best lobster dishes she had ever had. While both of us are pie-and-cookie gals, and not the type to order fluffy, filigreed desserts, the raspberry mille-feuille with red coulis and the warm apple feuilleté with rosemary-and-vanilla sauce sparked a conversation as intense as any we'd had over food on this trip. In the background, Debussy laid the soundtrack for our whispers of admiration. Unlike Didier Corlou's cuisine, which excited us with its virtuosity and an acrobatic sense of adventure, Chef Huong's moved us with its underpinnings of tradition. The food was as quietly debonair as the atmosphere.

Because Julie and I do not live lives in which pampering is a part of the daily experience, we take a special pleasure in being spoiled, particularly when it comes to food and all of its attendant elements. We basked in the gentility of our meal, while our waiter added to the feeling that we had walked into an early twentieth-century novel of manners, one by Edith Wharton or Henry James, perhaps. He was everything a good waiter should be, courteous and handsome and dignified, just like the establishment he worked in. And like the Palace, he made us feel special and at home at the same time.

Handsome Men

Our morning tour of the Dalat Market with Chef Huong, the hotel's executive chef, got off to a late start. In all fairness, Linh's itinerary was not to blame. Julie and I were out at the hotel's back entrance on time. Chef Huong arrived on time. The van that was to transport us, though, was nowhere to be seen. This was our first encounter with Chef Huong, and while we waited, making precaffeine small talk about how much we had enjoyed our meal at Le Rabelais the night before, Julie and I sat on the steps, enjoying the cool morning air. Although some of the clouds in the sky were gray, they were high, and it didn't look as if it was going to rain. In a bush beside the steps, yellow hibiscus floated in thin, watery sunlight.

Finally, after an hour of waiting, the van rambled up, and as it poked along around the grounds of the Palace, Chef Huong and I talked about the uniqueness of Dalat's produce and how it lends itself to a rich blend of cuisines. He was nearing fifty, and while there were traces in his demeanor of the sobriety that underscored the food at Le Rabelais, his smile was boyish and adorable. Since this was not my first crush on the trip, I was beginning to wonder if I just had a thing for chefs.

Anchoring the town's main Hoa Binh Square when it was first built in the 1920s, the central market now sat down the slope from its original location, its contemporary college-dorm-style architecture reflecting what is often described as Art Deco in Vietnam. I had been in this market many times, buying a hat or scarf or gloves, and once a shawl as a birthday present for a friend's mother, not really paying much attention, focused only on what I needed at that time. As for the food sold there, my memories were of strawberries and artichokes, perhaps because they came as such a surprise back then, during my first months in Vietnam.

Now I saw just a few baskets of mealy-looking out-of-season strawberries and plenty of dried but few fresh artichokes. Instead, there was autumnal October produce: navy beans, snow peas, squash blossoms, and baskets of persimmons everywhere we looked, the enlightening color of a monk's new robe. As we walked the aisles we saw jars of pickled eggplant; fish prepared with lemongrass, chili, and salt; and *banh cuon* ready to be taken home and steamed. In one stall, a woman sliced a few wilted artichoke stalks for her husband's lunch. The vendors in their long sleeves, wool caps, and heavy, waterproof boots were smiling and friendly, with none of the reserve you would expect in such chilly weather.

"It's funny how every market has its own mood," Julie noted. In Hanoi, there was a certain coolness among the vendors that made her uncomfortable taking their pictures; in Hoi An, an indifference to her roving camera that gave her a sense of freedom; and here in Dalat, lots of laughter, which made taking photographs fun.

Chef Huong's was not a typical tourist tour, with a dog-and-pony pause at each stall to explain unfamiliar ingredients or exotic utensils for our culinary edification. A few days earlier, he had sent a packet of recipes to our room for the class that was to follow our visit to the market. I chose the dishes I wanted to make, with *ragu* at the top of my list. Now, we checked in with his regular vendors, as he did every week, shopping for ingredients we would need, plump beans and fresh straw mushrooms and a succulent cut of pork, building our anticipation for the lesson to come.

By ten our shopping was done and we were relaxing in the living room of the general manager's residence, which served as the site of cooking classes and private hotel events, as well as Antoine's home. With green, glass-paned front doors and a buttery yellow exterior, Villa #27 was right at home on Tran Huong Dao, a boulevard out of time, lined with preserved manors built mainly as summer retreats for high-ranking French officials in the early days of Dalat's development. Back then, the typical Dalat villa had a small kitchen, accessible from the basement staff quarters. Today, after a well-planned renovation, Villa #27 included a spacious demonstration kitchen in the former winter garden. In it, an assistant prepped vegetables and herbs, while a room away Chef Huong confessed, "When I was young, I didn't even know how to cook rice."

For a man from inexperienced beginnings, in a country that had been cut off for so long from outside culinary education, Chef Huong was in an impressive position. He was born in Dalat in 1958, and as a young man, he spent five years in the army. Then, while still in his twenties, he came to the Dalat Palace, which was more than a decade away from its present grand state. His sole training included assisting foreign chefs, six months with Saigon Tourism in Vung Tau, and some hands-on experience. From this, according to Antoine, "He can compete with and match many European chefs. His cuisine is an enhancement of the local produce, *mise en valeur* of what Dalat has best to offer. He has developed his palate for French tastes and techniques in a way that even a genuine French-born rarely achieves." He was one of the only Vietnamese head chefs at a luxury hotel in Vietnam.

Settled in a wing-backed armchair by the tall windows, wearing a teal dress shirt and black trousers, Chef Huong looked more like a man about to go out for a nice meal rather than prepare one. He said, "When I was young and worked for the government, I was sent into the mountains. I saw how the people there cooked food in bamboo. I smelled it, but I didn't eat it. I didn't think it was hygienic." He smiled an embarrassed smile. "Back then, I didn't know any better. Now I want to take the ingredients and techniques from this area and make an original cuisine.

"I am very interested in the origins of food. For example, traditional dishes like *pho* and *bun cha* are original to Hanoi. But food in the north is influenced by China and France, and to make these dishes …" He paused. "I got a book from Didier, and I go on the Internet, but the recipes are always different." He leaned forward, the way one instinctively does when edging deeper into a train of thought. "When I was a young boy, I would eat *banh xeo*. But two years ago I went to Hue, and *banh xeo* there is different from Dalat, even though they say Dalat *banh xeo* is from Hue. In Hue they use a different pan and different ingredients."

I asked, "So, do you think there is an original Vietnamese cuisine?"

"I don't know." He grinned, self-consciously. We were verging on sacrilege, challenging the originality of Vietnamese food. "Maybe not."

This was a question that had crossed my mind more than once since I had begun my research. What made a food original? How uninfluenced by other sources must a cuisine be to be considered original? How far back in time does it have to go? Did Vietnam have a national original cuisine? Did it have original regional cuisines? For example, of the bamboo meals Chef Huong mentioned, Antoine had written, "Very little is known about the culinary habits of the local tribes, aside from special herbs found in the forest and used for cooking or minority wine. There is a place where you can eat dishes cooked in bamboo, but I am not sure this is from the Montagnards [indigenous mountain tribes people], or rather if it is an old Cham influence, since the dishes are very similar to what is done in the Celebes Islands by the Tana Toraja Tribes."

One of the most intriguing things to me about Vietnamese food is how much it has been affected by outside sources, which I have already touched upon, and yet how distinctive it is. I am intrigued by how it is not Chinese and not Cambodian and not Thai and not French, despite the clear influences of these cultures. Most notably, the country's largest ethnic group, the Viet, owes the majority of its culinary traditions to the Chinese. Although habitation in the north of present-day Vietnam dates back to Paleolithic times, food and food-related customs did not enter the written record until the Chinese invaded Vietnam in the second century BC. During Chinese rule, the Viet were introduced to stir-fry, bean curd, shoots, sprouts, chopsticks, and most importantly, noodles. Although the Chinese were expelled after the 939 AD Viet uprising, which led to the creation of an independent kingdom and the founding of the royal capital of Hanoi, additional dishes arrived with later Chinese invasions, including hot pot and Mongolian beef. If the Viet offered anything culinary to the Chinese in return, I have found no documentation.

Meanwhile, the central and southeastern portion of what is now Vietnam was under Cham rule, until the Viet from the north took control in the 1400s. Because of their location between the Khmer Empire (present-day Cambodia) and the South China Sea, the Cham culture was also understandably sculpted by outside sources, from the oft-invading, Hinduized Khmers to seafaring

returned the boar's leg to the refrigerator, he told us, "With this kind of thing, with the new, I try to find the positive in everything and bring it all together. I don't believe in teaching what not to do, but what to do. And in the end, it's up to them." By them, he was referring to the Vietnamese who worked for him. "It would be rude of me to impose my culture."

I felt at home because he made us feel at home, as he helped to set out plates and bowls while the rest of us put food on the table. We sat down together, Antoine, Chef Huong, Julie, me, and the quiet assistant in her funny white headscarf, passing plates of grilled pork and caramelized fish, talking, laughing, no one the boss, no one an employee, although Antoine was certainly the host as he hopped up, disappeared, and reappeared with a bottle of 1999 Chateau Serilhan Bordeaux, which was heaven in a glass.

The moment Antoine tasted the *ragu*, he was rapt, thrilled by the way the meaty flavor of the pork played off the nuanced result of the simmered-down tomatoes. He'd had local versions before, but never Chef Huong's. He asked, "Can we have this next Friday?" Then he told Julie and me, "Every Friday night we serve a special dish at Larry's Bar. Something homemade and hearty. We have about twenty expatriates here in Dalat. I send out an email to alert them."

Oh, how I longed to be an expatriate in Dalat on a Friday night.

Eventually, our plates were empty but for some scrapings of sauce that we were all too polite to lick up. Our glasses held only the last skim of wine. Antoine lit a cigarette, leaned back with satisfaction, and said, "When I first came here in 1992, I loved this country. I knew I would return."

I said, "I know what you mean. I can't explain it, but I felt as if I belonged the day I first arrived."

As for that *ragu*, what can I say about any dish that is served in a sun-warmed dining room with good wine and good conversation, in the company of my lovely sister and two handsome, creative men? It was wonderful. It was rich and fresh. It is the freshness I remember most. When I returned home, I made *ragu* according to Chef Huong's recipe. The vegetables were a little different; I couldn't find the right beans, and I used crimini mushrooms instead of straw. But it was satisfying, although I will confess that part of the satisfaction had to do with the company I kept: the memory of our afternoon at Villa #27 in Dalat.

Chef Huong's Dalat *Ragu*

Because the key to this recipe is fresh vegetables, you can play around with it, substituting different kinds of beans and mushrooms, or perhaps adding white pearl onions, depending on what is in season. The one ingredient that is essential is tomatoes. You must get the freshest, best tomatoes you can find. It is the liquefied tomatoes combined with the fish sauce that creates the buttery flavor of this dish.

INGREDIENTS:

1 lb. pork shoulder, cut into 1-inch cubes
1/4 lb. carrots, cubed
1/4 lb. potato, cubed
1/4 lb. taro, cubed
1/4 lb. fresh beans (cranberry, fava/broad, lima/butter)
1/4 lb. fresh straw mushroom (button or crimini can be substituted)
1 small shallot, minced
1 clove garlic, minced

2/3 lb. fresh ripe tomatoes, skinned and thoroughly seeded, chopped. I blanch the tomatoes for easy peeling. Don't overdo it with the tomatoes or the sauce will be sour.
1 French bay leaf
2 tbsp. vegetable oil
6 cups vegetable stock
Salt and pepper to taste
1 tbsp. + 1 tsp. fish sauce
Loaf of crusty French bread for dipping

DIRECTIONS:

1. Cut pork into cubes, and marinate with 1 tbsp. fish sauce and pepper for 30 minutes. Do not marinate in the fridge.
2. In a medium frying pan, brown pork in 1 tbsp. oil. Salt to taste.
3. In a separate medium frying pan, sauté shallot in 1 tbsp. oil, and then add garlic.
4. Add tomatoes to shallot/garlic, and sauté on low heat, reducing until it is almost liquid. Reduce thoroughly to remove sourness. There should be no trace of tomato left in the pan.
5. While tomatoes are simmering, remove pork from the pan with a slotted spoon (to keep as much grease in the pan as possible), and put in a bowl.
6. Pan-fry carrots in pork grease for flavor. Remove, and add to pork bowl.
7. Pan-fry potatoes in pork grease for flavor. Remove, and set aside.
8. Pan-fry taro in pork grease for flavor. Remove, and set aside.
9. Pan-fry mushrooms in pork oil with a little salt, for flavor. Remove, and set aside. (As you fry the vegetables, you may need to add a little oil and even a tad of fish sauce. You can also add the juices draining from the pork in the bowl.)

10. While simmering tomatoes and pan-frying vegetables, blanch beans to remove acid from the skin. You should use fresh beans. If using dried beans, let them soak overnight. If you must use canned beans, don't stress over it. This dish will still be terrific.
11. While the last of the veggies are frying, pour tomato liquid in a large soup pot, and add pork, beans, and carrots. Stir in 1 tsp. of fish sauce.
12. Add stock and bay leaf. Cook for 1 hour on low heat, covered, until meat is tender.
13. Add potato and taro, and simmer, covered, for 20 more minutes.
14. Add mushrooms, and simmer, covered, for 10 more minutes. Keep an eye on the taro/potatoes to make sure they don't get too soft.
15. Serve hot with a fresh, crusty French bread.

Serving: 4 as a main dish.

Phan Thiet

Southern Vietnam

" *Woe to the cook whose sauce has no sting.* **"**

Geoffrey Chaucer

Hanoi•

•Hue
•Hoi An

•Nha Trang
•Dalat

•Saigon   •**Phan Thiet**

Afishionados

In his 1936 travel book, *The Land of the White Parasol*, Sidney J. Legendre wrote, "At noon we arrived at Phan-Thiet ... Here you would smell the cool invigorating salt air, if the Annamites had not arrived first ... they have erected a factory for the preparation of Nuoc-Man [sic] ... Until my arrival in this little village I had thought that I knew the smells of the world ... but here was something entirely different ... it dominated our nostrils and left them incapable of picking up any smell less powerful than that of a dead buffalo stewing on the plains in a hot sun."

Many changes may have occurred in Vietnam in the seven decades since that was written, but one thing remained the same. Undiluted by a breeze, intensified by the tropical heat, the late afternoon Phan Thiet air still reeked of *nuoc mam* (fish sauce). It was within this stink that Julie and I were introduced to Jon Bourbaud, executive chef of the Novotel Ocean Dunes Resort, on a verandah that overlooked the sea. I had discovered Jon by way of an essay he wrote about fish sauce. We began corresponding via email, and his fast-and-loose enthusiasm for Vietnam's pungent condiment captivated me. Lanky, fair, and nearly my age, Jon turned out to be just as his emails foreshadowed, in that rank of people who seem, upon first meeting, like a long-lost friend. In less than ten minutes of our introduction, we were sprawled in planter's chairs, squinting against the downwind draft from the *nuoc mam* factories, gossiping about a mutual acquaintance, an old Vietnam hand with a reputation for crazy, to whom Jon had given informal asylum recently at the resort.

Just six hours earlier, Julie and I had left Dalat, corkscrewing our way down the mountain toward Phan Thiet, on the shore of the South China Sea, two hundred kilometers east of Saigon. We were going to learn about *nuoc mam*, even though Phu Quoc Island is hailed as the fish sauce capital of the country. But Phu Quoc, off the southwest tip of Vietnam, did not fit into our itinerary, and my lengthy correspondence with Jon gave me confidence that Phan Thiet was a perfectly fine place to study the most essential ingredient in Vietnamese food.

Built for the area's hydro projects, the mountainous road out of Dalat was too new. Even though our driver was mellow, a trait not common in drivers in Vietnam, it made no difference. This was a vertiginous, hairpin, little-traveled road whose not-yet-tamped dirt and gravel caused the van's back tires to skid at every turn, no matter how slow we were going. We tried to ignore the possibilities of crashing down the mountainside as we talked with Jan Vail, our trip's burly, bearded patron saint, sans saintliness, who had met up with us in Dalat. He had set up the majority of our hotel stays, as well as connecting us with some of the country's best chefs. But conversation stalled. We were too lethargic from a breakfast of bacon and eggs at Le Rabelais and good food and wine from the previous night at Y Nhu Y, the restaurant where Chef Huong was experimenting with local recipes. We gazed silently out the windows at the steep, forested slopes, unspoiled except for this road and the sharp cut of a sluice that seemed to rise into the sky.

Gradually, the trees gave way to hillside coffee plantations, which flattened into small, family-owned dragon fruit orchards. As the world leveled out, persimmon stands dotted the sides of the road, like the berry stands that sprout on American country back roads during summer months. I remembered the small groves of dragon fruit from my first trip to Phan Thiet with Sam nearly a decade earlier. We loved dragon fruit. We kept it in the freezer and ate it after meals for dessert, and we had gotten a kick out of seeing our favorite scaly pink fruit hanging heavy among the tentacles of the prehistoric-looking trees.

That was so long ago that Phan Thiet had no hotels, and we had stayed with Vietnamese friends, crashing on cots and in hammocks in a mosquito-net-draped pavilion just steps from the beach. In the mornings, a boy scaled trees to bring us coconuts, whose milk was as thin and cool as the predawn air. Years later, when the Novotel opened, we stayed there too, on business trip weekends, which meant golf on Sam's part and reading in the sun on mine. Strange, but I didn't remember the smell of fish sauce in the air on either of those trips.

Our schedule of a fish market tour, a fish sauce factory tour, various fish meals, and a fish sauce tasting began with the fish market of Mui Ne at 5:00 a.m. the morning after our arrival in Phan Thiet. But our early start was made less painful by the quiet night that preceded it. And to get up with the sun meant to enjoy a few pre-fish-sauce hours, even though it would have been so much fun to take a deep breath of *nuoc-mam*-infused air and, à la Robert Duvall, announce, "I love the smell of fish sauce in the morning."

The windows were rolled down a few inches, and sea air flapped into the van as we traveled along the coastline from Phan Thiet to nearby Mui Ne, a fishing village best known on the backpack circuit for its cheap beachfront guesthouses. Hoa, the resort's twentysomething assistant food and beverage manager, was driving. He was Jon's physical opposite, with intense, dark eyes. As quiet as Jon was gregarious, he rounded out our fish sauce quartet.

As the four of us wandered along Mui Ne's little beach, we chatted about the fishing industry—squid and shellfish mainly for export, mackerel and smelt for local restaurants, and anchovies for fish sauce. It was a shabby beach, with its muddy shore and colorful but timeworn fishing boats, many wedged in the muck of low tide. Despite the grit of mud and broken shells, and plastic bags caked like scabs in the sand, the scene was picturesque. Women trotted along with baskets of seafood balanced on poles over their shoulders. Fish shimmered in the morning light. Charming *thung chais*—traditional round basket boats woven from wide strips of bamboo and sealed with pitch—lazed on the calm water.

On a sopping patch of beach, people were bargaining over plump pink fish piled in yellow plastic boxes, which had just been hauled in from a newly arrived fishing boat. It was a ragtag-looking group, the men bareheaded or wearing baseball caps, or in one case a motorcycle helmet, and the women in traditional conical hats. Their synthetic tops and trousers looked as if they were paired by the color-blind, and their sturdy, single-strap Biti rubber sandals were the kind that could be bought for less than a dollar at any local market. As we watched the haggling, I thought back to Nha Trang and all we had learned about the hand-to-mouth lives of the fishermen there. Mui Ne was no different. Individually, these people made just enough to get them to the next day. Collectively, though, many of them contributed to one of the country's most profitable industries.

Literally, *nuoc mam* means "fish water," and it is something Vietnamese food cannot exist without. Contrary to commonly held prejudices, it is not the product of rotting fish. As Jon wrote to me:

> Rinsed fresh fish and salt are layered into large earthenware jars or wooden vats lined with sea salt, then topped with a layer of sea salt before a woven bamboo mat is placed over the fish and weighted down with rocks to keep it from floating. It is covered with mosquito netting and a lid, and left in a sunny location for the duration of the process—up to two years.
>
> From time to time the vats are uncovered to air out and let the fish be exposed to direct sunlight. This periodic "sunning" is said to be the secret to producing a sauce of superior quality, with a more fragrant aroma and a richer color. After eight months, the liquid is removed and placed in another clean vat and allowed to air out in the sun for a couple weeks, to dissipate any strong fish odor. Then it is re-strained and ready for bottling.

I have heard variations on this process, since there are as many subtle aspects to the preparation of fish sauce as there are opinions about the best producers. You must factor in the type of wood used for the barrel, the temperature, the length of fermentation, and of course the quality of the salt and fish—long-jawed anchovies are preferred for their delicate flavor and high degree of protein. All of this can cause variations, but essentially, *nuoc mam* comes down to just two elements: fish and salt. Nothing more, nothing less. Such a humble combination, and yet the result of the first extraction, or *nuoc mam nhi*, is compared to the first pressing of an olive oil. It is dark and rich-flavored and used directly on a dish, while second and third pressings are mixed into marinades.

In the West, the once popular *garum* is considered the distant cousin of *nuoc mam*. This viscous liquid is made from the innards of a fatty fish, such as mackerel, which is macerated with salt and blended with aromatic herbs. It is generally traced back to classical Roman times, although there are claims that the Romans got it from the Greeks (Sophocles wrote about "stinking *garos*"), and in the heyday of the Empire, the finest versions were said to have come from Spain. But the Romans were the ones who had the greatest passion for it, and their Empire owed more than a small degree of its success to a profitable *garum* trade. *Garum* shows up in nearly every recipe, including those for sweets, in *De Re Coquinaria*, a first-century collection of recipes by Apicius, one of the world's first gourmets. Poor Romans mixed it into their porridge, just as the Vietnamese mix *nuoc mam* into their rice, and the rich spent thousands of dollars at today's prices for just a few liters of the best-quality *garum*.

Trading in *garum* can be traced back to the fifth century BC and crystallized deposits that were found in amphorae from shipwrecks around the Gulf of Lions in the Mediterranean. Although it is undoubtedly related to *nuoc mam*, there is no evidence that the West brought it to Southeast Asia, or the other way around, even though Jean Anthelme Brillat-Savarin casually suggests in *The Physiology of Taste* that *garum* was "perhaps that *soy* which comes to us from India and which is known to be the result of letting certain fishes ferment with mushrooms."

Didier Corlou claims that *nuoc mam* dates back thousands of years in Vietnam, and if anyone would know, he would. Unfortunately, the Vietnamese do not have the kinds of detailed written records like the Romans have, no ancient cookery books to give us a thorough account, and if you investigate what is commonly known about the history of *nuoc mam* production in Vietnam, you won't get very far, lurching to a halt with producers such as Hung Thanh, a fourth-generation company on Phu Quoc Island, which has been using traditional methods since it was founded in 1895.

While few specifics are known about the evolution of *nuoc mam* over the centuries, one thing is certain: unlike *garum*, which is now a culinary footnote in the history of ancient Rome, *nuoc mam* has staying power. It survived the domination, colonization, and flat-out bullying of the Chinese, French, Japanese, and Americans. Surviving the Chinese and Japanese wasn't that remarkable of an achievement, but surviving the French and Americans: impressive. In nearly every colonial narrative I have read, there is at least one complaint about the reek of fish sauce—it was often associated with savagery and mentioned as a way of separating civilized cultures from the uncivilized. As for the Americans, there are near-legendary tales about how the war was lost because the North Vietnamese smuggled arms in fish sauce barrels, thereby assuring they would never be searched.

That *nuoc mam* managed to survive is not simply a matter of taste. If it were merely because the Vietnamese liked its flavor, it's possible that it could have dwindled away long ago, just as *garum* did. *Nuoc mam* persists in large part because of its nutrients. The Vietnamese don't need the protein bars and shakes that we in the West use to supplement our diets. They have fish sauce.

High in amino acids, top-quality fish sauce contains 40 percent protein. It also supplies riboflavin, niacin, iron, and Vitamins B12 and B5. It is considered a preventative for parasitical worms, and because of its calcium content, it is even good for the teeth. Best of all, it doesn't need refrigeration. It is easy to imagine what an ingredient like this could mean during times of hardship, and how fortunate a hungry person would be to mix some into a small dish of rice. As an aid to survival, *nuoc mam* has endured.

Sadly, that endurance has not helped Vietnam's signature condiment find a home outside the country. Because of embargoes after the American war in 1975, Vietnam stopped selling *nuoc mam* to Europe. Thailand leaped to fill the void. Most exported Thai fish sauce is inferior, often diluted and containing sugar, but even though Vietnam returned to the market in the 1980s with a much better product, Thailand had staked its claim. Not only was its fish sauce familiar, it also had a good angle: branding that uses Vietnamese names, along with the designation *nuoc mam*, rather than the Thai word for fish sauce, *nam pla*. Even today, in California's Little Saigon, home to more than three hundred thousand Vietnamese, I have not been able to find a fish sauce that, despite all of the Vietnamese words on the label, does not say *Product of Thailand* somewhere on it.

In addition, fish sauce from Thailand is often disguised so that it appears to be from Phu Quoc Island, since Phu Quoc is considered the standard bearer when it comes to quality. The island's 55,000 inhabitants produce six million liters of fish sauce a year, and this fish sauce is so highly regarded, at least inside Vietnam, that it is protected by the Ministry of Culture, which has made it illegal to put the Phu Quoc label on any fish sauce not from the island. In a country not known for its respect of copyrights and trademarks, as my visits to Dalat's farms revealed, this is a strong statement.

According to the World Trade Organization on intellectual property rights, "A place name ... does not only say where the product was made ... It identifies the product's special characteristics, which are the result of the product's origins." Outside Vietnam, most people, even gastronomes, know little about the special qualities of Phu Quoc fish sauce that are being maligned by generic labeling. It would be a shame for the rich, umber-colored, traditionally made "*phu quoc*" to become interchangeable with any old quality of fish sauce that cares to don the name. Of course, it wouldn't be alone. Trademarking products according to their region of origin has always been difficult, as is proven by Darjeeling, Roquefort, Champagne, and so on.

So, is there any hope for authentic *nuoc mam* to take its rightful place in the world? France is working to help Vietnam protect its fish sauce in the EU, that noble champion of culinary heritage, and even went so far as to register Phu Quoc as a brand in 2002, in order to keep fakes off the market. But that is only one small step. And there are other problems besides trademarking.

At the time of my trip, only two producers were recognized by the EU for meeting food hygiene standards. There is also the issue of odor. Because it is diluted, most Thai fish sauce is not as pungent as Vietnam's best-quality stuff—at first whiff it is less frightening to the uninitiated. According to a rumor, *nuoc mam* was actually banned from Vietnam Airlines' flights after a bottle broke on a plane and the smell was impossible to get out. On a practical note, pure Vietnamese fish sauce is more expensive to produce, which means it has a hard time competing with economical, watered-down rivals.

Aside from safeguarding a reputation, the reason it is so important for Vietnam's *nuoc mam* to be fairly represented is that the global market for fish sauce is estimated at $300 million a year. While this is a trifle compared to the international rice and coffee trades, where Vietnam is a leader, it is still a substantial market to be left out of, especially for the country considered to produce the finest quality in the world.

I am fortunate. I don't know why, but there is something about the smell of fish sauce that appeals to me. A meatiness that I find appetizing, even though I had to squint and hold my breath at times as I walked through the Fisaco fish sauce factory. The odor was dizzying, but this was to be expected from four hectares housing dozens of dimly lit, mildew-singed cement warehouses filled with hundreds of gargantuan wooden barrels: five thousand kilograms of fish and two thousand kilograms of salt, resulting in seven thousand liters of fish sauce each. As residents of Phan Thiet, Jon and Hoa did not even seem to notice the smell. Julie found it nauseating, but persevered—overcoming not only her aversion to the odor but also her fear of the giant spiders weaving their webs in nearly every darkened crevice—in order to take photos of the rustic barrels. Our patron saint, Jan, who had just taken us to lunch at a wonderful café overlooking the water, spent most of his time outside while we were guided through the miasma by the factory's manager, Mrs. Nguyen.

A small, middle-aged woman wearing a pale yellow shirt, tan pants, and owlish eyeglasses at least twenty years out of date, she was, thanks to the fashion egalitarianism left over from Communism's heyday, unidentifiable as the manager of such a large company. From looking at her I would not have been surprised to encounter her behind a desk taking messages for her boss, and yet she informed us, "I can tell from just one sniff how much protein a fish sauce contains." Along with a panel of expert quality control tasters, she was charged with making sure that each batch of fish sauce upheld the company's standards.

Just as you cannot discern the position of many workers in Vietnam by what they wear, you cannot always tell the status of a company merely by walking into its buildings. To the rudimentary kitchen of Hanoi's historic Cha Ca La Vong restaurant and the modest office of Dalat Wine's forward-thinking chairman, I add the warehouses of the Fisaco fish sauce factory. Outside, the paint had long ago flaked off the cement walls, and the corrugated metal roofs were streaked with moss. Inside, the peaks of salt were dingy, the network of spider webs an industry of its own, and I was allowed to climb—barefoot!— onto the edge of an open cask of fish sauce, in order to peer into the top of one of the barrels.

Each barrel was more than six feet tall, elevated off the ground on a foot-high platform, and paired with a smaller cask. I clambered on top of two casks, balanced precariously with Hoa at the ready to catch me if I fell, and looked into a barrel, at a woven mat weighted with rocks, which pushed the liquid beneath it down. The cask and barrel were arranged so that the small cask caught the "sauce" dribbling out of the enormous barrel's spigot—if I did fall and Hoa didn't catch me, I would tumble straight into a cask, and I wondered if I would ever be able to get the smell of fish sauce out of my hair. Tightly gripping the edge of the barrel, I eased my way down and saw that what looked like mold around the casks' rims was in fact a crusting of salt. The liquid the casks contained was as thick and dark as motor oil. We were told that the contents of the barrels sat for a year in the cool of the warehouse, before being exposed to the finishing touch: the sun.

Despite its lack of prettiness, which it certainly made up for in character, Fisaco considered itself to be the producer of Vietnam's best fish sauce, honored not only inside the country with medals at various trade fairs but also regarded highly enough to be exported to France. I was sure the producers on Phu Quoc Island would disagree, but I saw no reason to argue. One reason for the excellence, Mrs. Nguyen told us, was the location.

"Why?" I asked. "What's so special about Phan Thiet?"

Mrs. Nguyen waited for Hoa to translate my question, her expression pursed, perhaps a side effect of working so closely with fermented anchovies over the years.

"I have been asked this question many times," Hoa said. "I don't need to ask Mrs. Nguyen. I can answer it."

Hoa joked with the best of them. We had been punning around about our role as "afishionados" all day. But essentially he was a serious young man. His family was among the local fishing community whose fishing boats were confiscated by the government after 1975. How hard he must have worked to rise beyond the stigma of enemy of the state to reach his position at the hotel. Yet he was still proud of Vietnam, and I admired his loyalty to his hometown as he explained, "The sea in Phan Thiet is different. Special." Nodding at a cask of fish sauce, he said, "It's the water."

I was reminded of an old advertisement for Olympia beer, which was brewed in the state where I grew up. *It's the water, and a lot more.* "The water?" I asked. "That's it?"

"Yes, the water," he said with pride.

"What about the water?"

But he just smiled.

It turned out, according to Mrs. Nguyen, that there was also a "secret ingredient." What it was, of course, she could not tell us. Later, over drinks at the hotel, Jon and I speculated. Since the mash inside the barrels was nothing more than salt and fish caught in Phan Thiet's "special" water, we finally concluded that it was the barrels themselves that lent the crucial element. Crafted from the wood of the *bang lang* tree, they were used year after year, batch after batch. We imagined the salt and anchovies absorbing into the wood, caramelizing in the heat. Over time their residue would mellow and bring depth. In return, the wood would impart its own distinctive flavor, the way oak barrels contribute to the tenor of wine.

As if a secret ingredient weren't enough for the *nuoc mam* connoisseur, Fisaco also produced small, individually crafted batches, aged on a plot at the back corner of the factory grounds. Here were rows of waist-high, sun-kissed earthenware vats, each wearing what looked like a traditional conical hat. These jars were prepared for private customers, and I envied the discriminating palates that received such distillations.

While I was curious to learn more about the people who were privileged to own these special batches—high-ranking party officials, or restaurant owners perhaps—the undiluted smell of fish sauce was taking its toll after an hour of touring the factory. Even though she was still taking photos, I suspected that Julie had fallen into a coma, and I was beginning to feel light-headed. When I told Jon, he revealed his fish sauce theory. "About twice a month, it seems like everything goes wrong. No one can get it together. The entire city falls apart. I've decided it has something to do with the fumes of fish sauce in the air."

Perhaps it was the stinkiness of the afternoon, but Jon's speculation made me giggle.

Then Hoa said, "That's fishy," and Julie declared, "You're just fishing for compliments." High on the fumes of special-reserve *nuoc mam*, we all giggled and couldn't stop. Thus is the fate of afishionados.

After Jon and Hoa had purchased a few different grades of Fisaco fish sauce for our tasting the next day, we returned to the hotel and found chairs on the terrace in a fresh sea breeze. We gulped the clean air along with our late afternoon drinks. I had bought a few bottles of Fisaco's top grade, and when our waiter spotted them on our table, he asked if he might take a sniff. "Of course," I said.

He twisted off a lid, inhaled, smiled dreamily, and declared, "Good smell equals good taste." He added that this fish sauce was good enough to deserve its own cocktail. He was joking. I think.

Later, heading back to our room, Julie said in a hushed tone, lest she be overheard offending a national treasure, "I don't think I could ever tell the difference in smells. It all smells rancid to me."

Fish Sauce Snob

When I told a few friends, both Westerners and Vietnamese, that I was going to do a fish sauce tasting, I felt as if I were telling them I was planning to suck on dirty old socks. First came the *ugh* factor. Then the *why?* And then, even though I had explained my reasons, which made perfect sense to me, I was the target of the *you-should-be-committed* raised eyebrow. Who in her right mind would voluntarily do such a thing? It is like volunteering to be poked in the eye with a salty, fishy-smelling stick.

The hotel dining room had just emptied of the breakfast crowd, and I felt daring, a bit of a culinary rebel, as our fish sauce quartet gathered in front of a table whose wineglasses contained shallow, golden wells of fish sauce. Then Jon told me that he had already done this three times before, including once with Salma Abdelnour, the travel editor of *Food & Wine*. "She really got into it," he said, admiringly. His words pinched my heart, as if he had told me that not only was I not the first girl he had loved, but also that first girl was a supermodel with a Nobel Prize in literature.

In preparation, Jon had arranged four rows of ten glasses each, with every row containing various gradations within a selection of brands. Using the same principle that is applied to wine tasting, the glasses were set out on a white tablecloth so we could see the subtle difference in colors, which ranged from pale amber to a burgundy-tinged cognac, depending on the quality of the extraction. Other important elements I was told to look for were related to the protein level. Higher protein content produced a slight viscosity, and less protein yielded a smellier liquid.

The glasses were for Jon, Hoa, Julie, and me. Politely, Julie bowed out. "I need to take photos," she explained, her excuse fooling none of us. Jon called in Dong, a young member of the hotel's food and beverage staff, who was impressively overjoyed at the prospect of tasting fish sauce at ten in the morning. With a gloss of Tiger Balm rubbed under her nose to ward off the pee-yew, Julie stood as far out away from us as possible, as if we were blind people making bottle rockets. "I love you," she muttered to her telephoto lens.

Jon raised a glass from the first set. "This one is from a local producer. Not Fisaco. Ready?" he asked with a grin.

Hoa, Dong, and I followed suit. Studiously, we peered at the color. We took healthy sniffs. Then, we sipped. Mmm, yummy, nothing like the flavor of fermented anchovies before noon. Admirably, no one—and by no one, I mean me—gagged.

"It's a later pressing," Jon said. "Not much protein. I can taste the fish guts."

Julie scowled.

My stomach turned.

"It's to be expected," he explained. "Last pressings wind up with lots of leftover bits."

Hoa scornfully declared it "*nuoc muoi*," or "salt water." Dong agreed earnestly with all criticisms. I could taste the salt (but how, I wondered, did they know it was too much?); I couldn't taste the guts (at least, that's what I assured myself); and I wondered if I had what it took to evaluate the refined soupçons in fish sauce.

Rather than the water and crackers associated with wine tastings, a swig and swish of Coca-Cola was used to cleanse the palate between tastes of fish sauce. "I don't know why," Jon said, "but with *nuoc mam* it's the best thing for rinsing the taste buds." What this said about fish sauce, I wasn't sure I wanted to know, as I recalled an experiment I once did in grade school, where I dropped a penny into a cup of Coke and watched the proprietary blend of high-fructose corn syrup, phosphoric acid, and caffeine eat the coin away over the course of a week until it looked like Swiss cheese.

Coca-Cola and fish sauce. I could not imagine a more unappetizing combination. But I had made a commitment, and if *Food & Wine*'s Salma could get into it, so could I. I guzzled some Coke and tried the second sample, which was from Fisaco, with a 30 percent protein level. The moment I tasted it, I could see the flaws in Sample #1. This one was smoother and didn't smell nearly as fishy.

Along with the olfactory barrier, there is a logical reason for why a fish sauce tasting is such a strange thing to do. Fish sauce is a condiment. It is not meant to stand on its own, and it is never, ever sipped alone, like wine, as we were sipping it now. You would not even dunk a crusty chunk of ciabatta in it, as you would a good olive oil. It is umami, part of that fifth flavor sense, taking Vietnamese food to a higher level—and taking on a miraculously inoffensive quality, but only when it is mixed with other flavors. And yet, as we moved from #2 to #3, my appreciation for the nuances of *nuoc mam*, in and of itself, grew.

Sample #3 came from the controversial, $1 million bottling plant that the multinational food corporation Unilever opened on Phu Quoc Island in 2002—not to be confused with Phu Quoc's traditional family businesses. Branded under the Knorr label, it was just under 24 percent protein, and it had a chemical taste that was disturbingly familiar. I had been told that Knorr added MSG to its fish sauce. Whether or not this was true, it did not account for the revolting artificial flavor that stirred in the recesses of my memory. I rinsed with Coke, suddenly glad for its dubious cleansing qualities, and made my way to Sample #4. Another one from Fisaco, this had 20 percent protein. It was too salty, which was just one of the many distinctions my taste buds were learning to discern. Rinsing again, I tried #5.

Gorgeous, I thought, surprising myself with a word I never thought I would use to describe fish sauce. A 40-percent-protein Fisaco first pressing from the giant barrels that were made from the wood of the *bang lang* tree, this was a slightly sweet liquid, with a hint of smoky prime tenderloin. It had a caramel color, and a discreet, satisfying odor. Once I had swallowed, it left a pleasant molasses aftertaste in the back of my throat. I looked around at my fellow tasters. Jon had picked up the bottle and was studying the label with a smile. Dreamily, Dong murmured, "This could make me an addict." He turned to Hoa, and as they held their glasses up to the light and tipped them gently from side to side, they discussed the merits of this particular fish sauce, murmuring reverently in Vietnamese.

It was satisfying, not only to be able to distinguish this *nuoc mam*'s superiority, but also to be with these two young men who were so enthused about something that had been part of their daily lives since they were born. Hoa and Dong were in their twenties in twenty-first-century Vietnam. The world was offering itself to them in exciting new ways. MySpace and Kentucky Fried Chicken were just the beginning. And yet they still got excited about fish sauce. I admired them, and I also envied them, because I could not imagine this conversation in America, among people of any age.

We Americans do not have an ingredient like fish sauce that holds our cuisine together. From the clam chowder of New England to the Tex-Mex of the Southwest, our regional food traditions run deep. But *nuoc mam* goes beyond a single dish. It goes beyond a single region. It is pervasive, reaching into every corner of every kitchen in the country. While I wilt at the thought of life without my family's pies, they are not integral to my daily meals. Were there any dishes in Vietnam that could exist without fish sauce? Certainly, every person in the country has tasted it, if not eaten it every day of his life.

Fish sauce has a kind of devoted following that few ingredients know, and Vietnam's reliance on it for protein as well as flavor is disturbing, in light of *nuoc mam*'s trajectory into the industrialized world. In one of his first emails to me, Jon wrote, "Some fish sauces are now being made by the process of hydrolysis, in which a kind of enzyme or acid is added to hasten fermentation, while others have artificial color or are being diluted with salt water flavored with sugar or MSG." What this said about the future health of Vietnam, I didn't want to consider. Nor was I making any accusations, but when I tried the 20-percent-protein-level Sample #6, also from the Knorr factory, Jon's correspondence came to mind. The artificial flavor I detected before was now overpowering, and I was finally able to identify it. It was the awful dry-rubber taste that I got in my mouth when I blew up a balloon.

After a 20 percent Fisaco sauce that left a telltale debris of salt in the bowl of the glass and a 15 percent Knorr that strangely had no fish smell at all, we reached the grand finale: a tasting of Fisaco "private reserve." This sample, which contained the optimum 40 percent protein, had fermented outside in the sun-bathed days and temperate nights of Phan Thiet, in one of the individual earthenware jars. Jon and Hoa had to beg for just a dribble of it, and we raised our glasses in anticipation. Julie and her camera ventured closer.

The liquid's flushed hue smoldered in the muted, late morning light. Hoa peered into his glass, his expression almost fierce, as if seeking the answer to the meaning of life. I wondered if this would be a turning point, one in which my taste buds finally acknowledged my desire to be a great connoisseur. We inhaled. Dong sighed and said, "Friendly," and we laughed at the accuracy of this description. Eagerly, but with the reverence the moment deserved, we sipped.

I searched for the acidity, but there was none. I measured the brine, which was present, but as an undercurrent, influencing but not defining the flavor. A roasted essence culminated in a slightly nutty aftertaste. When I lowered my glass, there was no residue around the rim. But what was most noticeable about this fish sauce, as I took a second sip, was its balance between salty and sweet.

Two hours had passed. It was almost noon. Our discriminating judgments had been imposed. All ten samples had been tried. Every possible fish idiom had been exhausted—*fishy business*, *a fine kettle of fish*, *fish out of water*, *big fish in a small pond* ... it was amazing how many we came up with once we got started. The tasting was over, but I returned to the remaining splash of private reserve in my glass. I took one last sip and confirmed, to my great joy, that I had become something I had not even known existed: a *nuoc mam* snob.

Inspired by the waiter's comment the day before, Jon had the bar concoct a celebratory drink: one shot gin, one shot vodka, and a dash of fish sauce. We christened it the Phantini, and we all belted one down. Even Julie, who at least wanted these bragging rights. Unanimously, we declared the Phantini the foulest thing any of us had ever tasted.

In her classic cookbook, *Pleasures of the Vietnamese Table*, the chef Mai Pham writes, "In our family, my sister Denise was the only person entrusted with the task of making the sauce ... To this day, whenever we get together she's still the *nuoc cham* master. She usually begins the ritual by smashing garlic cloves. Using a stone mortar and pestle, she pounds them with chilies and sugar until they become a paste ... Then she juices the lime, gently scraping off the pulp, making sure the inner white flesh doesn't get too bruised and make the sauce bitter. The lime juice is then combined with the fish sauce and chili mixture for an interesting balance of sour and sweet."

A simple concoction that relies on fish sauce, *nuoc cham* is Vietnam's staple sauce. Because it is served uncooked as a dipping sauce, when making it you should always look on the fish sauce bottle's label for *nuoc mam nhi*, which means a first extraction. In its classic form, it goes beautifully with grilled beef, pork, chicken, seafood, and even a plain bowl of rice. It is also modified in countless ways to enhance specific dishes.

After our fish sauce tasting, we gathered at one end of the metal prep counter in the Novotel's kitchen. Because our visit to Phan Thiet was all about *nuoc mam*, Jon explained that the emphasis of our class would be on pairing each dish with a complementary sauce made with the base of a classic *nuoc cham* sauce. A menu of local recipes had been chosen by the staff, which was led by Chef Yen, irresistible in her cornflower blue bandana. Even though Jon told Chef Yen and her team that Julie and I probably didn't need another lesson in fresh spring rolls, they refused to omit their "Phan Thiet Special," a spring roll made with steamed grouper.

From the affectionate way that Chef Yen and her assistants discussed the food as we prepared it, it was clear that they had a strong allegiance to their local cuisine, whose gems are rarely hailed on the typical traveler's circuit. They reminded me of an older gentleman who had been sitting on the hotel verandah the afternoon we arrived. Overhearing Julie and me chatting with Jon about the purpose of our trip, he handed me a scrap of paper, on which he had written: "Phan Thiet food to try: Muc 1 Nang (squid w/ 1 sun), Tom Vo (local Phan Thiet lobster), Goi Ca Mai (local fish salad), Toan Duong (near Novotel), Cay Bang (Mui Ne)." He was not shy as he offered me his recommendations for local specialty dishes and restaurants. He knew he was doing me a favor.

As we started working on spring rolls, I realized that I had nearly neglected the food of Phan Thiet. It wasn't that I hadn't tried some, but I was so distracted by my fixation on fish sauce that I had failed to acknowledge it. In fact, I had had some excellent dishes, including the day before's notably fresh lunch of fish salad, steamed fish in rice paper, and sun-dried squid dipped in a sweet chili sauce at the open-air Dung Su Da One Dia restaurant overhanging the sea. The dishes had not made me breathless, like clam rice (literally that first time, and figuratively every other time after that), but the narrow strips of squid had a memorable tang, drawn out with each drizzle of chili sauce, and the cleanness of the fish salad was boldened by its bitter, minty herbs.

With these dishes suddenly in mind, my appetite grew. "What do you think sets Phan Thiet food apart?" I asked Jon, as Julie and I chopped, stirred, and shuffled around the kitchen's narrow cooking space, getting in Chef Yen's way.

"Too many people try to overcomplicate food. When the ingredients are fresh, keep it simple."

His case was proved by the Phan Thiet spring roll, which consisted of steamed grouper, mild white onions cut into thin wedges, slices of dank Chinese mushroom, translucent strips of ginger, sprigs of celery leaf, and just enough salt and pepper. These basic, unadorned ingredients were wrapped in sheets of rice paper and became something remarkable simply by the addition of the sauce.

This particular sauce had begun as the standard *nuoc cham* of fish sauce, lime, sugar, garlic, and long, sweet chilies cut into thin, round slices. To this Chef Yen added more sugar, more lime, and crushed pineapple, creating a tart-sweet slurry that played on the neutral flavor of the grouper, the woodiness of the mushrooms, and the sting of the ginger. With Jon and Hoa looking on, Julie and I ate our spring rolls standing up at the counter, surrounded by cooks prepping meals for hotel guests. We ignored the sauce that dripped down our wrists, dipping and devouring as we did at home, alone or with someone we knew well, when food was so good that we couldn't even be bothered to toss out a couple of plates and sit down at the table.

Nor did any of the other dishes make it into the dining room. Nibble-sized, Italian-style ravioli were made with rice flour dough and a filling of prawns and garlic. Gently, Chef Yen tossed them with deep-fried shallots and the sautéed greens of a "not too fat" spring onion. We dunked them in an uncomplicated *nuoc cham* and popped them into our mouths with the satisfaction that comes with any food that can be eaten in just one bite. Splashed with a *nuoc cham* sauce whose guest star was minced ginger, a dish of snowy white steamed squid served as the palette for strokes of chili, cilantro, and lemongrass and was eaten just as quickly as the ravioli, although with less finesse.

By the time our impromptu meal was over, we had eaten six different dishes with six different sauces, all of which were built upon *nuoc cham*, which in its turn owed its existence to *nuoc mam*. What could have been monotonous was instead made inventive. My appreciation for fish sauce grew. As with a rare breed of performers—not celebrities, but true artists—the show could not go on without it, even though it was fated to forever play a supporting role.

Phan Thiet Spring Rolls

While this version is ideal—simple and fresh—when it comes to spring rolls, you can use any ingredients you want, from traditional favorites such as cooked pork and shrimp to mango, grilled tofu, or roasted red peppers. Once you get the hang of them, get creative. Spring rolls are great as a party appetizer cut into bite-sized pieces, for a light lunch with soup, or as a side dish for a larger meal.

INGREDIENTS FOR SPRING ROLLS:

1/2 lb. halibut
1 white onion, halved and cut into slivers
1/2 lb. wood ear or shiitake mushrooms, julienned
Large chunk of ginger, julienned
Sprigs of cilantro
4 oz. rice vermicelli, also called rice sticks, prepared per package instructions and cooled
Rice paper, 10-inch round (read the ingredients to make sure they are made of just rice and water)

INGREDIENTS FOR PINEAPPLE SAUCE:

1 Thai chili, minced
1 clove garlic, minced
1 tbsp. sugar
2-1/2 tbsp. fish sauce
2-1/2 tbsp. lime juice
1/2 cup warm water
4 tbsp. crushed pineapple

PREPARING THE SPRING ROLLS:

1. Steam the halibut, and then cut into thin slices.
2. Set each ingredient out on a table so that it is convenient to reach. Also set out a large bowl or flat pan of warm water to soften the rice paper. In the middle of the ingredients, put a large wooden cutting board.
3. Dip a piece of rice paper in the warm water to soften it.
4. Lay the rice paper flat on the cutting board.
5. Lay out a small handful of noodles at the lower center of the rice paper, in the shape of a log.
6. Lay some mushrooms, onion, ginger, and cilantro on the noodles.
7. Fold the bottom fourth of the rice paper up over the noodles.
8. Fold the right edge of the rice paper in a fourth of the width of the paper, as if you are making an envelope.
9. Fold the left edge of the rice paper in a fourth of the width of the paper, as if you are making an envelope.
10. From the bottom, roll fast and tight to make a spring roll. If the roll is loose and floppy, don't feel badly. I've been making spring rolls for years, and mine are still haphazard!
11. Repeat until finished with your ingredients.
12. If you want to cut the spring rolls into bite-sized appetizers, wrap each roll in a piece of dry paper, and cut it with a sharp knife. Discard the dry paper.

Recipe

PREPARING THE SAUCE:

1. Mash chili, garlic, and sugar in a mortar and pestle.
2. Put the mix in a dish, and add water, lime, and fish sauce.
3. Add pineapple to make a slurry.

Saigon

Southern Vietnam

"So it happens that when I write of hunger, I am really writing about love and the hunger for it, and warmth and the love of it and the hunger for it ... and then the warmth and richness and fine reality of hunger satisfied ... and it is all one."

M. F. K. Fisher *The Gastronomical Me*

Daughter Number Four

Reunited at the Caravelle Hotel in Saigon, Julie, Huong, and I climbed into the back of a cab on an overcast Sunday morning. We were going to Bac Gai's house. Of all the cooking lessons I took on this trip, Bac Gai's was the one I looked forward to most. She is my Vietnamese mother, and I am her Con Tu, her Daughter Number Four. My Vietnamese sisters, Duyen, Dung, and Diem, are her Daughters Two, Three, and Five, respectively. In keeping with tradition, to throw evil spirits off the trail of the firstborn, there is no Number One, and Diem was demoted when I joined the family, because she is eight years younger than I.

As the cab drove past the old French opera house, skirting the post office and the cathedral modeled after Notre Dame, I was excited to reunite with Bac Gai, but I was also sad that I would not be seeing my sisters all together, as they had been when I first met them, living under their parents' roof on the edge of downtown Saigon. Dung is now married to a Chinese-Cambodian in Fort Wayne, Indiana, and Duyen is married to her high school sweetheart in Santa Ana, an hour's drive south from Los Angeles. The narrow, three-story building they inhabited before Dung and Duyen left the country was their childhood home, which had been confiscated by the Communists in the late 1970s when the family was caught trying to escape the country and sent to reeducation camps—even baby sister Diem, who was only three years old at the time. Bac Gai spent years trying to reclaim it, and by the time I arrived in Vietnam, she had succeeded. It was just around the corner from my morning English classes, and only five blocks from The Cave, where I lived for almost two years. So much had changed between then and now. Not only were two of my sisters living in America but I had to take a taxi, unlike the days when I lived nearby and could wander over any time I felt like it.

Beyond the honey-colored French colonial buildings of the city's main district, there is nothing exceptional about the suburbs of Saigon. They are a Honda-ridden tangle of low-lying, Eastern Bloc–influenced, Asian city sprawl, and they look the same for miles. But as our car crawled beneath the sullen gray sky, through the glut of traffic, a sweet melancholy nuzzled me. It was the kind of romantic sentiment I imagine many travelers associate with a return to their beloved vineyards of Tuscany or lavender fields of Provence.

I was hungry, thinking back on all of the meals I had had at Bac Gai's over the years. Despite the house's complicated, painful history, my own history with it was all about lunch. Working in Saigon as a teacher, I ate lunch there every week. Afterward, I would put on the pajamas that Bac Gai had sewn for me. They were the same kind of calico PJs with girlish, cap-sleeved blouses and appropriate-for-a-six-year-old shorts that Vietnamese women typically wear around their homes. Then I would curl up with my three sisters in the big king-size bed in the air-conditioned bedroom on the top floor, and we would gossip until we fell asleep.

This family, in this house, had saved me from homesickness during my first year in Vietnam. When my birthday came around, and I couldn't get a phone call through to my parents in the United States, the sisters threw a party for me. They had known me for just a few months, but not only were there cake and balloons, there was also a traditional *ao dai* tunic and trousers, sewed by Bac Gai with the skill that had once gained her work for the South Vietnamese president's wife. Whenever the family celebrated, whether Tet or the first anniversary of Bac Gai's father-in-law's death, I was included. Not just invited, like a guest, but dressed for the occasion in my *ao dai* and standing between the sisters in my place as one of the family.

Dung was the sister who brought me into this world. She was a student in one of my classes, learning English in preparation for her arranged marriage in America. I kept a diary during that time, and of the first day that Dung took me to meet Bac Gai, I wrote that she had said, "When I told my parents about you, they thought about me. They know I will go far away from home and miss my family. My mother is worried that you miss your family. Please think of us as family. Please come here any time you feel lonely."

This was all that Bac Gai had ever asked of me. That I come over when I felt like it and eat. And if I needed to, I should sleep, as well. She didn't care that I was a foreigner. She didn't care that I didn't speak Vietnamese and she didn't speak English. She only cared that I was fed, and that I did not feel alone.

These memories swam through my thoughts as our cab driver swung a risky U-turn through the morning upheaval of motorcycles and pulled to the curb in front of Bac Gai's house. Opening onto the sidewalk, the downstairs front room was occupied by a lingerie shop. Over the years, the space had also been used as a tailor shop, bookshop, music shop, and trendy clothing shop where Bac Gai would sometimes pull a blouse from the shelves and offer it to me as a gift. I never figured out if this space belonged to the family or if it was still the property of the government, as was sometimes the case with reclaimed houses. This question should have been easy enough to answer, but we were in Vietnam, so it remained one of life's great mysteries.

Julie, Huong, and I squeezed through the lingerie shop, passing displays of Triumph International bras and panties, delicate lace goodies for delicate Vietnamese bodies. An opening in the back of the shop revealed the dining room where Diem—Daughter Number Five—was waiting to greet us. Her spiky-haired infant son was asleep in a crib in the kitchen, and her five-year-old daughter clung shyly to the back of her black-and-white polka dot culottes.

I couldn't help laughing as I hugged her. "*Troi oi*, mama, look at you. Two kids! How is that possible!"

Diem is a giggler, and she giggled as she greeted Julie, whom she had met a few times, and was introduced to Huong. At thirty, Diem still had a baby face, and it felt strange to be welcomed by her in the role of a matriarch.

In all the time I had known the sisters, she was the *em gai*, the little sister, more than ten years younger than Duyen and Dung. She would sit slouched on a chair off to one side of our conversations, wearing jammies the color of cotton candy and sipping some sugary drink, while Duyen, Dung, and I talked about our lives, love, and politics. Inevitably, Diem would roll her eyes and sigh, heavily. "I'm bored," she would complain in her little girl voice. Now, her body was round with the voluptuousness that comes with a healthy marriage and motherhood, and she was the one who was talking to us of life, as we waited for Bac Gai to return from church.

It was difficult for me to think of Diem as anything other than the baby of the family—any family—despite her having two babies of her own. Acknowledging her as an adult meant acknowledging the passage of time. Duyen and Dung had gone from Vietnam. Nearing forty, I was no longer a part-time schoolteacher with all the time in the world to write a great American novel. Returning to this house, I felt tender. It was a reminder that life moves on.

In my diary, of my first visit to Bac Gai's, I also wrote about the meal, which included a lotus stem, shrimp, and pig ear salad. "My mother likes to cook special food," Duyen had told me, lifting a rubbery pig ear with her chopsticks. Crab soup was garnished with what I described as "an egg that looked like the bulbous, watery eyeball of the dog." Said dog was a scruffy mutt that lay sprawled under the table, and that once, mysteriously, was dyed blue for an entire week. There were also fresh spring rolls, whose unique flavor I will always associate with those first world-is-my-oyster months in Vietnam.

Also known as summer or salad rolls, spring rolls are ubiquitous in Vietnam. One particular version, *goi cuon*, are a favorite with foreigners, because they are familiar, and because they are consistently fresh and good, with their soft rice noodles, sprigs of cilantro, and slivers of pink shrimp. I love that you can turn anything into a spring roll, including grilled pork, fresh mango, and even chunks of steamed fish, as the chef at the Novotel showed us in Phan Thiet. Just add fresh herbs, perhaps some marinated wood ear mushrooms or pickled carrots, and tuck it all into a sheet of rice paper. At the end of meals, I often find myself picking at the bits of *rau ram* herb and green banana slices left on the communal plates, rolling them up in fragments of rice paper, and munching idly, no matter how full I am.

A spring roll's flavor can reflect the region where it is made. Its ingredients can even shed light on the type of celebration for which it is being served, or the history of the person making it. For example, Bac Gai's *bi cuon chay* reflect an element of her life story. A Catholic who migrated from the north of Vietnam with her family when she was a girl, she received the recipe from her Buddhist in-laws, so that she would have something special to serve on religious occasions when only vegetarian food is acceptable. These spring rolls were the kind I had eaten that first meal, and that I wanted to learn more than any other Vietnamese dish.

Back from church, Bac Gai hugged me tightly as she did every time I saw her, murmuring words of affection that I did not understand and rocking me from side to side, as if I were a little girl. She squeezed Julie hello and welcomed Huong and then got down to business, organizing the ingredients for *bi cuon chay*. As I watched her arrange pans and instruct her two housemaids, I thought, as I often did, that she must have been a queen in a former life. She gave instruction comfortably, yet graciously. She had the cheekbones of an aristocrat. And although her hair was swept into a plain bun and her tropical blouse and trousers were modest, "simplicity is the ultimate sophistication," as Leonardo da Vinci wrote. Of course, I could no longer look at her without prejudice. I admired her for fighting for her family when it would have been so much easier to give up. I respected her for surviving with dignity. And I loved her for the generosity she showed to not only me but also everyone I had seen her with.

As she prepared her kitchen, she chatted with Huong, who drifted along beside her, wearing a variation on her daily uniform, a white denim miniskirt and black camisole, despite that it was not even noon on a Sunday morning. Although they had never met before today, and were almost forty years apart, there was an ease between them. I could tell from their body language and the intimate tone of their voices. Part of this had to do with their dispositions, but I knew that part of their companionability also had to do with me. Huong accepted Bac Gai as the respected "mother" of her best friend. Bac Gai accepted Huong as the beloved friend of her Daughter Number Four. I was touched.

With each new ingredient, Bac Gai pulled out one of her many kitchen knives, to julienne, chop, or mince. I paid close attention, as her knife cut swiftly through mushrooms, manioc, and tofu. This process had been absent in all of the lessons we had taken, because the prep work was done for us, before we arrived. While this was efficient, it also did students a disservice, since there is something essential, especially when first learning to make Vietnamese food, about chopping your shallots, garlic, chili, and herbs by hand. There is an emotional attachment, a commitment, that can only be made to a dish through chopping. When I press a clove of garlic between my thumb and coiled forefinger, snapping the knife into the flesh of the clove and releasing the aromatic sting, I am meditating on the evolution of my creation.

I trailed Bac Gai as she moved swiftly through her kitchen, each act of preparation melding seamlessly into the next. She cut the end off a cucumber and rubbed it over the exposed section, to draw out the bitterness. Then, holding a crude, oiled vegetable slicer in her elegant fingers, she sliced the cucumber into nearly translucent strips with more finesse than if she had used a grater. As she picked up the next one, I asked if I could help. She handed me the slicer and held my hands in hers as we slipped the blade down the length of the cucumber. Then she released my hands and let me work on my own.

Many years earlier in Bac Gai's kitchen, I sat in silence and observed its dented pots, daggerlike knives, and faded plastic spice containers. I had written, "It is the sort of place that daily industry has made into a shrine." Above a tile tray built into the floor, which served as a sink, one corner of the cluttered room had been exposed to the sky. There was a way to cover it when it rained, but mist still leaked through. Today, the ceiling was permanently sealed, the clutter contained in attractive cupboards, and the tray replaced by a built-in, two-basin sink. But the decades-old pots and hefty knives bought at local markets still prevailed. Just as the mint-colored mixer, received as a wedding gift in 1964, has prevailed in every one of my mother's kitchens for more than forty years. Just as the aluminum roasting pot prevailed for decades in my grammy's kitchen in Carnation.

There was a history in Bac Gai's kitchen, of feeding a family during times of prosperity and times of great need. To be at home in it was one kind of privilege—a privilege I had long enjoyed. To prepare a meal in it, in this kitchen of one of the best cooks I had ever known, was quite another. Even though I was just slicing cucumbers, I was nervous. I wanted Bac Gai to be proud of me. But I was foolish to worry. Unskilled as I was with the unfamiliar knife, she muttered only "good, good" at my awkward efforts and smiled happily when I presented her with a bowl of pulpy, uneven cucumber slices.

Gai, the loyal housemaid who had been with the family since the early 1970s, fried carrots, manioc, cabbage, and mushrooms until they were tender, and then sautéed them in vegetable stock and sugar. A second, unfamiliar housemaid flash-fried sweet potato and baked tofu to a crispy brown. The smell of hot oil filled the kitchen, drifting upstairs, where Diem's husband and Bac Trai, my Vietnamese father, were hidden away, napping or watching TV as most Vietnamese men do while the women are cooking. Julie and I crumbled sheets of dried bean curd into a bowl. Bac Gai dry-roasted sticky rice in a frying pan until it became a deep, dark yellow. To my surprise, she ground it in a mini Cuisinart and explained that the traditional method of using a mortar and pestle was just too labor intensive. Although I consider the mortar and pestle to be a supremely romantic kitchen utensil, who was I to protest? I bought roasted rice powder in a jar at the Bangkok Market in L.A.

As the battered frying pans hissed with oil and the rice slowly roasted, my hunger intensified, which should have been impossible after more than four weeks of exhaustive eating. But when it comes to the aromas of cooking, rice is among my favorites. While being steamed, it releases a buttery fragrance that clings to the humid air throughout Vietnam. Dry and roasting, it becomes something else entirely. You can smell its pragmatism, its ability to nourish. As its dusty incense filled the kitchen, I could also smell my first meal in this house.

On top of spread-out newspapers on the low wooden table where we were going to prepare the rolls, Bac Gai mixed all of the fried ingredients in a big blue plastic bowl. There was also a square plastic basket with basil, mint, *rau dap ca*, and cinnamon-flavored *rau tia to* (perilla), which Bac Gai informed us is good for curing headaches. Like Miss Vy up in Hoi An, she knew the healing properties of every herb and vegetable she ate. A thick wooden chopping block was set out, its hard surface necessary for making the rolls as tight as possible.

Julie, Huong, Diem, Diem's kindergarten-age daughter, and I stood at the end of the table, watching Bac Gai, who was squatting on a small plastic stool. As we got ready to make the spring rolls, Huong had been translating the names of ingredients and techniques, but for this, translation was not necessary. Bac Gai laid a sheet of pliable round rice paper on the chopping block. At the base of the paper, she arranged a mosaic of greens and covered it with a layer of filling. She folded the sides of the rice paper in, as if she were making an envelope. She pulled the paper taut and rolled as fast as possible so that rips would not matter.

With the mindless mindfulness that comes from years of practice, Bac Gai made half a dozen spring rolls, uniform in shape and size. After lining them up on a plate, she stood and offered me the stool. I wished that someone else would follow her perfect example, but I was the one who insisted on learning to make her special spring rolls, so I was the one to go first, naturally. I laid out my rice paper, greens, and filling, which left a grit of roasted rice on my fingers. Easy enough. But although I maneuvered the paper as quickly as I could, my spring roll was scrawny and loose. I held it up, and it flopped to one side. Diem giggled. Julie snapped a photo. Huong said, "Don't worry, it's your first try."

With Bac Gai at my side, gently coaxing me, my second one was a little bit better. I made a few more, some sloppy, some not so bad, and she consoled me with the adage that a person must make at least a hundred spring rolls in a row in order to master the technique. She was not the least bit troubled that Daughter Number Four was not a spring roll expert.

I was willing to sit there all day and make a thousand spring rolls, if that's what it took, but the others wanted their turns. Julie set her camera aside, and with Bac Gai advising, she arranged a piece of rice paper on the wooden block. Competitively, as I had felt when making fresh rice paper in Hoi An, I wondered if she was going to out-roll me. Back home, her food was tasty *and* attractive. Mine was usually just tasty. Unlike me, she had patience when it came to the aesthetics of a dish. But her first roll was on par with mine, and although hers improved faster, I was satisfied. She hadn't shown me up right out of the starting gate.

As for Diem's rolls, I had already decided that they wouldn't count in the little contest I was holding in my head, because she hated to cook. "Boring," she would say, and then yawn, dramatically. She was only doing this because I had insisted—because I wanted her rolls to make mine look good in comparison. They didn't. They were competent, which she was quick to point out, giggling.

Then came Huong, with confidence enough to choose only the greens she liked and ask Bac Gai if she could make a few rolls to set aside for herself. She had less experience in the kitchen than even Diem, the hater of all activities kitchen related. Huong's mother cooked for her when she wasn't eating in restaurants. Yet on her first attempt she produced a superb spring roll.

Smiling with delight, Bac Gai clapped her hands.

"How?" I sputtered.

Knowing perfectly well that her skill bugged me, especially since she had once considered packaged ramen and canned corn a "home-cooked" meal, she grinned, shrugged, and said, "I am a Vietnamese girl."

The food was too good, and we ate too much. Bowls of vegetarian soup and all of the spring rolls, which are more filling than they appear to be. We dawdled around the dining room table, our gestures slow and our postures limp. Bac Gai and Huong chatted quietly. Huong had stopped translating, and Bac Gai had stopped asking her to. I caught a few words here and there. *Heo*—pig. *Suc khoe*—health. When I worked up enough energy to ask, "What are you talking about now?" Huong glanced at me listlessly and said, "Sometimes, I only feel like speaking Vietnamese."

On my own, I deduced that they were discussing why Buddhists are vegetarians. Exiled from the finer points of their conversation, I studied the walls. I was familiar with the trio of tinted wedding photographs that hung above a dry erase board. A bright red calendar with gold Chinese letters was typical of a Vietnamese house. The Jesus clock from the Flamingo casino in Las Vegas, where two of Bac Gai's sisters lived, was new. It was dumping rain outside. "*Mua mua*," I muttered to myself. Rain rain. The baby was asleep in a mosquito-net-shrouded crib in the kitchen. Diem and her husband looked ready to fall asleep in their chairs. Bac Trai, who had joined us for lunch, had already retreated back upstairs. Julie's camera had fallen to the wayside, and it was only a matter of time before she would succumb to a nap.

As if we weren't already drowsy enough, Bac Gai served homemade *mo* wine, for our digestion. From a recycled Courvoisier bottle she poured the pinkish syrup over ice. Huong broke her translation moratorium to explain, "*Mo* fruit is from the north. The Japanese love this one, but the government doesn't export it because it's a national treasure. Bac Gai says it's good for the blood." Its flavor reminded me of overripe peaches.

We were drifting in a mellow, postprandial haze when the phone rang. It was Duyen, calling from California. She wanted me to know that her art exhibition closed the week I returned to America. Could I make it? I could barely hear her over the revving motorcycles out in the wet street, through the open front of the lingerie shop on the other side of the dining room wall. As I pressed the receiver against my ear, to shut out the noise and isolate her voice, I thought about how strange life was, tipping us so randomly into one another's worlds. How far we had come and gone and come again, since that first lunch with Bac Gai, ten years before.

Eventually, reluctantly, Huong left to catch a flight. Since we last saw her in Hoi An, she had been given a promotion. She was now a producer, and her first assignment was a shoot in Singapore. While she would miss a couple of cooking classes with us, she would be back in time for our final meal with Hoang Anh, the granddaughter of the chef of the last emperor. Julie and I napped most of the afternoon away in Bac Gai's bedroom. Hours later, when it was time for us to leave, it was dark. The streets smelled clean from the rain. Bac Gai hailed a cab. I hugged her and began to cry.

I hadn't seen Bac Gai in four years. Since that time, my beloved aunt Judy, my sweet grammy, and my first adult love had passed away. Bac Gai's mother had died, and her husband was sick and frail. We didn't know when I would be coming back to Vietnam, and when or if we were going to see one another again. Using the only language we shared, we wrapped our arms around each other and held on, valuing the moment. Valuing the gift of a meal with family and friends. The blessing that is the opportunity to teach and learn, and to sit down one more time together over a plate of *bi cuon chay*.

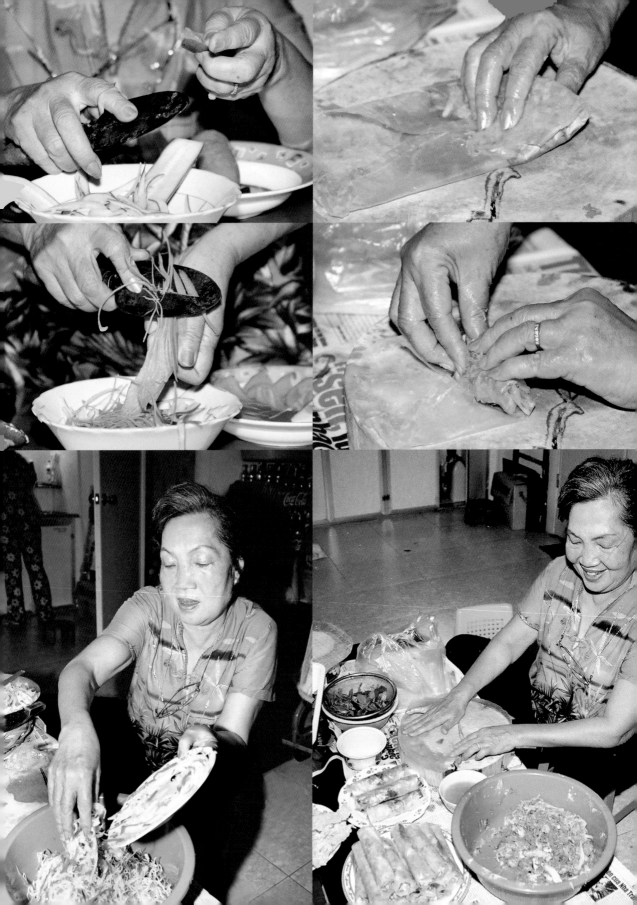

Bac Gai's Vegetarian Spring Rolls
(*Bi Cuon Chay*)

Having never worked from written recipes, Bac Gai honored me by helping me get her *bi cuon chay* down on paper. If the recipe seems intimidating, keep in mind that in the end, all you are really doing is mixing the filling ingredients together and then rolling them with herbs in sheets of rice paper. Although it took me a day to shop for and make these spring rolls, it was worth it.

INGREDIENTS FOR FILLING, PART ONE:

2 cups carrot, peeled and julienned (about 2 medium carrots)

2 cups manioc (also called yucca), peeled and julienned (about 1 small manioc)

1 cup shredded cabbage

1 cup shiitake mushrooms, julienned

1 tbsp. sugar

2 tsp. vegetable bouillon powder or concentrated liquid

3 tbsp. vegetable oil

INGREDIENTS FOR FILLING, PART TWO:

3 cups sweet potato (white flesh), julienned, mixed with 2 tbsp. white vinegar and 1 tbsp. sugar and set aside (about 1 medium sweet potato)

8 ounces baked tofu, unflavored, thinly sliced

3 tbsp. vegetable oil

INGREDIENTS FOR FINAL MIXTURE OF FILLING:

2 ounces green (mung) bean vermicelli (about 2 cups), prepared per package directions and cooled

4 sheets dried bean curd skin (*tau hu ky*), crushed into small pieces (about 3/4 cup)

3/4 cup toasted peanuts, finely chopped

1/2 cup roasted rice powder

Rice paper: 1 packet 10- or 12-inch rice paper, made with just rice and water (12-inch pieces are easiest to work with for this recipe)

Herbs: Fresh mint, Thai basil (Italian basil is fine), *rau dap ca*, *rau tia to*, and other Asian herbs (if you can find only mint and basil, these rolls will still be terrific)

DIRECTIONS FOR FILLING, PART ONE:

1. Heat oil in a large frying pan.
2. Fry carrots, manioc, and cabbage. Do not let the mixture get too soft. Test the manioc to make sure it remains al dente by the end of the following process.
3. Add mushrooms, and fry a bit longer.
4. Add sugar and vegetable bouillon to taste, and fry just a bit longer still.
5. Remove from heat, and set aside to cool. Drain any liquid.

DIRECTIONS FOR FILLING, PART TWO:

1. Heat oil in a large frying pan. Flash-fry the sweet potato until it is yellow-brown and crispy. Remove from pan and set aside to cool.
2. In same pan, flash-fry the baked tofu until crispy. Remove from pan and set aside to cool. (This step is optional. You don't need to fry the tofu.)

DIRECTIONS FOR FINAL MIXTURE:

Once all the cooked ingredients have cooled, mix them together in a large bowl with the rice vermicelli, peanuts, roasted rice powder, and crushed bean curd skin.

DIRECTIONS FOR MAKING SPRING ROLLS:

1. Using a hard surface, such as a wooden cutting board, lay out a piece of dampened rice paper. You can dampen (soften) the rice paper in a wide bowl of warm water. Remove as much excess water as possible (let it drip off) before making the spring roll.
2. Line the lower center of the paper with herbs.
3. Lay 1/3 to 1/2 cup of the mixture into a cylinder shape on the herbs. The amount can vary depending on how large you want your spring rolls.
4. Fold the bottom fourth of the rice paper up over the mixture.
5. Fold the right edge of the rice paper in a fourth of the width of the paper, as if you are making an envelope.
6. Fold the left edge of the rice paper in a fourth of the width of the paper, as if you are making an envelope.
7. From the bottom, roll as fast as you can.

INGREDIENTS AND DIRECTIONS FOR DIPPING SAUCE:

1. Mix 1/4 cup carrot, peeled and shredded; 1/4 cup cucumber, peeled and shredded; and 1 tbsp. sweet white vinegar. Set aside to marinate. (Do this at the beginning, as you are preparing the spring roll ingredients.)
2. In a bowl mix the following:

   Simple syrup of 1/2 cup water and 1/8–1/4 cup sugar
   1/2 cup soy sauce
   1/4 cup sweet white vinegar
   Juice of 1 lime
   2 red Thai chilies, seeded and minced
   2 tbsp. toasted peanuts, finely chopped

3. Cut the carrots and cucumber into small pieces.
4. Mix carrot and cucumber blend with remaining ingredients. Top with peanuts.

Serving: 10–15 spring rolls

Pickled Onions

For Saigon I had scheduled two official cooking classes. The first was at the Saigon Cookery Centre, which was popular with expatriate housewives and tourists. The class included a tour of the city's main Ben Thanh Market, followed by an enjoyable lesson in a quaint, well-decorated practice kitchen, where Julie and I got another chance to work on fresh spring rolls and clay pot fish—though not masters, we were finally getting the hang of both. We finished early in the afternoon, spent a few hours shopping on Dong Khoi Street, and then caught a cab to Emily's place.

A Canadian who had arrived in Saigon a few months before me, Emily was the first friend I made in Vietnam. I met her just a few hours after my flight landed, at the Lotus Café across the street from my hotel on Pham Ngu Lao Street. This casual joint was where "the crew" from my language school and their friends hung out morning, noon, and night, planning road trips on their geriatric Minsk motorcycles, listening to Merle Haggard, and inexhaustibly reliving the night before—among expatriates in a place like Saigon, there was always a night before. It was the kind of place where everybody knows your name, and the house special, "egg in the hole," was a cure-all for hangovers, hunger, and all manner of homesick blues.

When I lived in Saigon, Emily was one of my few foreign friends who regularly had others over to eat. Dinner parties were not common among the expatriates I knew, with the exception of those few couples whose gorgeously remodeled French villas or gated compound abodes were paid for by Philip Morris, Johnson & Johnson, or whatever other corporation the husband worked for. Their houses came complete with real stoves, and cooks and maids to prepare food, serve it, and clean up afterward. It was like having a restaurant in your home. But among us common folk, with our meager hot plates, odd school schedules, and immersed-in-Vietnam lifestyles that necessitated sanctuaries verboten to the trespass of others, dinner parties just weren't done. Besides, the entire city was a twenty-four-hour dining room.

Emily, though, was different. Although we ate out together at the Lotus Café, Red Rhino, and Buffalo Blues, I loved it best when she invited a few girlfriends over to the little, partially al fresco apartment where she used to live. These low-key gatherings were cozy and informal, with smart conversation and spring rolls, maybe some pizza and beer, those being the days when the quality of available wine was unreliable outside big restaurants.

Emily's get-togethers had been special because she didn't care about impressing. In her old apartment she never worried that part of one wall was missing and the rain was coming in, or that she didn't have enough chairs for everyone to sit on—and that one of the chairs had been pilfered from a neighbor's garbage pile. This attitude was demonstrated once again as Julie and I helped her put out quiche, a green salad, a basket of sliced baguette, and bowls of olives for nibbling with the French wines we had bought at a new, glossy wine store on Le Thanh Ton Street. Emily had not seen us in years, since Julie and I took refuge in her house, trapped midtrip after 9/11, and the lack of pretense in this meal for long lost friends was more flattering than any haute offering could ever be. It declared that the invitation to make ourselves at home was not just lip service.

Candles flickered on the patio around the table. A mosquito coil burned, its smoke spinning like incense in the mild night air. Sen arrived. She and Emily had known one another for a decade, since they met at the Lotus Café, where Sen once worked. Emily was almost fifty, and Sen somewhat older (the reverse of Huong and me), and they had one of those wonderful sisterlike friendships. Emily was straightforward and irreverent as a sailor. Sen had a schoolmarm gravity. Both were intense with curiosity and a sense of humor. Most Vietnamese are short by Western standards, and Sen was no exception, but she was still taller than Emily. While I didn't know Sen well, I always liked seeing her. She was smart, and she kept me on my toes with her out-of-the-blue statements. Once, in the middle of a casual conversation whose subject I have forgotten, she commented, "I like Pearl S. Buck. She really knows how to write about the feelings of an Asian girl."

Minh the cat sidled among our legs as we ate. In a voice launched by a thousand cigarettes, Emily caught me up on people we once had in common—their marriages, their divorces, two tragic deaths that seemed inevitable as soon as I heard the news. There was a party happening somewhere in the lane, and we heard distant music and occasional bursts of laughter. The salad was crisp, the quiche filling but light, as dishes made with the fresh eggs of Vietnam always are, and the wine was better than any I could have dreamed of—or afforded—during my first days in Vietnam. Although this was a meal I could easily have had in the States, it stood out, not only because I was sharing it with good friends, but also because I had come halfway around the world to spend this evening on Emily's patio. Her home was a harbor, and a harbor acquires its meaning from the voyage that takes you to it. A voyage to this table from my old life in Vietnam, by way of my new life in Los Angeles, through the banana flower salad of Hanoi, clam rice of Hue, fried eggplant of Hoi An, clay pot fish of Nha Trang, *ragu* of Dalat, fresh fish spring rolls of Phan Thiet, and *bi cuon chay* at Bac Gai's that had brought us there that day.

Inevitably, Julie and I regaled Emily and Sen with the culinary discoveries we had made.

"Clam rice is honest-to-God the most original dish you will ever eat," I declared.

"I'm still trying to decide if my favorite hotel restaurant is at the Metropole or the Dalat Palace," Julie said.

"Have you ever had snacks in Hue?" I asked.

"Snacks?" Sen asked.

I struggled to recall the Vietnamese words for each of the different nibbles.

"I never thought I'd like squid," Julie declared, "but Phan Thiet changed my mind. Just steamed and drizzled with sweet chili sauce."

"What about strawberry wine?" I asked. "Have you ever had strawberry wine? When I get home, I'm going to make my own strawberry wine."

"I have lots of friends who make it, but I've never done it myself," Sen confessed.

"Pshhh," Emily hissed. "Don't sound so apologetic. What about your pickled onions? That's what they should try. She makes the best pickled onions."

I knew instantly what Emily was talking about. Although I hadn't had them in years, I remembered the small, glistening bowls set out alongside dishes of tiny dried shrimp to nibble on at Bac Gai's house during the Tet holidays. As if I had eaten them only yesterday, my mouth watered at the thought of the sweet, prickly sensation that accompanies each bite. We were well into our second bottle of Bordeaux, the red wine swimming pleasantly through our bloodstreams. I was full from the quiche and salad, but starving for pickled spring onions. "You have to give me the recipe," I demanded, scrounging for a piece of paper. I would serve it with drinks before my meals.

Emily didn't need to be asked twice. "You start with as many fresh spring onions as you can get your hands on. It takes a lot to make each jar."

"You must peel the onions to get to the bulb," Sen cut in, enthusiastically. "Cut off the green, cut off the root, then peel. And when you get to the white center, make sure it's clean. Put the bulbs on a bamboo tray, and leave them out to dry in the sun for at least three or four hours, or maybe a day. Take them into the house, rinse them quickly, and dry—"

"The secret is that they must be dry," Emily interjected. "Really, really dry."

"Mmm, yes, dry." Sen nodded, vigorously.

I dutifully scribbled this imperative.

"Never use a hair dryer," Sen warned, in a way that made me wonder if she was speaking from experience. "You might cook them."

Julie sipped her wine and murmured, "No hair dryers. Got it."

"Next," Sen said, "put them in a dry glass jar."

"It must be completely dry," Emily said, as if imparting this information was her life's sacred duty.

"Do you think it needs to be dry?" Julie asked me.

"An airtight jar," Sen added. "You can use plastic, but glass is better. Now it's time to put the sugar in the jar ..."

As Emily and Sen continued, their voices overlapped, their years of friendship giving them the same ability that Julie and I had, after a lifetime together, to start and complete one another's sentences, as well as read one another's thoughts. *Use your hands, we use our hands, fine-grained sugar, yes, it has to be fine-grained, very dry, use your hands, do not use a spoon, three layers of bulbs, one layer of sugar ...*

"How much sugar in a layer?" I managed to break in and ask.

"A bulb's worth," Sen said. "Maybe a little less. Leave about an inch of space at the top of the jar, and put the lid on tight. You might even wrap some tape around it."

I waited for Emily to pounce in with the order to make sure the tape is dry, but she just sat back in her chair as Sen finished up, explaining that the jar should be left in the corner of a balcony, in the sun but not direct sun all day, for three weeks. "You should start watching it after two," she added. "When you begin to smell it, it's ready. Drain the liquid, and share the bulbs into twenty small jars, but only open one at a time. Every time you open the jar some of the good smell will go out. You can keep the jars in the refrigerator for up to a year. If you want, you can use the leftover liquid instead of lime to make *nuoc cham.*"

Exhaling deeply, Sen looked at the three of us, who were watching her as intently as if she had been juggling fire. Our craving for pickled spring onions was palpable. "I think I've got it," I said, showing her my scribbled notes, which were a bit of a mess, given the wine.

She took the paper and nodded as she lowered her glasses down the bridge of her nose to examine my scrawl. I realized this was probably the first time she had seen the process she knew by heart written down. She was well-educated, well-read, and had been to Paris, but she was still a Vietnamese woman of a certain generation. "This one," she said, handing the recipe back to me, "I learned it from my grandmom."

As Julie and I walked up Emily's quiet lane to the main street to hail a cab, I heard the sound of a *mi go*—a noodle knocker, someone who knocks two pieces of bamboo together to let the neighborhood know that soup is available for delivery from a nearby cart or shop. Late at night when I lived in The Cave, I would lie in bed and just listen to the silence of the city. It was broken rarely, and only then by the night sweepers or the bamboo tap tap tapping of the *mi go* passing in the lane, its echo drifting through the vents at the top of my living room wall, up to the air-conditioned bedroom, beckoning with the comfort of a midnight bowl of soup. Despite my many relationships, it was easy for me—for any foreigner—to feel alone at times in Vietnam, but never at night, when the *mi go* passed through the hush, like the spirit of an ancestor whispering assurances into my dark, cool room.

Sen's Magical Spring Onions

For this recipe, I am not going to offer specific amounts for the ingredients, which are only spring onions and sugar. The amount you need depends on the size of your jar. Keep in mind that it takes a lot of onions just to fill an eight-ounce jam jar—I used over one hundred. But once you make a batch, you'll be addicted. So just toss *Scent of Green Papaya* or *Vertical Ray of the Sun* into the DVD player, and start peeling and chopping.

DIRECTIONS:

1. Peel the onions to get the white bulb. Cut off the roots and the green stems.
2. Clean the bulbs.
3. Lay the bulbs on a flat tray, and dry in the sun for three to four hours or up to one day.
4. Take the bulbs into the house, and rinse and dry quickly. The onions MUST be dry before you continue.
5. In a dry, airtight glass jar, place bulbs in a layer in the bottom of the jar.
6. On top of the bulbs, spread a layer of fine-grained sugar, up to the same thickness of the bulbs.
7. On top of the sugar, lay three layers of bulbs, pressing them tightly together.
8. From here, continue with one layer of sugar and three layers of bulbs until you are within an inch of the top of the jar.
9. Put the lid on the jar, and make sure it's tight. Wrap tape around it if necessary.
10. Put the jar somewhere where it will get direct sunlight during part of the day.
11. After two weeks, start smelling it. When you can smell a strong odor, open the jar, drain it to keep the bulbs from getting soggy, and put the bulbs into a new, dry jar.
12. Keep the jar in the fridge. Serve bulbs as nibbles with drinks.

Tiny Food

At the head of a lane that would lead us to our second official cooking class in Saigon, two men were working on a motorbike. One was bare-chested. The other wore a faded shirt that looked as if it might disintegrate at any moment. Julie and I walked past a warren of houses, flanked by walls painted in the typical chipped-and-chalky shades of eggshell blue, buttercup yellow, and mint green. In Vietnam, neighborhoods are not segregated into rich and poor, with the exception of dedicated foreign compounds and new suburban residential developments, and so it was among a few shacks and some upscale houses, their gates topped with barbed wire, that we came to a nicely kept, three-story home with a small sign out front: *Dzoan*. The door was answered by a woman who pressed delicate, prayer-folded hands to one cheek, smiled warmly, and said, "It's so good to meet you." Her voice was as soft as a bird's downy wing.

I had expected the chef so often described as "the Julia Child of Vietnam" to be taller, and to have a more resonant voice. With visions of PBS's *The French Chef* in my head, I was surprised by this woman who could only be described as petite, even by Vietnamese standards. Mrs. Cam Van did not look any different from the Vietnamese grandmothers I knew, even though she had a popular restaurant, had authored more than ten cookbooks, and had hosted a TV cooking show for twelve years. She was the closest I had found in Vietnam to the American culinary personalities that populate the Food Network. But whereas there was something about Julia Child that made her seem as if she had always been an adult, it was easy to imagine what Mrs. Cam Van looked like as a girl, despite her silvered dark hair drawn back into a demure bun. Her eyes were bright, and her skin glowing, which she attributed, she later told us, to a morning elixir of pomelo juice and plain yogurt.

She led us through a humid covered patio and sparsely furnished living room, into a kitchen where three middle-aged couples from Orange County, California, were gathered for the cooking lesson that was a part of their package tour of the country. The couples milled around, exploring the kitchen, which was one of the reasons this class was so popular. It offered not just a chance to cook with a famous chef, but to cook in that chef's private kitchen. With a rolling island at its center containing six gas burners, this one was larger than the standard Vietnamese home kitchen, but otherwise it was typical: tall, scuffed, water-stained walls, white tile counters, plastic baskets filled with vegetables and herbs, half a dozen strainers of different sizes, plastic shopping sacks, gas canisters, an old tea thermos, and rustic cleavers and papaya peelers. Most typical of all, though, was the austerity, that defining hallmark of Vietnamese decor that is exacerbated by the fluorescent lighting used to save energy and keep a room cool. This was a kitchen in which Mrs. Cam Van cooked foremost for her family; next, for her restaurant, as was evident by the industrial-size pot of oxtail soup simmering on a back stove; and finally, with her classes.

As Mrs. Cam Van rounded us up around the cooking island, I realized, without the flash of illumination that such a moment deserved, that for the first time on this trip, preparing to cook, I felt as if I was on known territory. After so many lessons and my day at Bac Gai's house, the tools of the traditional Vietnamese kitchen had become familiar, as well as the objects that may have seemed to the uninitiated like nothing more than meaningless knickknacks. A metallic plastic cat, three kitchen gods on a mirrored plaque, and the fisherman La Vong casting his line down from a high shelf. All intended to bring good luck to the household. When I tasted the iced tea served by Mrs. Cam Van's tall, handsome son, I smiled with recognition at the flavor of *mo* fruit, the Hanoi plum from which Bac Gai made her liqueur.

Unlike five weeks earlier, I now knew how to shop for banana flower and how to caramelize fish in a clay pot. I could make without measuring a fair *nuoc cham* sauce. Despite my imperfections as a chopper and slicer of vegetables, Bac Gai still loved me. Without my being aware of it—without my knowing when or why—something inside me had shifted, and I felt at ease with the country's most popular chef, even when she revealed the dishes we were going to make. Among them was *banh xeo*—a crispy rice batter crepe stuffed with shrimp, pork, and bean sprouts—which required some of the same tricky and innate skills we'd had to employ when making fresh rice paper in Hoi An.

Banh xeo is a quintessentially southern dish. It captures the warmth of the region's flavors with its turmeric and coconut milk. It is common, but seems as if it would be complicated, just as omelets and roast chicken had once seemed to Americans, until Julia Child set them straight. Although Mrs. Cam Van did not have Julia's commanding gestures or robust voice, she had her same can-do spirit. She made a dish accessible, as she stirred the *banh xeo* batter ... from a mix. Yes, a mix!

My first instinct was to cry foul. Then I looked around the island, at how happy the couples were when they realized that they were about to make the very dish they had in a restaurant the night before. Shrimp sizzled in their frying pans, while batter was vigorously stirred. Everyone laughed as the husbands floundered with the tricky dual action technique for *banh xeo*: pouring the batter over the shrimp, pork, and bean sprouts with one hand while whirling the hot pan with the other, to spread the batter evenly. "Nice job! That's terrific! Good for you!" They teased one another's lumpy attempts and took lots of photographs, cheering when anyone succeeded in producing *banh xeo* that wasn't a great big clump of fried batter.

Like most of the cooking class students I had encountered down the length of Vietnam, their goals were so different from mine, their attitudes unhampered by the ambition that had at times nearly paralyzed me. The couples had come to this class just to have fun, something that did not seem to offend Mrs. Cam Van at all, and something that had not occurred to me. Not that I didn't want to have fun, of course, but it should be fun with a purpose.

That's when it happened, with my guard down, as such things do. The proficiency I had been so desperately seeking. Holding my frying pan at a tilt over the gas burner, I poured the *banh xeo* batter in a small, steady stream, not fearing that it might burn or glop ... and it didn't. Instead, it rewarded me as it began to bubble around the edges of the shrimp and pork. I set the pan onto the burner and sprinkled bean sprouts over the surface of the crepe, until just the right moment, when I slipped my spatula beneath it and quickly folded it in half, revealing its crispy golden shell.

Mrs. Cam Van passed behind me with a small cluck. "Very nice."

I set the pan aside, to be kept warm until it was time for lunch. Then I tackled our next dish: fresh spring rolls. In the center of a dampened sheet of rice paper, I arranged a collage of cold rice vermicelli, icy pink shrimp, pork, cilantro, and chives. I tucked and rolled, perhaps not perfectly, but even better, effortlessly, as if I had been doing it all my life.

The couples from Orange County left to tour Reunification Palace, and Julie went off to shoot Saigon's street food scene. Mrs. Cam Van and I sat on the covered patio at the front of her house, drinking iced tea, and I discovered that she had yet one more thing in common with Julia Child. She, too, had come to her cooking career inadvertently, and late in life.

Born in Hanoi and raised in Saigon, Mrs. Cam Van had graduated from college with a degree in literature. "At first I am a teacher in the high school, not a cook." Her voice was hoarse from a lingering cold, and her apple cheeks were flushed from the warm cocoon of the patio. Although October in Saigon does not have the crisp weather associated with fall in the West, she evoked autumn with her burnt-orange blouse, patterned with falling maple leaves. "I never go to cooking school. But every day, at home when I am a girl, my mom teaches me how to prepare food. In my family, we have six daughters. When my mom makes the meal, she asks us, 'Do you know what's in this dish?' So she teaches us slowly, drop drop drop ... one drop, two drops, so many drops, every day, until we become full. Excuse me." She smiled, and her eyelids fluttered shut. "Sometimes I close my eyes, and I can imagine my mother teaching me again."

I listened to passing motorcycles and the neighbor's barking dog while she drifted through her reverie. When she emerged, it was as if she had been swimming through time. She leaped ahead decades, to 1989, when she had to take her second son to Australia for surgery. She had been a language teacher for sixteen years, but because she was going away for an indefinite period, her contract with the high school was terminated. She returned after just a year, but she could not get work at the school again.

"But you know," she explained, "I can make cakes. Wedding cakes, chocolate cakes, many, many kinds. When I am young, every day I help my mom and my sisters make cakes. I love it. So I make cakes for parties, weddings, birthdays, meetings. People know me for this, and one day the television station is looking for a teacher to decorate cakes. They also ask me if I can cook a little.

"The first time they ask, I say no because I'm afraid. When you appear on TV, a lot of people will see you. And I don't know how to do anything like one gram, two grams. This is very difficult for me, because I can cook many dishes, but only by my feelings. I can taste and know, put in one handful, easy. For example, when I am teaching my son to cook, I tell him, 'Oh, Bi, I smell the water boiling.' He laughs. 'You cannot smell it,' he says. 'No, really,' I say. It's true, I can smell if a dish is too salty, but on TV, I must talk about one kilogram this, or we must use one teaspoon that. Finally, a friend advises me on how to do this, so I say yes. I am successful from the first program. Everybody, they love me so much."

Some people can acknowledge their own popularity without seeming boastful. Their acceptance of being admired is even part of their appeal. Mrs. Cam Van was in that circle. She sounded surprisingly humble as she continued. "In Vietnam the people don't call me the chef or the cook. They call me, how do you say, 'the good woman,' yes, 'the warmest woman.' Because when I appear on TV, they feel like I am their older sister, like their grandmom, or mother. Before, I am a teacher, so maybe this is natural for me. But they trust me, because when I teach, it is heart to heart. When I go around the city, people say, 'Hello Co Van.' Do you know Co Van? It means Aunt Van. And sometimes the child, they want to kiss me. Sometimes at night, the mother calls and asks me to tell the old story. I don't know how you say ... long, long ago."

"Like a fairy tale?" I asked.

"Yes, a fairy tale."

"They call you at home?"

"Yes, and I talk with the baby, about fifteen minutes. Then I say, 'hello, hello,' and if I don't hear anything, it's okay, so I hang up."

Coming from a country that places such value on privacy, I was intrigued. "You don't mind that people call your house?"

"I feel very happy, you know, because I can help the child sleep."

Despite the affection that Julia Child stirred in her viewers, despite the hominess of her Cambridge kitchen and its inviting copper pots and pans, I could not imagine her appreciating random calls from strangers, especially strangers who wanted her to sing their babies to sleep. But when I tried to explain how unusual this was to Mrs. Cam Van, who had lived in Australia and traveled extensively, she just looked puzzled and said, "But why? The housewives, they call me before they go to the market. 'Hello, Madame Cam Van, I want to buy something for my family today, but I don't know how.' Or, 'I just came back from the market, and I bought this fish. Please tell me, how can I cook this fish?' And I tell them."

It would have been a dream come true, being able to call up Laurie Colwin or M. F. K. Fisher when I was a young cook in my twenties and ask for just a little of their hallowed advice. "You're very kind," I said.

She shook her head softly, as if to say that kindness had nothing to do with it. "It makes me happy. Very, very happy to share what I know. I tell the young women, every day I go to the market so I can see the food. I can see by my eyes if the food is not fresh. This means the color is no good, the smell is no good. And how can I say, the touch, the sticky, if it's not sticky, I don't buy it. I see the vegetables and I think, no worm, this means no good. No worm means they use a lot of chemicals. The worm you can throw away, but the chemicals." She scowled. "And I don't like big fruit. The spring onions, the scallions, when they're small, they're very nice and safe. Small is sweet."

I smiled, thinking back to my very first lesson on Vietnamese produce, in the Hanoi market with Didier Corlou.

"The watermelon, bigger is no good," she explained. "It can be confusing, I know. The price of this one is ten dollars, but the price of that one, the bigger one, is five dollars. People think, oh, very small but very expensive, and very big and only five dollars. Why don't I buy the big and cheap? They don't understand. The guava, do you know? *Oi*? When I was in Hanoi, I saw *oi*, and I thought oh, what's wrong, it's so little. But now I know that the smaller is crunchier and sweeter."

As the afternoon waned, she compared big tarragon to small tarragon, big bean curd to small bean curd, big chili to small chili. I should have grown tired of it, but I didn't. Instead, her words were like the lullabies she used to quiet the babies of the women who called her house. She was the Julia Child of Vietnam, but she was also much more, and as she talked I closed my eyes and grew hungry for all the tiny food of the world.

The Real Thing

On our final night in Vietnam, Huong was back from Singapore, and Julie was down to her last roll of film. Our cab crawled through downtown's evening traffic toward Phu Xuan restaurant in District Three. The streets were tight with motorcycles snaking expertly around sedans and Toyota Mekong SUVs. Exhaust uncoiled, violet-blue, into the warm air. At roadside stands, noodle soup simmered, the salty broth mingling with gasoline fumes. Fluorescent signs advertised *Nha Sach*, *Nha Thuoc*, *Quan Ao*—Bookstore, Pharmacy, Clothing Store—above wide-open facades that revealed a living theater of shoppers purchasing books, aspirin, and clothes.

We were feeling sentimental, and not just because this was going to be the final meal of our trip. Phu Xuan was more than a last task to accomplish. The restaurant was owned by Ho Thi Hoang Anh, the granddaughter of Ho Van Ta, leader of the group responsible for preparing meals under Emperor Khai Dinh and later Emperor Bao Dai, the "Playboy Emperor," Vietnam's last sovereign, who had died in exile in France in 1997. Born and raised in Hue, Hoang Anh had inherited a legacy of classic imperial recipes, and she and her scholar husband specialized in the history and food of Hue, amassing perhaps the largest private collection of Hue food documents in the world. Her recommendations had served as our guide to Hue's culinary treasures. She was a link back to our beloved city, which we already missed, for its calm, grace, sleepy river, lousy weather, clam rice, and *bun bo Hue*.

Our taxi deftly dodged a Honda Dream motorcycle with a six-foot potted palm wedged between its suave male driver and stylish female passenger, who wore a tweed newsboy cap and lavender opera gloves. I was reminded of the time I had ridden across town on the back of a vintage Triumph, a bookcase balanced on my lap. I loved the improvisational nature of Vietnam, which showed itself in its streets, in its people, in its food.

Preoccupied with our upcoming meal, Huong asked me, "Do you think Hoang Anh knows where *bun bo Hue* comes from?"

Still blue that she had been too sick to join us at the snack café in Hue, Julie asked, "Do you think she serves snacks?"

Answering them both at once, I said, "I hope so."

Phu Xuan is the original name for Hue: *phu* means wealth and *xuan* means joy. These auspicious words welcomed us twice above the restaurant's front door, in classic gilded relief on an ornately carved wooden sign, and beside that in red fluorescent tubing on a metal lattice, as if the restaurant were a crossroads between past and present. We entered beneath a pair of yellow silk lanterns. Just inside, Hoang Anh greeted us, and we took turns clasping her hands. She was stunning in a black silk Chinese-style blouse and trousers. Like the fabric, her black hair was so glossy that it reflected the room's lamplight. A thick red bracelet ringed her wrist. Hers was the pale, radiant skin that the women of Hue are famous for.

Given her reputation, I had expected her to be old. "She's so young," I whispered to Huong, just as Hoang Anh whispered something, as well. I asked, "What did she say?"

"She thought you were going to be old."

"She's very beautiful," I said.

"She thinks you're very beautiful."

It was one of those nights, balmy outside, softly lit within, perfect for mutual admiration and flattery. Hoang Anh was moved by how much we loved her hometown. We were touched by how happy our love for Hue made her.

A waiter closed the front door behind us, but the sounds of the street seeped through. That muffled, inescapable ebb-and-flow buzz of motorcycles and honking horns. Still, the mood was tranquil, underscored by a flutter of piano music coming from the stereo. There were just a handful of tables, a few occupied. Although the chairs were handsome with their carved wooden backs, and a few important-looking documents hung in regal frames on the walls, no attempt had been made to turn the space into a replica of a grandiose imperial dining room. As we sat down, another waiter poured fresh green tea boiled with ginger in the traditional Hue style in simple porcelain bowls rather than cups.

Talking about our delicious four days in Vietnam's former imperial city, Huong and Hoang Anh seemed like sisters. Their voices intertwined, high and light. I was carried back to Hue as I caught a word here and there—*mui* (rain) and *muoi* (salt). That soft, powdery salt purchased from our *coc* vendor in the pouring rain. I sipped around the seaweedlike leaves that floated in the tea, listening with happiness to *com hen* and *bun bo Hue* buoyant on the surface of their conversation. I heard my name, Co Kim Fay, or Miss Kim Fay, which was what Hoang Anh called me, despite my insistence that she call me Kim. It sounded so sweet, and for some reason, every time she said it, "Co Kim Fay," Julie and I giggled.

But before I was completely swept away by the mood of the evening, I still had questions I wanted answered. "So," I said, eagerly, "*bun bo Hue*. It was everyday food, right?"

Huong rolled her eyes, and I knew what she was thinking: all work and no play ...

Hoang Anh, who understood a little English, nodded.

"Did the emperors ever eat common food?" I asked. "Did they ever eat *bun bo Hue*?"

"Of course," Huong said, as if this was a question she could have answered without Hoang Anh's expertise.

"Out in the streets?"

For this one she had to refer to Hoang Anh. Huong told me, "No, food like *bun bo Hue* comes from the queens. Because the queen is just a normal person. When she gets married, she brings the normal food, you know, like *bun bo Hue*, to the royal family. Hoang Anh says that when we talk about the emperors, we think they have special dishes made just for them, but actually, they don't. When Hue was the capital of Vietnam, everything regarding culture, all the art, poetry, and music, it all had to go to Hue. The food, too. When it gets to Hue, they make it better, they refine it. That is true imperial cuisine."

"So how does *com hen* fit into all of this? Did the emperors ever eat clam rice?"

"Oh," Huong said, smiling, "this one, it's very interesting. *Com hen*," she murmured to Hoang Anh, who grinned at my obsession with clam rice. "Hoang Anh says *com hen* is the most normal dish of all, for the poor people, because the rice, the *com*, usually it's left over from the day before, and the vegetables are already in the garden. They just get the *hen*, the clams, from the river and cook it, so it's very cheap, you know. But one of the queens, she went into the palace and the only dish she remembers is that thingie. So that's why they have it there."

Softly, Hoang Anh added, "Bao Dai. Tell Co Kim Fay about Bao Dai."

"Oh, yes," Huong said. "You will like this. Emperor Bao Dai, he loves *com hen*. There was one time when he was at his villa in Dalat, he was going to have a party and he really wants to have clam rice. So they get the helicopter to go to Hue and get the *hen* from the river and bring it back. But because the king only uses a little of the clams, you know, just enough for that night, they have a lot left over, so they put it in the lake. So now they have *com hen* in Dalat, too."

I could not believe my luck. Because the key to *com hen* is the clams from Hue's Perfume River, I assumed that it could only be had in Hue. But it turned out that my new favorite dish from my new favorite city could also be found in the first city I had fallen in love with in Vietnam. I could not help dreaming of my next trip. This time, properly bundled up against the mountain chill, I would eat *com hen*—a dish of the common people, but adored by kings—made with Hue's tiny river clams harvested from Dalat's beautiful, freezing alpine lake.

We talked about *com hen*, *bun bo Hue*, and the way that the salt of Hue is baked in a brick kiln so that it is as fine as talc, until our stomachs quivered with hunger. Eventually, Hoang Anh asked if we were ready to eat. We were ravenous, but also on our guard. We were crazy about Hue food and crazy about Hoang Anh. But we had been so let down by our imperial meal in Hue. When Huong mentioned our disappointment, Hoang Anh declared that such dinners were solely for tourists and had nothing to do with real imperial food. In any case, her dishes did not include red chilies decorated like koi fish. Nor did they include such legendary ingredients as rhino skin and deer sinew. Rather, they followed the fundamental imperial principle that had been passed down to her: the refinement of the everyday. We would start, she told us, with fresh spring rolls.

Julie and I exchanged discreet glances. We had overdosed on spring rolls over the past five weeks. A Vietnamese dish couldn't get any more everyday, and although we knew how it could be customized, we were unsure about its potential to be refined.

How satisfying it is to be pleasantly surprised.

A small white plate was set in the middle of the table, and on this plate, four perfect cylinders. Four delicate round spring rolls, each wrapped not in a sheet of rice paper, but in a leaf of lettuce the color of early summer, and tied with a strand of a green onion. Were it a Cézanne—for it reflected the artist's love of the casually but perfectly arranged—it would have been called *Still Life with Cilantro and Rose*. The small moist rose being a delicately carved carrot.

It was impossible for these spring rolls to be any more uncomplicated. Lettuce, cold rice vermicelli, cilantro, and shrimp. The lettuce was crisp, the noodles chewy. The shrimp was brisk without the distraction of the pickled vegetables that usually fill a spring roll. The dipping sauce was sweeter than usual, light and playful.

"Do you like this one?" Hoang Anh asked.

"Mmm," we murmured. "Uh huh."

Satisfied with our primal, inarticulate response, she nodded and lifted her hand to let the waiter know that we were ready for our next course. He brought two more plates, containing *banh beo thien mu* and *banh la cha tom vi da*, versions of the snacks that Huong and I had eaten in Hue. The first was a tiny steamed rice flour "pancake" topped with minced shrimp and served with a pale sauce. The second was a thin steamed rice flour "pancake" filled with minced shrimp and wrapped in banana leaf. Both were chewy and creamy, salty and smooth.

"Oh, heaven," Julie murmured. "Are these like the ones in Hue?"

"Better," I said.

"They were really good at the snack place," Huong said, "but this ..." She searched for the right words until finally, at a loss, she settled on, "This is really, really good."

"Lucky emperors," Julie said, wistfully.

Hoang Anh spoke softly to Huong in Vietnamese. Translating, Huong said, "She says that the food, it's about where you put your heart and soul. The emperor went away, and we had the wars with the French and America and this and that, so there was no imperial cuisine for a while. Then after the war, we were poor, so none then either. But now the lifestyle is changing. The markets are full again. From her memory, Hoang Anh can remember what her grandfather's food tastes like, and because of the love, she can bring it back."

I thought of the local chefs I had spent time with on our trip. Mrs. Loc safekeeping her family's "secret" recipe at Cha Ca restaurant in Hanoi; Miss Vy ardently passing along her knowledge of Vietnamese food traditions in Hoi An; Chef Huong researching the indigenous cuisine of Dalat; and now Hoang Anh resurrecting the food of the emperors. All of them relying on the precious gift of memory—a gift so at risk of being wiped out during the country's lean years—to keep Vietnam's culinary traditions alive. All of them understanding that *terroir* is as much in the heart as it is in the land.

Next came a house specialty, *nghieu xuc banh trang me*. Hoang Anh did not serve *com hen* at Phu Xuan because she could not get the clams fresh, so I had chosen what sounded like the next best thing: sautéed clams and noodles. I told myself that I was not expecting anything as spectacular as clam rice. I would never put that kind of pressure on another dish. Still, in my heart of hearts I wanted it to be unforgettable.

Following Hoang Anh's lead, Julie, Huong, and I each scooped morsels of clams and noodles onto a piece of sesame rice cracker. Just a mouthful, so that it could be eaten in one bite. I chewed and swallowed and looked across the table to see Huong and Julie nodding approvingly at their plates. The noodles were sweet in the nectar of the chopped, steamed clams. The white onions had been caramelized until they were tender but still crisp. Fresh snippings of *rau ram* lay cool against the nutty, roasted crunch of the cracker. The garlic was fragrant, the chilies sharp, and the fish sauce as light as a sea breeze. *Nghieu xuc banh trang me* was as sophisticated as clam rice was fundamental, and because of this the two dishes provided a perfect balance, reflecting the richness of Hue.

"May I have this recipe?" I asked.

"Of course," Hoang Anh said.

Julie whispered, "It will be perfect with banana flower salad."

Too soon, the night—and our journey—came to its end. We lingered on the sidewalk in front of the restaurant, reluctant to leave. As Julie, Huong, and I took turns hugging Hoang Anh good-bye, the soft, warm rain of autumn in Saigon began to fall. Next door a woman squatted over a vat of *mien ga*, and steam rose toward the dark sky. I could smell the heat of the chicken simmering in the broth. The traffic had faded away. The city was quiet. I was happy. Once again Vietnam had given me everything I had hoped for and more.

Hoang Anh's Clam Noodles

As much as I wanted to replicate clam rice at home, it relied too heavily on one ingredient that I cannot buy in the United States: the tiny clams from Hue's Perfume River. Instead, I am offering this recipe for clam noodles, from Hoang Anh's Phu Xuan restaurant in Saigon. There are numerous keys to the success of this recipe: caramelizing the onions to just the right balance of tender and crisp, using fresh clams, tossing in fresh herbs at the very end of the process, and serving the finished noodles on *banh da* (toasted sesame rice crackers).

For the clams, choose the smallest that you can find. The weight in this recipe is for clams in their shells. Buy extra, in case some of the clams don't open when you steam them. The coolness of the *rau ram* herb serves to counterbalance the chili. I recommend chopping extra, in case anyone wants to add more to their own serving. The same goes for the chili. *Banh da* can be purchased pretoasted. Otherwise, you can toast them in your oven at 400 degrees for just a few minutes until golden brown.

INGREDIENTS:

2 lbs. Manila or littleneck clams

2 oz. rice vermicelli, also called rice sticks, prepared per package instructions

1 tbsp. vegetable oil

1 small white onion, sliced

1 clove garlic, finely chopped

1/4 cup coarsely chopped *rau ram* (cilantro may be used as a substitute)

Banh da crackers for scooping

MARINADE FOR CLAMS:

2 tbsp. fish sauce

1 pinch fresh ground pepper

1 red Thai chili, finely chopped

1 small shallot, finely chopped

DIRECTIONS:

1. Prepare marinade.
2. Set bamboo steamer (or colander) over a pot of boiling water. Place clams in steamer. Steam clams until shells open, 5–10 minutes. Do not use clams if their shells do not open.
3. Remove clams from steamer. Remove clam meat from shells. Dice meat, and mix into marinade. Allow clams to marinate, 15–20 minutes, while you prepare the rest of the ingredients. Marinate at room temperature, not in the refrigerator.
4. Cook noodles until al dente, per instructions on the packet, approximately 3–5 minutes. Drain noodles, and rinse in cold water. Cut into 2-inch lengths.
5. Sauté onions in vegetable oil on low/medium heat until translucent. Make sure they do not get soggy. You want the onions to retain their crispness.
6. Add garlic to onions, and sauté about 1 minute, "for fragrance."

7. Add clams with marinade to onions and sauté, so that the liquid penetrates and the mixture takes on a caramelized texture, about 3–5 minutes. Keep heat low, so that the mixture doesn't dry out. If you need to, you can add a teaspoon or so of water. Do NOT add extra fish sauce, since this can make the dish too salty.
8. Raise heat, add noodles, and stir-fry quickly.
9. Remove pan from heat, and stir in *rau ram*.
10. Serve with *banh da* (toasted sesame rice crackers). The crackers are broken into pieces and used to scoop up the noodles.

Serving: 2 as a main dish.

Epilogue

When Julie and I returned to America, we immediately began practicing the recipes we had collected. She tackled banana flower salad. I set my sights on clay pot fish. We took turns with Miss Vy's crispy fried eggplant, and we continued until between us we mastered the recipes that are in this book. Certainly, we are not experts on Vietnamese cuisine, but we have enjoyed our small accomplishments.

As for my dream meal for my family and friends, it is still coming together in its own roundabout way. Rather than start small, within six months of our trip, Julie and I found ourselves catering a holiday party for more than fifty at my friend Connie's house in Venice Beach. And at the invitation of our friends Joel and Dagny, we threw a dinner party for twenty-five winemakers and wine lovers in Paso Robles. Miraculously, both overly ambitious events were successful. People still talk about the banana flower salad.

Generally, though, our efforts have been simpler. One sunny afternoon in Seattle, I practiced making steamed fish spring rolls with West, the seven-year-old son of my best friend Bette. I rolled a couple before he took over, making dozens with the kind of patience children are not usually known for. Because I was in the experimenting stage, he gave me plenty of good advice, such as making sure the rolling surface and my hands stayed dry. Those hours together, concentrating on keeping the filling intact, laughing as West tried out new shapes (the square "pillow" was our favorite), are precious among my memories. On that same trip to Seattle, my friend Janet and I scoured the International District for a clay pot so she could test the recipe I'd perfected for clay pot fish. She liked it so much she tried it again with shrimp, which she decided is her favorite.

Since our trip to Vietnam, Julie has gotten married. We served *ragu* and the fish spring rolls to her new husband Clive and friends Hilary and Michelle one warm summer night here in L.A. And when I got up the nerve to finally tackle Bac Gai's vegetarian spring rolls, I made them in the kitchen of Julie and Clive's new house on Mount Washington and shared them with the newlyweds, my cousin Jeanne, and her son Connor, sitting around the living room with plates balanced on our knees, overlooking the San Bernardino Mountains. Each of these times, I felt great pride in being able to offer this part of my life in Vietnam. Sharing the flavors of the country I love, I felt closer to the people I love.

Clearly, when it comes to cooking Vietnamese food, the recipes in this book are just a starting point. If you are interested in learning more about making Vietnamese cuisine, I suggest purchasing Mai Pham's *Pleasures of the Vietnamese Table*, Ann Le's *The Little Saigon Cookbook*, and Andrea Nguyen's *Into the Vietnamese Kitchen*. Nguyen's website, Viet World Kitchen, is also a valuable resource.

As for traveling to Vietnam, do it now. The country is changing quickly. Saigon becomes more of an international city every day. Up in Hanoi, Didier Corlou has moved on from the Metropole hotel, although thankfully he has not left town. You can now find him at the head of his own restaurant, La Verticale. Antoine Sirot is no longer in charge of the Dalat Palace, a situation I find tragic, even though he is still in Dalat, and the hotel is still my favorite in the world.

As the pioneering chef James Beard noted, "Food is our common ground, a universal experience." Through its exploration of Vietnamese cuisine, I hope this book gives you a greater understanding of that experience.

Glossary, Acknowledgments & Credits

Glossary

American War: The name given to the war between the United States and Vietnam by the Vietnamese.

ao dai: Traditional tunic and trousers worn by Vietnamese women.

banh cuon: Rice paper "pancake" filled with minced pork and wood ear mushrooms.

banh khoai: Small, crispy, cassava flour pancake filled with shrimp and bean sprouts. A Hue specialty.

banh vac: Also known as "white flower." Steamed rice paper dumplings stuffed with minced shrimp.

banh xeo: Crispy rice flour "pancake," made with turmeric and coconut milk and filled with shrimp, pork, and bean sprouts.

bun bo Hue: Beef, pork, and crab sausage soup with lemongrass and chili. A specialty of Hue.

bun cha: Grilled pork and pork patties on a bed of rice vermicelli. A specialty of Hanoi.

bun rieu cua: Minced crabmeat with rice vermicelli soup.

bun thit heo nuong: Grilled pork on a bed of rice vermicelli.

cao lau: Pork noodle soup. A specialty of Hoi An.

cha ca: Grilled, fried fish with turmeric and dill. A Hanoi specialty.

cha gio: Fried spring rolls.

Cham: Ethnic minority in southern Vietnam

cyclo: Three-wheeled vehicle pedaled by a driver who sits behind a bucket seat for passengers.

Dalat: Highland city in southern Vietnam.

doi moi: Government policy of economic reform instituted in the mid-1980s.

dong: Vietnamese currency.

expat: Also: expatriate. A person who lives in a country other than his or her homeland.

goi cuon: Fresh spring roll.

Hanoi: Vietnam's capital, in northern Vietnam.

hoanh thanh: Wonton soup.

Hoi An: Old Chinese port town in central Vietnam.

Hue: Former imperial capital in northern Vietnam.

mien ga: Chicken and glass noodle soup.

mi quang: Pork, shrimp, and egg noodle soup.

nem lui: Minced pork on sugarcane.

Nha Trang: Port/beach city in central Vietnam.

nuoc cham: Dipping sauce made with fish sauce, chili, lime, garlic, sugar, and water.

nuoc mam: Fish sauce made with fermented anchovies and salt.

Phan Thiet: Beach town in southern Vietnam.

pho: Noodle soup usually made with beef (*bo*). A specialty of Hanoi, although it is popular throughout Vietnam.

rau ram: Staple herb in Vietnamese cuisine.

Saigon: Former capital of southern Vietnam, officially known as Ho Chi Minh City.

Tet: Lunar New Year, usually at the end of January. Vietnam's most popular holiday.

thung chai: Basket boat made of bamboo and pitch.

tom lui: Minced shrimp on sugarcane.

umami: The palate's fifth food sense, created by an amplification of the basic four: salty, sweet, sour, and bitter.

Viet Cong/Viet Minh: Both groups fought against the Americans and joined forces during the American War. Viet Cong refers to the National Liberation Force of South Vietnam. The Viet Minh were nationalist soldiers in the north led by Ho Chi Minh.

Acknowledgments

Along with the many people written about in these pages, I would like to thank the following friends and family for their commitment to helping me make this book the best it can possibly be. For reading the manuscript in its various forms, my mom, Bette, Ann, Joy, Meagan, and Natasha, and especially Janet and Connie, my loyal, thoughtful, committed, and wise readers. For moral support and pancakes, my dad, Jerry. For pies and countless desserts over the years, my aunts Wilma, Janice, Judy, Norma, and Pat. For generously sharing the fruits of her kitchen, my cousin, Jeanne. For loving Vietnam as much as I do, and capturing its flavors in her photographs, my sister, Julie. For her appetite for Vietnamese food, my dear friend Huong. For Janet M., for her talent and patience, and designing a book that captures the spirit of Vietnam. And for his belief in my work, my publisher, Albert. Special thanks to Jan Vail for helping arrange so much of this trip.

To prepare for my trip and write this book, I researched countless books, magazines, scholarly papers, and websites. I am particularly grateful to the following publications and organizations:

Articles, books, and websites

Glutinous-Rice-Eating Tradition in Vietnam and Elsewhere, by Nguyen Xuan Hien, White Lotus, 2001.

Impasse, by Nguyen Cong Hoan, Red River Press, 1983.

Into the Vietnamese Kitchen, by Andrea Nguyen, Ten Speed Press, 2006.

The Little Saigon Cookbook, by Ann Le, Globe Pequot Press, 2006.

"Rice Paddy Dike Construction," by Bill Herod, 1987, www.country-data.com/cgi-bin/query/r-14676.html.

Vietnamese Cuisine, by Didier Corlou, Department of Publications, Vietnamese Ministry of Culture and Information, 2003.

"Vietnamese Fish Sauce," by Mary Nguyen, Trade & Environment Case Study, 2004, www1.american.edu/TED/vietnam-fish-sauce.htm.

Vietnam Investment Review, www.vir.com.vn.

Viet Nam News, http://vietnamnews.vnagency.com.vn.

Viet World Kitchen, www.vietworldkitchen.com.

Organizations

French Ministry of Foreign Affairs. International Union for Conservation of Nature. The Library of Congress Country Studies and the CIA World Factbook. Ministry of Agriculture and Rural Development, Vietnam. World Health Organization.

Credits

As well as using the following publications for research, I have also quoted from their pages and would like to express my appreciation. Page numbers listed below refer to the location of quotations in this book.

"The Art and Science of Grafting," by Adam Wheeler, University of Vermont, www.uvm.edu/~mstarret/plantprop/grafting.pps (pg. 195)**.**

The Book of Salt, by Monique Truong, Houghton Mifflin Company, 2003 (pg. 157).

"Cao Lau & Crispy Pancakes in Central Vietnam," by Graham Holliday, *Noodlepie*, www.noodlepie.com, 2004 (pg. 123).

The Cuisine of Viet Nam, by Annabel Jackson (ed.), Ham Chau (ed.), and Van Chi (ed.), The Gioi Publishers, 2005 (pg. 95).

"From Indochine to Indochic," by Eric T. Jennings, *Modern Asian Studies* 37, Cambridge University Press, 2003 (pg. 187).

The Gastronomical Me, by M. F. K. Fisher, North Point Press, 1943 (pg. 252).

Home Cooking, by Laurie Colwin, Alfred A. Knopf, 1988 (pg. 64).

Land of the White Parasol and the Million Elephants, by Sidney Jennings Legendre, Dodd, Mead & Company, 1936 (pg. 233).

Life in the Forbidden Purple City, by Ton That Binh, Da Nang Publishing House, 2003 (pg. 95, 96).

"A Maritime Logic to Vietnamese History? Littoral Society in Hoi An's Trading World, 1550–1830," by Charles Wheeler, 2003 (pg. 122-123).

Paradise of the Blind, by Duong thu Huong, Penguin Books, 1994 (pg. 36, 108).

The Physiology of Taste, by Jean Anthelme Brillat-Savarin, Counterpoint, 1949 (pg. 9, 117, 236).

Pleasures of the Vietnamese Table, by Mai Pham, HarperCollins Publishers, 2001 (pg. 246).

A Room of One's Own, by Virginia Woolf, Harcourt, Brace & World, Inc. (pg. 10).

"Saigon Favorites: The Rest of My Bests," *Eating Asia*, http://eatingasia.typepad.com, by Robyn Eckhardt, 2005 (pg. 199, 201).

Shadows and Wind, by Robert Templer, Penguin Books, 1998 (pg. 68).

"Street-free streetfood stunna," by Graham Holliday, *Noodlepie*, www.noodlepie. com, 2004 (pg. 51).

"Transitions in Taste in Vietnam and the Diaspora," by Mandy Thomas, PhD, *The Australian Journal of Anthropology* 15:1, 2004 (pg. 37).

The Unprejudiced Palate, by Angelo Pellegrini, The Modern Library, 2005 (pg. 69).

The Vietnam Guidebook, by Barbara Cohen, Harper & Row Publishers, Inc., 1990 (pg. 37, 122).

World Food: Vietnam, by Richard Sterling, Lonely Planet, 2000 (pg. 123).

Photo References

11, Street café in Hanoi. **12**, Didier Corlou at the December 19 Market with chili, dragon fruit, sliced banana flower, rice, root vegetables, and star fruit. **19**, Fresh herbs. **20**, Metropole hotel cooking class with Madame Hai. **27**, Banana flower salad, sliced banana flower, and fresh banana flower. **28**, Didier Corlou's herb, spice, and sauce experiments. **34**, Street traffic in front of Restaurant Bobby Chinn. **42**, *Pho* soup cart. **47**, Sidewalk café. **48**, Clams and chili, stall vendors, and tamarind crab at Ngon. **53**, Stall vendor at Ngon. **54**, Fresh dill, Mrs. Loc, and simmering *cha ca* at Cha Ca La Vong. **63**, Dining room and kitchen of Cha Ca La Vong. **65**, Huong eating soup. **66**, Vietnamese countryside. **71**, Fresh squash. **72**, *Bun bo Hue*. **77**, Architectural detail at the emperors' tombs. **78**, Clam rice. **85**, Kitchen and clam rice ingredients at clam rice restaurant. **86**, Cyclo at night. **91**, Traditional vegetable peelers. **92**, Kim and Huong bicycling into the Imperial City. **99**, Gate inside Imperial City. **100**, Julie and Huong on the Perfume River. **105**, Bicycles. **106**, Detail of tomb of emperor Minh Mang. **111**, Sugar cane juice cart. **112-113**, Boat kitchen on the Perfume River. **114**, Ba Roi's *bun bo Hue* stall. **119**, Miss Vy at the Cargo Club Cooking School. **120**, Lanterns outside an old Chinese shop house. **125**, Vinh Hung Hotel. **126-127**, Typical Hoi An street scene. **128**, Red Bridge Cooking School classroom. **135**, Fresh spring rolls. **136**, Minh Mi Quang restaurant. **145**, Door in Hoi An. **146**, Making spring rolls and turmeric fish in banana leaf at the Cargo Club Cooking School. **155**, Crispy fried eggplant. **156**, Vegetable and seafood at the Hoi An Market, and harvesting water spinach. **163**, Local fisherman in Nha Trang. **164**, Catching lobster. **171**, Lobster farm. **172**, Fishing boat details and fishing boat pilot. **177**, Fishing in Nha Trang Bay. **179**, Clay pot fish. **181**, Picking greens at Golden Garden Produce. **182**, Dalat landscape. **189**, Dalat landscape. **190**, Grafting tools and Mr. Bui at the Valley of the Peach Blossoms nursery. **197**, Pineapples limes, bananas, and cinnamon. **198**, *Ragu* at Doan Doan. **207**, Dalat vegetables at Golden Garden Produce and Organiks. **209**, Dalat strawberries. **210**, Bottling wine at Vang Dalat. **219**, Vang Dalat wine. **220**, Antoine Sirot and Chef Huong investigating fresh boar leg. **227**, Beans, shallots, and Chef Huong preparing *ragu*. **231**, Clay pot fish. **232**, Mui Ne beach and fish sauce vat at Fisaco fish sauce factory. **241**, Special reserve fish sauce vats at Fisaco. **242**, Hoa examining fish sauce. **249**, Fish sauce tasting samples, Jon, Kim, and Jon and Hoa. **251**, Ingredients for Phan Thiet Spring Rolls. **253**, Bac Gai. **254**, Making spring rolls in Bac Gai's kitchen. **263**, Bac Gai preparing ingredients and making spring rolls. **266**, Spring onions. **272**, Mrs. Cam Van. **278**, Phu Xuan restaurant, Hoang Anh, Hoang Anh teaching Kim about salt meals, spring rolls, and tea. **285**, Fresh rice noodles. **286**, Street vendor in Hanoi. **289**, Market vendors in Dalat.

Julie and Huong

Julie Fay Ashborn

Julie Fay Ashborn's travels through Southeast Asia inspired her photography in *To Asia With Love*, *To Vietnam With Love*, and *The Little Saigon Cookbook*. She was raised in the Pacific Northwest and now lives in Los Angeles with her husband Clive, daughter Charlie, and son Oliver.

Nguyen thi Lan Huong

Raised in Saigon, Nguyen thi Lan Huong loves food and travel. When not off on her next adventure (England, Australia, the United States, and countries throughout Asia)—making sure to sample the local cuisine—she is a producer and partner for Fatman Films Asia.